In Memory Of

Elsie Swanson Scheibe '26

Dedicated by the
Carleton College
Alumni Association

Oscar Wilde in the 1990s

Melissa Knox

Oscar Wilde in the 1990s

The Critic as Creator

CAMDEN HOUSE

First published 2001
by Camden House

Camden House is an imprint of Boydell & Brewer Inc.
PO Box 41026, Rochester, NY 14604–4126 USA
and of Boydell & Brewer Limited
PO Box 9, Woodbridge, Suffolk IP12 3DF, UK

ISBN: 1–57113–042–x

Library of Congress Cataloging-in-Publication Data

Knox, Melissa, 1957–
    Oscar Wilde in the 1990s: the critic as creator / Melissa Knox.
        p. cm. — (Studies in English and American literature, linguistics, and
    culture. Literary criticism in perspective)
    Includes bibliographical references and index.
    ISBN 1-57113-042-X (acid-free paper)
        1. Wilde, Oscar, 1854–1900 — Criticism and interpretation — History —
    20th century.   I. Title.   II. Studies in English and American literature, linguis-
    tics, and culture (Unnumbered). Literary criticism in perspective.

PR5824 .K54 2001
828'.809—dc21
                                                                2001025587

A catalogue record for this title is available from the British Library.

This publication is printed on acid-free paper.
Printed in the United States of America

For Sylvia Maynard Sturgis

Contents

Acknowledgments

I would like to thank my husband, Josef Raab, for making it possible for me to write this book, and our son, Leopold, for giving me much joy. Thanks also to Alexander Greiffenstern for creating the index, and to my editors, James Hardin and James Walker, for their help and their patience.

Melissa Knox
Eichstätt, Germany
23 April 2001

Introduction

"I WAS A PROBLEM for which there was no solution" (*Letters*, 685), Oscar Wilde remarked, and indeed he remains a Gordian knot. The relationship between his life and work — a central critical question since his death in 1900 — continues to dominate writing about him. Picking at these tangled strands, critics make cases for Wilde as a literary or cultural figure devoted to a cause (gay rights, Irish identity, aesthetics, literary theory), and then demonstrate that he lived out this cause in his life and expressed its relevance in his work. Because his life's relationship to his work continues to spark heated debate, intensive biographical scrutiny remains indispensable. If one uncontested and in-contestable truism about Wilde exists, it is that the facts of his life do not speak for themselves. They can be counted on to contradict themselves, and they benefit from extensive analysis.

Like other books in the Literary Criticism in Perspective Series, this study focuses primarily on the critics, not on Wilde himself. But unlike the other books in the series, the present study lists Works Cited alphabetically rather than chronologically since only a single ten-year span is covered.

Contemporary critics reiterate the idea that whatever one says about Wilde, the opposite is always true. In a *New Yorker* article from May 1998, "The Invention of Oscar Wilde," Adam Gopnik remarks that "one of two sure things that can be said about Oscar Wilde is that he would not read any of the books being published about him today," since "all books that try to prove anything" were books Wilde considered not worth reading. The other sure thing, Gopnik surmises, after complaining about the "burden of proof, point-scoring, thesis-making, and, you often get the feeling, thesis-winning" books among the recent vast Wilde literature, "is that he would read them all."[1] The critic's degree of biographical insight frequently determines the value of current Wilde criticism.

What seems to annoy contemporary literary critics committed to particular ideologies is that Wilde had none. Above all, he proved an unsystematic thinker: spontaneous, brilliant, impulsive, willfully self-contradictory. Unlike many contemporary critics, he did not devote himself to the idea that nothing can ever be definitively known, or bemoan the ways in which the cultural background and personal bias of the critic distorts or colors everything he or she discusses. Instead, Wilde thought that the way to truth led through these distortions, that the critic's personality equaled "an element of revelation." "Truth" remained a concept he respected, even, or especially, when referring to it as "one's last mood."

Intensely intellectual but not logical, Wilde perceived and indeed believed in the importance of subtle personal influences and intuitions in literary criticism, remarking that by "intensifying his own personality" the critic "can interpret the personality and work of others, and the more strongly this personality enters into the interpretation, the more real the interpretation becomes."[2] Wilde's Dorian Gray remarks that "the true object" of life is the creation of artistic worlds, and that in his search for new and delightful sensations he adopts "certain modes of thought that he knew to be really alien to his nature, and abandoned himself to their subtle influences" (CW, 105). Wilde's intellectual affinities with Hegel, Nietzsche, Freud, and William James show his grasp of the importance, indeed of the necessity, of powerful irrational and unconscious forces in thinking and judgment.

I found, therefore, that critics who maintained, like Wilde, a flexible attitude, who were willing to abandon logic for intuition, and who interested themselves in the mind and in human behavior, wrote more original and insightful books. My own 1994 book, Oscar Wilde: A Long and Lovely Suicide, is a psychoanalytic biography, a form not in the vanguard of Wilde criticism, or literary criticism generally, during the period up to and including the 1990s. Although many exciting and innovative developments have occurred in recent years, newly intensified scrutiny of biographical details and an interest in their extensive interpretation occurs rarely enough to be considered anything but a trend. Old beliefs die hard, among them that the lives of artists exist separately from their art; that biographic details, especially those that biographers or their audiences deem personally uncongenial or even disgusting, endanger the status of the art; and that biography has less to offer than literary theory, especially forms of literary theory regarding personality as a function of culture and society primarily. As a biographer, I see personality as a collection of internal forces upon which society and culture have an impact. Culture and society do not, however, cause or create personality, no matter how much they influence its expression.

In the case of Oscar Wilde, who called attention to the relationship between his art and his life, and between art and life in general, biographic interpretation ought to top the list of theoretical modes of investigation. It is an old story that Wilde's plans for his tragic fall line the plots of his plays, which read like blueprints for just the catastrophic degradation he endured. The importance of Wilde's own perception of the relationship between his art and his life demands far greater attention than it has received, especially in recent literary criticism.[3]

Not surprisingly, the earliest Wilde criticism consisted almost exclusively of biographies and personal reminiscences. In recent times, particularly the last ten years, literary critics have, however, de-emphasized the importance of biography. One reason for this is that no one who knew Wilde remains alive today, whereas in the early decades of this century, his voice, his face, and his peculiar "elephantine" walk, as his close friend Robert Ross called it, lived in the memories of many. Biography also has a history of being considered nonliterary and noncritical. A famous warning — one of many — came from Coleridge, who in his *Biographia Literaria* translated Gotthold Lessing's (1729–81) *Briefe, antiquarischen Inhalts* No 57 as follows: "The critic must know, what effect it is his object to produce; and with a view to this effect must he weigh his words. But as soon as the critic betrays, that he knows more of his author, than the author's publications could have told him; as soon as from this more intimate knowledge, elsewhere obtained, he avails himself of the slightest trait *against* the author; his censure instantly becomes personal injury, his sarcasms personal insults." A writer who dares to appropriate additional biographical material is not even a critic, Coleridge argued, but instead "the most contemptible character to which a rational creature can be degraded, that of a gossip, backbiter, and pasquillant . . . he steals the unquiet, the deforming passions of the World into the Museum; into the very place which, next to the chapel and oratory, should be our sanctuary, and secure place of refuge; offers abominations on the altar of the muses; and makes its sacred paling the very circle in which he conjures up the lying and prophane spirit."[4]

Coleridge might have been pleased to know that some of the best books about Wilde were written when much less biographical material or scholarly apparatus, like annotated editions and manuscript material, was available, that is, before the 1960s. During this period of scant resources for research, Wilde's reputation remained in eclipse. Biographers relied on ingenuity and creativity to flesh out a life from the few known facts, while today, the exhaustive mountain of growing data has the potential to overwhelm all but the hardiest.

Hesketh Pearson's biography, *Oscar Wilde: His Life and Wit* (1946), offers many useful stories and anecdotes, and presents Wilde as a brilliant man. When Pearson began his biography, however, Bernard Shaw advised him not to write it, claiming that other biographers had already said all there was to say. "Sherard has done the hero-worshipping, Ransome the respectable, and Harris the vivid portraiture," argued Shaw in a conversation with Pearson (Pearson 1). In Shaw's view Wilde was a "raconteur, conversationalist, and a personality, and these points cannot be reproduced" (1). Pearson objected that "no one had yet attempted to reconstruct Wilde as a great character," and that "Wilde's genius as a talker was by no means dependent on his manner" (1–2). Pearson's work is one of the first biographies to stress the literary and intellectual originality of Wilde's writing.

A few critics recognized Wilde's genius, but influential ones often ignored him: F. R. Leavis, for example, says almost nothing about him. The New Critics demonstrate little interest in him, perhaps because of their belief that the text alone, without biographic or cultural background, had to speak for itself. Such a position would be almost untenable for a critic attempting to understand Wilde's thought. Wilde makes not so much as a cameo appearance in I. A. Richards's *Practical Criticism* (1929), although both Matthew Arnold and T. S. Eliot are there, nor does he appear in the Cleanth Brooks and Robert Penn Warren anthology *Understanding Fiction,* nor in the Brooks, Warren, Purser anthology, *An Approach to Literature.* In *A History of Modern Criticism,* René Wellek condescendingly opines that Wilde's "sordid tragedy" and the "myth" that grew up around him as a martyr "gives to [his] ideas on art and literature a historical position which they may not deserve in a history of criticism, apart from the personality and pitiful fate of the man." He added that "obviously" Wilde's ideas were "anything but new," but admitted to finding "solid brainwork under the glittering surface of Wilde's prose" (Wellek 407–9).

Until the 1950s, most critics offered moral evaluations of Wilde, and many saw him as a minor figure who spouted amusing, but ultimately trivial, epigrams. There existed numerous biographical reminiscences of an entertaining or a tragic Wilde, but few critical appraisals that did him any justice. This attitude began to change in the 1960s, and as more and more information about Wilde and his thinking became available, his reputation as an artist and a thinker grew. A breakthrough occurred in 1989 with the publication of Wilde's *Oxford Notebooks,* collected and commented on by Philip E. Smith and Michael Helfand, who demonstrate that Wilde, far from being a frivolous dilettante, involved himself deeply in philosophic and scientific discoveries of his day. Richard Ellmann's masterful biography of Wilde appeared the previous year, and explored important connections between Wilde's intellectual and artistic growth and his emotional development — for example, his dread of syphilis and his defenses against this dread in his novel, *The Picture of Dorian Gray*.

Ellmann's insights did not always receive the credit they deserved, perhaps because theoretical developments, which asserted that information about authors' lives should not enter discussions of their work, have influenced contemporary literary criticism since 1969, when Michel Foucault wrote an article entitled "What is an Author?"[5] Foucault argued that cultures, not individual personalities, produce novels. The idea was then advanced by Roland Barthes, who wrote "The Death of the Author,"[6] and widely accepted by literary and cultural critics, though not by the common reader, for whom biography remains popular. (Biographies of all types routinely top bestseller lists.)

Admittedly, Foucault and Barthes cannot be exclusively credited or blamed for the diminished status of biography as a tool of literary critics. In 1993, Ian Small, who painstakingly finds, catalogues, and evaluates rare Wilde books and manuscripts from a traditional literary critical perspective, dismissively discussed early Wilde studies by Arthur Ransome and Arthur Symons, who wrote in 1912 and 1930 respectively. Small concludes that these authors are only "interesting in the manner of most of the early biographical material, in that they are written by individuals involved in some of the events which they describe, and hence are clearly partial in their judgments" (174). To be partial in judgment is, incidentally, the defining virtue of the literary critic according to Wilde, a point to which we shall return, because his critics have often assumed that Wilde must have been merely ironic, or affecting a pose. This tendency not to take Wilde seriously, or to fail to see when he is serious, also defines much of recent criticism.

Wilde himself asserted the importance of studying his life as a work of art, and his attempt to craft his life as art, when he asked André Gide, "Would you like to know the great drama of my life?" and answered, "I've put my genius into my life and only my talent into my work."[7] With these remarks he practically mandated biography as a form of literary criticism, though he tried to throw everyone off the track by calling biographers Judases and the "mere body-snatchers of literature."

This book explores the forms of resistance to biography as well as its successful use in criticism of the 1990s. I believe criticism of this decade, the centennial of Wilde's rise and catastrophic fall, captures the essence of perennial critical questions, and especially anxieties, about Oscar Wilde. We return to Wilde's fin de siècle as a key to understanding our own; we attempt to define his identity as a way of understanding who we are, where we have come from and where we are going at the end of the twentieth century. The current explosion of popular interest in Wilde provides ample evidence for this claim. In May 1998, two new books of literary criticism about Wilde were advertised in the *New York Review of Books;* Ken Ruta's one-man show, *Oscar Wilde: Diversions and Delights,* was just finishing a run in Boston; *Gross Indecency,* the Moises Kaufman play about Wilde's trials, was enjoying an eighteen-month run in New York City; Liam Neeson was playing Wilde in *The Judas Kiss* on Broadway and in a soon-to-be released film; Stephen Fry's film, *Wilde,* had just opened in New York City. In the May 11, 1998 issue of *New York Magazine,* John Simon observed, "A century after his fall from grace into penal servitude, penniless exile, and premature death, Oscar Wilde is more famous and feted than in all his years of glitter and glory." He then asked, "Does even a month go by without a new book, movie, or play about him or at the very least an article of critical appraisal?"

In a similar vein, Don Shewey wrote in *The Advocate,* a nationally known gay and lesbian news magazine, "Wilde is all over the World Wide Web . . . You can even find his astrological chart on-line" (57). Popular culture continues to embrace and reinterpret Wilde: the 1998 movie *Velvet Goldmine* represents Wilde as a child, who announces, "I want to be a pop idol," and who grows up to be just that. The character announces his bisexual relationships and quotes Wilde frequently, in just the style that Wilde quoted other writers, that is, without attribution. The pop idol's identity remains more mysterious than the real Oscar Wilde's, for in the movie Wilde is an alien foundling, abandoned by a "luminous green spaceship" leaving "a cloud of pink smoke."[8]

There exists a curious — perhaps a Wildean — paradox in recent criticism about him, especially that written in the 1990s. While eschewing biography, for the most part, current criticism tries hard to establish his identity — as an Irishman, gay man, philosopher, journalist, poet, or visionary of one particular cause or another. Perhaps we feel his affinity for us. His personal life revolved around the types of uncertainties that are associated with the fin de siècle. He never stopped revising the national, religious, personal, class, and sexual aspects of his identity, and at the end of the twentieth century his critics continue this revision. The writer credited with the most thorough and well written

Wilde biography of our time, Richard Ellmann, pinpoints perhaps the chief reason for our interest in Wilde: "He belongs to our world more than to Victoria's" (Ellmann 553). But a literary critic influenced by mainstream ideologies, Lawrence Danson of Princeton University, follows the Foucauldian path of the "death of the author," asserting that Wilde's fate "was a fate he helped to make: his own paradoxes, after all, also perform the decentering of meaning and of its authorizing agencies, which presages the postmodernist author-as-text" (Danson 10). Without commenting on Danson's prose or speculating on his meaning, I point to a common trend among antibiographical literary critics of the 1990s — the propensity to "read" the author as a "text" of his culture rather than reading his personality. Unlike those from earlier centuries, such critics refuse to try to understand Wilde's emotions, or what in the nineteenth century would have been called his soul.

Wilde would not have gone along with current trends toward diminishing the emphasis on personality. Instead, he would have led the way to modern uses of biography as a method of literary analysis. This comes across in his psychologically precise apercus, for instance, "Wordsworth went to the lakes, but he was never a lake poet. He found in stones the sermons he had already hidden there." Wilde's apparent dislike of biographers exposes a fear of (and fascination with) the self-revelations that delighted and plagued him all of his life. Biography was a method of literary criticism, while exhibitionism and confessionalism proved to be unavoidable, and sometimes desirable, components of literary criticism: "The highest, as the lowest, form of criticism is a mode of autobiography" (*CW*, 17), he wrote. He defined "the highest criticism" as "the record of one's own soul" (*CW*, 1027). Naturally this insight filled him with conflict, and he swore that he lived "in terror of not being misunderstood" (*CW*, 1016), but he stuck to his principles, and as his critics in the 1990s frequently remark, he drew early blueprints for contemporary forms of criticism. As I hope this book will demonstrate, critics of the 1990s who value the biographical spirit expressed by Wilde in numerous epigrams write the best criticism about him.

Holbrook Jackson in *The Eighteen-Nineties* (1922), one of the first studies to define the literary and cultural importance of that decade, remarked, "With many writers, perhaps the majority, it requires no effort to forget the author in the book, because literature has effectually absorbed personality, or all that was distinctive of the author's personality. . . . But . . . the complete Oscar Wilde was the living and bewildering personality which rounded itself off and blotted itself out in a tragedy . . ." (81). Oscar Wilde's work was indeed the entry point to his life, though for many writers it is the other way around. Jackson, who had written biographies of George Bernard Shaw and William Morris, understood the importance of implementing biography in literary study. In Wilde's case, biography has proven to be instrumental in illuminating his work, but biographical studies of Wilde — and indeed, biography in general — have remained controversial in literary criticism for the following reasons.

First, early biographies of Wilde, especially Frank Harris's work, *Oscar Wilde: His Life and Confessions* (1916), have been criticized as mere reflections of the biographer's personality, or as having political or literary agendas of their own. Though Harris embroidered Wilde's life with incidents that might have happened, and in most cases probably did, these were events that Harris could never have witnessed. Thus, he was branded a liar. Most claims of inaccuracy should be taken with a grain of salt, however, since the accusers are sometimes relatives of Wilde who have — like all biographers — their own agenda. Merlin Holland, Wilde's grandson and holder of the copyright to his unpublished letters and manuscripts, has been known to censor critics who write about Wilde's homosexuality and his probable infection with syphilis.[9] But at this point, Wilde's view of the personal agenda of literary critics should again be considered. In his critical dialogue, "The Critic as Artist," he dissolved what the twentieth century has declared a false distinction between subjectivity and objectivity, saying that the difference between subjective work and objective work was one of "external form merely" (*CW*, 1045), and making it clear that the highest form of criticism was the personal impression. I believe Wilde had a strong intuition that the impressions of the unconscious mind and the experiences of the critic had to be considered along with the critic's conscious intent.

Biographical studies are also controversial because until the 1960s, insufficient Wilde material had been collected and organized to make possible the writing of scholarly biographies. Rupert Hart-Davis's editions of Wilde's letters, *The Letters of Oscar Wilde* and *More Letters of Oscar Wilde* (1962 and 1985 respectively), proved to be a major breakthrough. These letters display Wilde's conscious crafting of his life as a work of art. They also express his Freudian, or ancient Greek, feeling of predestination in reliving certain emotional attachments as he is driven toward an inexorable doom. In the letters, we find the following observations:

Our most fiery moments of ecstasy are merely shadows of what somewhere else we have felt, or of what we long some day to feel. So at
least it seems to me. And, strangely enough, what comes of all this is a
curious mixture of ardour and of indifference. I myself would sacrifice
everything for a new experience, and I know there is no such thing as
a new experience at all. I think I would more readily die for what I do
not believe in than for what I hold to be true (*Letters,* 185).

This is a profound confession of how and whom he loved, and of how
he planned to destroy himself — to go down with a whimper, not a
bang — like the main character in his fairy tale, "The Remarkable
Rocket." We also get Wilde's confession that in his novel, *The Picture
of Dorian Gray,* the three main characters — Lord Henry, the wit; Basil
Hallward, the portrait painter; and Dorian Gray, the beautiful young
man — are, respectively, who the world thinks he is, who he thinks he
is, and who he would like to be, "in other ages, perhaps."

The early criticism that recognizes Wilde's genius, including Holbrook Jackson's study, tends to stress the importance of using biographic data in order to understand the development of his various
literary and personal styles, as well as the impact he had on his culture.
For instance, early critical studies by "Leonard Cresswell Ingleby" (a
pseudonym for Cyril Arthur Gull), *Oscar Wilde* (1907) and *Oscar
Wilde: Some Reminiscences* (1912); by Thurston Hopkins, *Oscar Wilde:
A Study of the Man and his Work* (1913); and by Stuart Mason (a pseudonym for Christopher Millard), *Oscar Wilde and the Aesthetic Movement* (1920) are valuable because they were written by people who
knew Wilde well, and who had occasion to observe events in his life
that helped to transform his personal and literary styles. Ian Small rejects the studies' accuracy, insisting that they "tell the reader more
about the disposition of their respective authors than their subjects."
However, this begs the question of how he would know, since they did
know Wilde personally, and Ian Small did not (174).

In one of Wilde's best known critical dialogues, "The Critic as Artist," he made clear his belief that Matthew Arnold's ideal of objectivity,
"to see the object as in itself it really is," was both impossible and unde-
sirable. Wilde states that criticism should see the object "as it really is
not." This quality of telling the reader "more about the disposition of
their respective authors than their subjects" characterizes the criticism
that brings to light new insights about Wilde. Such insights can be seen
in the early biographies and critical studies of Wilde mentioned above,
as well as in George Woodcock's *The Paradox of Oscar Wilde,* another
influential work that appeared in 1949 and the first study to emphasize

Wilde's political interests. Woodcock has been accused of propagandizing Wilde as an anarchist — indeed, Woodcock wrote a whole book about anarchism — but without Woodcock's work, it is possible to imagine Wilde never having become a hero of gay political rights in the 1980s.

Another significant book, Christopher Nassaar's *Into the Demon Universe* (1974), is the first study to call attention to what has been called the "dark" side of Wilde, the Wilde who saw himself as a sinner and a tormented soul. Nassaar's book interprets Wilde's attitude towards his homosexuality as a "contagion" in his life, and contains many plausible interpretations of Wilde's works as evidence of a need to purify or cleanse himself. For instance, when Lord Arthur Savile in Wilde's "Lord Arthur Savile's Crime" takes a bath, he wants to wipe away the "stain" of "some shameful memory"; Nassaar points out that this is a symbolic baptism. Other such scenes exist, particularly in *The Picture of Dorian Gray*. (Wilde's terror of disease, especially syphilis, offers another reason for his preoccupation with washing away some distressing memory or event, as discussed in *Oscar Wilde: A Long and Lovely Suicide*.) Nassaar's book was criticized as too biographical, however. Ian Small, in summing up the prevailing disregard for biography, remarked that Nassaar's book had been one of the first attempts "to construct a coherent critical reading by exploiting, rather than merely rehearsing, the facts of biography" (177).

Other studies, admired more than Nassaar's, also tend to make biographical pronouncements — for example, that Wilde was an "individualist" or a "moralist." In this category are Philip K. Cohen's *The Moral Vision of Oscar Wilde* (1978) and Rodney Shewan's *Oscar Wilde: Art and Egotism* (1977). These books impress me as less specific in their biographical content, less informed, less original, and less precise than Nassaar's work.

In the year 2000, Wilde's reputation remains at an all-time high, but the criticism about him is often uninformative, jargon-ridden, or plagued by ideologies wed to a political cause that the author wishes to advance. This is a pity, since the last decade includes what ought to be one of the most fascinating areas in Wilde research, namely gay and gender studies, which should attempt to explore Wilde's ideas about his sexuality, and the intellectual and emotional constructs through which he and his age understood sexuality. But these books often fail to realize the potential of biography in illuminating Wilde, sometimes because they reject the importance of the concept of personality, preferring to understand Wilde as a product of his culture or an index of it. Wilde's own interest in — indeed obsession with — his own personality and the meaning of personality in general is often ignored.

In the following summaries and discussions of Wilde criticism of the 1990s, I hope to reveal the affinity of the best criticism to Wilde's own critical standards, and to show how less successful criticism deviates from those standards. Every book or essay I included means that I excluded another from the enormous quantity of writing about Wilde in the decade of the 1990s, but my attempt has been to include as much as possible of original thought — which frequently employs biographical criticism — and of thought representing critical theories common in the past decade.

Three useful essay collections edited by Regenia Gagnier, C. George Sandulescu, and Peter Raby are partially included. Gagnier's *Critical Essays on Oscar Wilde*, a collection intended as a "testimony to what Wilde represents for our time and place — late twentieth century life in the United States," offers a vision of Wilde as a figure who represents many things, but whether he is appreciated for his personality and writings, or for gay activism, or social theory, he stands for "freedom and toleration." This is a typically American value, and one of many explanations for Wilde's particular appeal to American critics.

Sandulescu's *Rediscovering Oscar Wilde,* a volume of 464 pages on subjects widely varying from Wilde in cyberspace, to Wilde's ethnic identity, to his sexual relationships, grew out of the May 1993 conference in Monaco, "Rediscovering Oscar Wilde," the fifth international conference of the Princess Grace Irish Library. Borrowing from Shakespeare studies the term "The Supreme Quartet," referring to Shakespeare's four tragedies — *Hamlet, Othello, King Lear,* and *Macbeth* — the editor, C. George Sandulescu, turns to Irish studies for an "analogous Quartet of Stars," and comes up with Yeats, Joyce, Beckett and Wilde (xv). The papers offered in this volume, he writes, are intended to remedy the fact that the work of Wilde is "one of the most inadequately charted by scholars," a complaint referring to the lack of a concordance and a facsimile edition. Peter Raby's *Cambridge Companion to Oscar Wilde* collects fifteen essays on a wide variety of topics under three main headings: *Context, Wilde's Works, and Themes and Influences.* The collection introduces various faces of Wilde, both personally and professionally. The book includes a number of illustrations, many of them scenes from Wilde's comedies in contemporary magazines, and a useful chronology of events of Wilde's life.

I have not reviewed my own biography, *Oscar Wilde: A Long and Lovely Suicide*, but have included a discussion of some of its central ideas in a summary of my biographic essay about Wilde's sister.

Notes

1 Adam Gopnik, "The Invention of Oscar Wilde," *The New Yorker,* 18 May 1998, 78.

2 Oscar Wilde, "The Critic as Artist." *Complete Works of Oscar Wilde,* ed. Vyvyan Holland (New York: Harper & Row, 1989), 1033. Hereafter references to this work will be cited in the text as CW.

3 An excellent short summary of the history of critical response to Wilde can be found in Zhang Longxi's "The Critical Legacy of Oscar Wilde," reviewed below in chapter one.

4 Samuel Taylor Coleridge, *Biographia Literaria* (1817). Ed. J. Engell and W. J. Bate. See vol. 7 of the *Collected Works of Samuel Taylor Coleridge,* ed. Kathleen Coburn. (16 vols., Bollingen Series 75. Princeton, NJ: Princeton UP, 1983): 109–11. The Lessing translated and quoted by Coleridge can be found in *Sämmtliche Schriften* (1784–96) 12: 160–61.

5 Michel Foucault, "What is an Author?" (1969) *Language, Counter-Memory, Practice.* Trans. D. F Bouchard and Sherry Simon. (Ithaca, NY: Cornell UP, 1977).

6 Roland Barthes, "The Death of the Author." *Image — Music — Text.* Trans. S. Heath. (New York: Hill and Wang, 1977): 146. "We know that a text is not a line of words releasing a single 'theological' meaning (the 'message' of the Author-God) but a multidimensional space in which a variety of writings, none of them original, blend and clash."

7 André Gide, *Oscar Wilde.* Trans. Bernard Frechtman. (New York: Philosophical Library, 1949): 16.

8 Todd Haynes, *Velvet Goldmine* (New York: Miramax, 1998): 3–4.

9 See an exchange in *Victorian Studies* 39:4 (Summer 1996) between Susan Balée, who reviewed my biography, *Oscar Wilde: A Long and Lovely Suicide,* and Merlin Holland. Balée remarked that Holland as literary executor both shaped and inhibited Wilde scholarship, by charging fees that I considered excessive for use of Wilde manuscripts and by refusing use to critics whose ideas he disliked. Holland admitted in his reply that he had told another Wilde biographer, Gary Schmidgall, that he would not grant permission for use of manuscripts "if you are intending to make as much out of the syphilis question as Ellmann did with as little evidence and some of it twisted to fit his own thesis." In my opinion, Richard Ellmann did not twist facts to fit a thesis.

Works Cited

Balée, Susan. 1995. Review of *Oscar Wilde: A Long and Lovely Suicide*, by Melissa Knox. *Victorian Studies* 38.2: 319–21.

———. 1996. "Reply to Merlin Holland." *Victorian Studies* 39.4: 542–43.

Barthes, Roland. 1977. "The Death of the Author." *Image — Music — Text*. Trans. S. Heath. New York: Hill & Wang.

Brooks, Cleanth, John Thibaut Purser, and Robert Penn Warren, eds. 1975. *An Approach to Literature*. Englewood Cliffs, NJ: Prentice-Hall.

Coleridge, Samuel Taylor. [1817] 1983. *Biographia Literaria*. Ed. J. Engell and W. J. Bate. Vol. 7, *The Collected Works of Samuel Taylor Coleridge*. Ed. Kathleen Coburn. Bollingen Series 75. Princeton, NJ: Princeton UP.

Danson, Lawrence. 1997. *Wilde's Intentions: The Artist in his Criticism*. Oxford: Clarendon Press.

Ellmann, Richard. 1988. *Oscar Wilde*. New York: Vintage.

Foucault, Michel. [1969] 1977. "What is an Author?" *Language, Counter-Memory, Practice*. Trans. D. F. Bouchard and Sherry Simon. Ithaca, NY: Cornell UP.

Gagnier, Regenia. 1991. *Critical Essays on Oscar Wilde*. New York: G. K. Hall.

Gide, André. 1949. *Oscar Wilde*. Trans. Bernard Frechtman. New York: Philosophical Library.

Gopnik, Adam. 1998. The Invention of Oscar Wilde. *The New Yorker*, 18 May, 78.

Hart-Davis, Rupert, ed. 1962. *The Letters of Oscar Wilde*. New York: Harcourt, Brace and World.

———, ed. 1985. *More Letters of Oscar Wilde*. New York: Vanguard Press.

Haynes, Todd. 1998. *Velvet Goldmine*. New York: Miramax.

Holland, Merlin. 1996. "Comments on Susan Balée's Review of *Oscar Wilde: A Long and Lovely Suicide*, by Melissa Knox." *Victorian Studies* 39.4: 539–41.

Holland, Vyvyan. 1986. Introduction to *The Complete Works of Oscar Wilde*. London: Collins.

Ingleby, Leonard Cresswell [Cyril Arthur Gull]. 1907. *Oscar Wilde*. London: T. Werner Laurie.

Jackson, Holbrook. [1913] 1966. *The Eighteen-Nineties: A Review of Art and Ideas at the Close of the Nineteenth Century*. New York: Capricorn.

Knox, Melissa. 1994. *Oscar Wilde: A Long and Lovely Suicide*. New Haven: Yale UP.

Mason, Stuart [Christopher Millard]. 1920. *Oscar Wilde and the Aesthetic Movement*. Dublin: Townley Searle.

Nassaar, Christopher. 1974. *Into the Demon Universe: A Literary Exploration of Oscar Wilde*. New Haven: Yale UP.

Pearson, Hesketh. 1946. *Oscar Wilde: His Life and Wit*. New York: Harper and Bros.

Ransome, Arthur. 1912. *Oscar Wilde: A Critical Study*. London: Martin Secker.

Richards, I. A. [1929] 1956. *Practical Criticism: A Study of Literature*. New York: Harcourt, Brace.

Sandulescu, C. George, ed. 1994. *Rediscovering Oscar Wilde*. Princess Grace Irish Library: 8. Gerrards Cross: Colin Smythe.

Shewey, Don. *The Advocate*, April 28, 1998.

Small, Ian. 1993. *Oscar Wilde Revalued: An Essay on New Materials & Methods of Research*. North Carolina: ELT Press.

Smith, Philip E., and Michael S. Helfand. 1989. *Oscar Wilde's Oxford Notebooks*. New York: Oxford UP.

Wellek, René. 1965. *A History of Modern Criticism*. Vol. 4: 1750–1950. Cambridge: Cambridge UP.

Wilde, Oscar. [1891] 1986. "The Critic as Artist." *Complete Works of Oscar Wilde*. Ed. Vyvyan Holland. New York: Harper & Row. (References to this work will be cited in the text as CW.)

Woodcock, George. 1949. *The Paradox of Oscar Wilde*. London: T. V. Boardman.

1: Geistesgeschichte

THIS CHAPTER CONCERNS close readings of Oscar Wilde that follow tenets of traditional literary criticism: they are intended to reveal a new way of thinking about Wilde, his times, and popular as well as scholarly perceptions of Wilde today. They belong not to any one theoretical category, but they borrow from different methods, especially New Criticism and "old" historicism. From New Criticism they take close attention to textual detail, and from "old" historicism the conceptualization of Wilde as a major figure. They use traditional forms of discussing literature — for example, attempting to show a line of intellectual influence from German philosophers through Wilde's thinking. Because the readings in this chapter reveal literary, philosophic, and cultural influences on the development of Wilde's thought and style, I have grouped them under the heading "Geistesgeschichte," meaning the history of ideas and intellectual history, a term for which there is no exact English equivalent.

Works summarized and discussed in the first part of this chapter are Zhang Longxi's "Oscar Wilde's Critical Legacy" (1988, rpt. 1991); brief remarks by Peter Raby summarizing current critical approaches from his preface to *The Cambridge Companion to Oscar Wilde*, a volume of recent Wilde essays that he edited (1997); Isobel Murray's essay on a new source for Wilde's *The Picture of Dorian Gray* (1994); Patricia Flanagan Behrendt's *Oscar Wilde: Eros and Aesthetics* (1991); Julia Prewitt Brown's *Oscar Wilde's Philosophy of Art* (1997); and Sos Eltis's *Revising Wilde: Society and Subversion in the Plays of Oscar Wilde* (1996).

In the second part, "Theater History and Criticism," I have included Kerry Powell's *Oscar Wilde and the Theatre of the 1890s* (1990); Richard Allen Cave's "Power Structuring: the Presentation of Outsider Figures in Wilde's Plays," Joel H. Kaplan's "Wilde in the Gorbals: Society Drama and Citizens Theatre," Peter Raby's "Wilde and European Theatre," and Gerd Rohmann's "Re-Discovering Wilde in Travesties by Joyce and Stoppard," all from *Rediscovering Oscar Wilde* (1994); Joseph Donohue's "Distance, Death and Desire in *Salome*," from *The Cambridge Companion to Oscar Wilde*; and William Tydeman and Steven Price's *Wilde: Salome* (1996).

Page numbers for Longxi's article are given from the volume in which it is most recently reprinted, *Critical Essays on Oscar Wilde,* ed. Regenia Gagnier (1991). Page numbers for Raby's remarks on Wilde criticism are from *The Cambridge Companion to Oscar Wilde.* Page numbers for Rohmann, Murray, and Raby's essay on "Wilde and European Theatre" are from *Rediscovering Oscar Wilde,* ed. C. George Sandulescu.

Part One: Close Readings

Zhang Longxi

Zhang Longxi's "The Critical Legacy of Oscar Wilde" provides a useful summary and analysis of critical evaluations of Wilde, particularly those of the late nineteenth and early twentieth centuries, and points out connections between Wilde and figures as diverse as Vico and Sir Philip Sidney. Zhang's study was originally published in 1988, the year after Richard Ellmann's landmark biography of Wilde appeared. Both works are among the first to take Wilde's literary criticism seriously and find value in it.

Zhang writes, "Most scholars and critics have either overlooked [the principles of art for art's sake] brilliantly formulated in Wilde's critical essays in *Intentions,* looked upon them with deep suspicion, or regarded them with condescending tolerance" (157). This is an important statement, for it accurately summarizes prevailing attitudes toward Wilde's literary criticism up to the late 1980s, when Richard Ellmann's studies of Wilde began to change (although by no means eradicate) these attitudes.

Zhang summarizes René Wellek's *History of Modern Criticism,* with its chapter on the "English Aesthetic Movement," in which Algernon Swinburne and Walter Pater, but not Wilde, are discussed. Wellek, Zhang observes, takes a "highly patronizing" point of view that "insufficiently acknowledges the independent value of Wilde's thought," and attributes the prominence of Wilde's ideas on art to the "myth or legend" surrounding him as a martyr (158).

Wellek is particularly critical, Zhang writes, of Wilde's ideas on creative criticism in "The Critic as Artist." Wilde maintains that "the highest Criticism, being the purest form of personal impression, is in its way more creative than creation" and "treats the work of art simply as a starting point for a new creation." Wellek appears to feel that this point of view "confuses criticism with creation and misleads the critic," rendering the critic too subjective. Wellek sees poetic criticism as "irrelevancy," citing as examples the Mona Lisa passage in Pater, the "ostentatious fireworks" of Swinburne, and the "charming reflections" of Anatole France," which Wellek portrays as now out of fashion and presenting no danger to the profession of literary criticism.

Zhang states that Wellek's remarks date from 1960 and are now passé. By the 1970s and 1980s, Wellek was growing more and more displeased with trends in criticism — deconstruction, reception theory, and reader-response criticism, which in his view were all a dangerous revival of Wilde's ideas of creative criticism (159). Wellek thought these Wildean developments represented the "breakdown or even the abolition of all traditional literary scholarship and teaching" (159).

Zhang's comment is astute: "This rather gloomy prognosis of the destruction of literary studies by contemporary criticism sounds ironically like Wilde's own prophecy perversely fulfilled. 'It is to criticism that the future belongs,' Wilde declares. If creation is to last at all, it can only do so on the condition of becoming far more critical than it is at present" (159). Wellek's gloomy, angry view, Zhang proposes, arises from "his awareness that his own concept of criticism, which fifty years ago was regarded as so radical that it was attacked by traditionalists as the destruction of literary studies, is now regarded as old-fashioned by the younger generation of critics" (159).

Zhang then summarizes views of various critics who attack creative criticism, and who regard the optimal mode of criticism as one that is a commentary arising "after and because of the primary text of literature." But the "essential problem" of Wilde's critics, he argues, is "condemnation of creative criticism without proper attention to Wilde's ideas and exposition" (160). He praises the "coherent and symmetrical" structure of Wilde's dialogues, reminding us that "The Decay of Lying" posits "the bold creed of the new aesthetics," namely Wilde's claim that "Life imitates art far more than Art imitates life" and that "Life holds the Mirror up to Art." This refers, Zhang observes, to the attempts of fashionable ladies to dress like the beautiful figures in the paintings of Rossetti and Burne-Jones, and also to the "far more profound truth that art helps to shape our own vision of the reality of life and nature and that we see things only as we have first created them" (160).

Zhang connects Wilde's thinking here with that of contemporary, particularly poststructural, criticism. He mentions Eugenio Donato's remark, that the germ of a poststructuralist idea can be found in

Wilde's notion, namely that Japan and the Japanese as presented in art are pure inventions — that "representation cannot function without generating within itself the pseudoscience of an 'object.'" Donato compares this idea to Flaubert's realization that art is illusion.

Zhang also looks back in literary history for antecedents. In Wilde's idea that things "are because we see them, and what we see, and how we see it, depends on the Arts that have influenced us" (161), Zhang finds a hint of Vico, even though no direct connection between the two could have existed. In Sir Philip Sidney's *Apology for Poetry* Longxi finds another similarity: Sidney emphasizes the meaning "of poet as maker who creates, like God his own Maker, ex nihilo," and "to the charge of lying, Sidney rebuts that if to lie is to affirm as true what is actually false, then the poet 'nothing affirms, and therefore never lieth.'" Poetry is overtly fictional, in other words (162). Wilde thus "joins Sidney in the long apologetic tradition in an ironical way, turning the opposition of truth and fiction into a paradox and an aphorism" (162). Echoes of Sidney can be heard in the Preface to *The Picture of Dorian Gray*, where Wilde asserts that "no artist desires to prove anything. Even things that are true can be proved" (162).

Zhang writes that if "'The Decay of Lying' expounds the idea of life imitating art, this idea is then paralleled by that of creative criticism set forth in 'The Critic as Artist,' where Wilde maintains that if we understand nature and life through art, then we understand art through criticism. According to Wilde's argument, we learn to appreciate the glorious sky at sunset because of Turner, but we admire Turner because Ruskin has taught us how to understand his paintings . . ." (162–63). Pointing to acceptance of this argument by W. K. Wimsatt and Northrop Frye, Zhang praises Wilde's more advanced views: "Wilde's idea goes much further than the famous intentional fallacy of the New Critics and even further than Frye [who dismisses authorial intention by arguing that only 'criticism can talk, and all the arts are dumb'], for Wilde conceives of criticism as purely subjective . . ." (164). Wilde's "plea for radical subjectivity" leads almost to "something like Roland Barthes's radical pronouncement of 'The Death of the Author'" (164). By this, Zhang means that the Barthean critic is interested not in defining the author's intention but in reacting with his own writing to that of the writer under discussion.

Zhang mentions also Edward Said's interest in Wilde's creative criticism, and his ready acceptance of Wilde's idea of criticism "as an independent creation" (165). Wilde and Nietzsche, Said remarks, help us to see the importance of the role of criticism in the production of literary meanings, and in this context Said mentions powerful misreadings, bringing Freud and Nietzsche in as examples. "This leads us naturally," Zhang infers, "to Harold Bloom's idea of creative misreading or 'misprision,'" which affects poetry, reading, and criticism (166). Bloom begins *The Anxiety of Influence* "by citing Wilde as a perfect example of how devastating poetic influence can be," and casting Wilde as a poet who failed by being unable to overcome his anxiety of influences (166). Frank Lentricchia interprets Bloom's career according to the theory of the anxiety of influence, showing it as "a prolonged warfare with his new critical fathers," and with "traces of Wilde's influence in his revisionary poetics" (167).

Zhang discusses Geoffrey Hartman's *Criticism in the Wilderness,* which attempts, in Hartman's words, "to view criticism, in fact, as within literature, not outside of it looking in," a Wildean view (167).

Carefully, Zhang points out ways in which Wilde differs from deconstructive critics like Bloom and Hartman: "In deconstructive criticism . . . the idea of creative criticism is perhaps pushed in a direction Wilde may not have expected and may not endorse. While the deconstructive critic takes great pains to pull the text apart by exposing its fissures or internal inconsistencies, Wilde's aesthetic critic is much more interested in the pleasure of the text, the enjoyment of the beautiful" (168).

Praising Wilde for recognizing that objectivity is an illusion, Zhang concludes, "Wilde's creative criticism . . . seeks to open the text of an artistic work and its inexhaustible meaning rather than close it once and for all with a seal of authority" (170).

Peter Raby

Peter Raby, editor of an introductory study, *The Cambridge Companion to Oscar Wilde* (1997), and author of *The Importance of Being Earnest: A Reader's Companion* (1995), sums up major themes of recent Wilde criticism: His "radical position as a critic has been re-evaluated. He has been identified as a key figure within gay criticism. He is now recognized as a highly professional writer, acutely aware of his readership at a variety of levels, and also one who deliberately and systematically explored the oral dimension. His position as an Irish writer gives him status in the context of postcolonial criticism. The centenary of his trial, and the approaching centenary of his death as we approach our own fin de siècle, gives him a special contemporary relevance." Raby finishes with the usual admission of one who, having studied Wilde, finds him more difficult to understand than ever: "In defiance of what might seem critical overkill, Wilde, both as a writer and individual, remains as elusive as ever" (xv).

Isobel Murray

In "Oscar Wilde in His Literary Element: Yet Another Source for Dorian Gray?," Isobel Murray arrives at a surprising and intriguing thesis. She suggests that Louisa May Alcott's sensational and often pseudonymous novels, in particular *A Modern Mephistopheles*, first published in 1877 before Huysmans's *À Rebours*, influenced Wilde's *Picture of Dorian Gray*. Wilde met Alcott in New York, where they were guests of honor at a reception in 1882. They shared a lifelong admiration of Emerson, who had been a friend of Louisa's father, Bronson Alcott. Murray suggests that by 1889, when Wilde was working on *The Picture of Dorian Gray* as well as a story with similar themes, "The Fisherman and His Soul," Alcott's novel's title must have appealed to him. In *A Modern Mephistopheles*, Murray finds in Alcott's character, Jasper Helwyze, a model for Wilde's Lord Henry Wotton (285).

Much of the article includes comparisons of scenes and situations from Alcott's novel, involving mind control or manipulation by Jaspar Helwyze — whose surname (sounding like "Hell Wise") certainly suggests intimacy with the devil — and his victims, especially a young man, Felix, who is in some ways comparable to Dorian Gray. Murray summarizes "Wilde's temporary engagement with and attachment to *A Modern Mephistopheles*," asserting that the "most important way in which the Alcott novel offers suggestion to the author of *The Picture of Dorian Gray* is in her development of the character of Jaspar Helwyze" (294). Like Lord Henry, he seems to have ideas borrowed from Walter Pater, he is a spectator of life, he likes to influence others, and he is obsessively curious. Her argument is convincing, original, and entertaining.

Patricia Flanagan Behrendt

Oscar Wilde, Eros and Aesthetics, by Patricia Flanagan Behrendt, is an extremely uneven book. Although generally well written, and including some perceptive close readings in the first half, it also contains misperceptions of the women in Wilde's plays, which appear to this reader curiously moralistic, rigid, and stereotypically "Victorian." A few basic plot errors also occur in Behrendt's summaries of these plays. For example, she states that Lady Windermere, of *Lady Windermere's Fan*, "is the product of an affair that her mother had conducted with an opportunist much like Lord Darlington," Lord Darlington being the man who tries to get Lady Windermere to run away with him.

There are two inaccuracies in Behrendt's statement. Lady Windermere is not the product of an affair, but of a legitimate union; we know this because Mrs. Erlynne comes across a goodbye note Lady Windermere has written in desperation to Lord Windermere, when Lady Windermere plans to run off with Lord Darlington. Mrs. Erlynne says, "The same words that twenty years ago I wrote to her father!" (408). She also indicates that Lady Windermere is leaving her husband the same way that Mrs. Erlynne left her husband, and for the same reasons.

The second inaccuracy lies in the characterization of Lord Darlington. He is much more than an opportunist. He loves Lady Windermere — impulsively but genuinely — and makes impossible demands, namely that she decide to go away with him immediately or not at all. But his saving grace is that he is as desperate as she — and that complicates the charge of opportunism. Most of Wilde's characters are complicated, and Behrendt occasionally oversimplifies them.

Other inaccuracies include misrepresentation of statements by Richard Ellmann, who wrote the definitive biography of Wilde for our time. These will be discussed later.

The book is divided into five chapters, each dealing with a main thesis concerning the relationship of Wilde's aesthetics to sexual themes as understood in classical Greek thought, that is, the struggle to maintain a balance between satisfaction of passion and self-control, when necessary (ix). This approach is entirely appropriate for Wilde, a deeply psychological thinker, always aware of feeling driven by inner, unconscious conflicts, and who used Greek concepts such as Nemesis to allude to them, similar to Freud, whose thinking often lay in the same direction.

Behrendt states that one of the "more overlooked aspects of the concept of Eros is the bisexuality of the original image, which essentially frees it from what we would today call gender specific stereotypes" (ix). This remark is well-taken. Exploring the bisexuality of Wilde and his literary creations is a way of exploring his deep ambivalence in many areas, an ambivalence that gave him pleasure and heightened his creativity, but at times caused him deep and insoluble conflicts. Behrendt's thoughtful, personal, and self-analytic preface explores the ways in which Wilde inspires ambivalence in his readers.

Chapter one, "Eros and Aesthetics," begins with an arresting observation, that "very little attention has been paid in scholarship to the relationship between Wilde's literary aesthetics and his complex sexual identity" (1). Behrendt discusses the difficulty of knowing Wilde's private life from firsthand sources, and mentions Richard Ellmann's life of Wilde as an account that "will probably assume the status of a definitive biography." However, she takes issue with Ellmann, asserting that he characterizes Wilde "as a writer whose literary accomplishments were achieved in spite of his homosexual entanglements and the uproar which they seemingly introduced into his personal life" (2). This misrepresents Ellmann. Discussing Wilde's first homosexual encounters with Robert Ross and the spate of journalistic writings that Wilde subsequently produced for the *Pall Mall Gazette,* Ellmann remarked that these articles "exhibit a freshness not often present in his earlier work, as if to suggest that running foul of the law in his sexual life was a stimulus to thought on every subject. At least he knew where he stood. His new sexual direction liberated his art. It also liberated his critical faculty" (Ellmann 270).

Despite this, Behrendt insists that Ellmann found it "impossible . . . to envision a positive, stimulating relationship between Wilde's homosexual nature and his aesthetic development" (2). She does not distinguish between destructive personal aspects of some of Wilde's relationships as discussed by Ellmann — Lord Alfred Douglas proved to be a huge emotional and financial drain on Wilde, egging him on to his fatal legal challenge against Douglas's insane father — and the curiously stimulating effect that all the fights with Douglas seem to have had on Wilde's creative powers.

Behrendt goes on to mention that in the last two decades a number of studies of Wilde have appeared "which attempt to analyze certain elements of his style in terms of a psychic conflict related to his sexuality" (3). She quotes Eve Kosofsky Sedgwick's ideas that parts of Wilde's *The Picture of Dorian Gray* were used "as a handbook of gay style and behavior," but goes into no particular details. Behrendt's point is that not enough has been said on the score of Wilde's sexuality and its relationship to his aesthetic development.

This focus on sexual subject matter in literary works is, she feels, "an almost entirely new avenue for critical discourse" (5), and perhaps she is right if one does not count the work of Freud and other writers in applied psychoanalysis. She makes the valid point that a scholarly approach to sexual themes and imagery in literature is "an intellectually and emotionally complex, as well as controversial, pursuit for the scholar on a personal level," and quotes Steven Marcus, whose pioneering work on Victorian attitudes toward sexuality inspired him to examine his own feelings about delving into the subject (6). Behrendt observes that it is more common for scholars to avoid the subjective aspects of research into sexuality, remarking that "in another study on Victorian sexuality, *Corrupt Relations* (1982), none of the collaborating authors acknowledges the subject matter as anything more than an objective area of inquiry which stands apart from the researching self." The "very stance of the literary critic," she writes, "implies that she or he brings to the subject an objective methodology which promises to produce authoritative understanding" (7).

She then makes a remark that is consistent with Wilde's own thinking on the subject of what we call objectivity: "every reader and writer knows that there is no such thing as an objective stance in either literary or scientific discourse in this area of inquiry as long as we all possess libido" (7). Treading lightly through Julia Kristeva, Michel Foucault, and Leo Bersani on the subject of discourse about sexuality, she concludes with the thinking of Havelock Ellis, namely, that sex and sexuality are "the central problem of life." She states, "To study the treatment of sexuality in a writer's work is, therefore, to study a central impulse in the development of his or her aesthetics and world view — an impulse which combines with the impulses of others as a central motivating factor in the development of culture" (8).

Her following section on the politics of sexual discourse in nineteenth-century England is among the most clearly written and perceptive that I have read. Behrendt begins with a striking thesis: "Since all discourse on sexual subject matter, including the literary and the scientific, contributes to public perceptions of sexual behavior and to the formulation of public policy or laws, the act of writing itself cannot be separated from the political, even when carried out in the sphere of literary criticism, which may seem, to some, remote from any sphere of influence other than the academic" (9). She points out that the political nature of discourse on sexuality was "never more clearly illustrated than in mid-nineteenth-century England, during the period which corresponds to Wilde's early childhood in England" (9). Discussing the physician William Acton's scientific discourse on prostitution, which resulted in the Contagious Diseases Act of 1866, and various writers who did not dare to write about homosexuality at that time, Behrendt proves her thesis well. She goes into detail about Jeremy Bentham's private documentation of his objections to the vicious prosecutions of homosexuals under English law in the 1770s, objections he dared not publish because his political opponents would then have had a powerful weapon for discrediting his whole program of Utilitarian reforms (10–11). She covers briefly but thoroughly the grisly history of English laws concerning homosexuality, starting in 1533 when male homosexual acts were declared by Parliament to be capital acts punishable by death, and ending with the 1885 Criminal Law Amendment Act that had been designed to protect underage girls taken into brothels, but also designated sodomy as a crime punishable by "ten years' penal servitude as a maximum." Some of her formulations about Wilde's attitude toward the law, however, seem naïve. Having made the point that several types of discourse about homosexuality were at odds politically, namely the scientific discourse of writers like Havelock Ellis and the discourse of *belles lettres,* Behrendt makes the following claim: Wilde, "in sacrificing himself to the atrophied language of the law, when he could simply have crossed the Channel, had forgotten or failed to realize that in the language of literature — like that used against him in court — and in the language of the law, themes and ideas which invoke 'the unspeakable' refer to entirely different concerns about the nature of homosexuality" (14). For instance, *belles lettres,* she says, idealized homosexual love in transcendent and sublime terms.

This oversimplifies Wilde's motivation for his strange, self-destructive behavior. She writes, "Wilde's political naïveté — which led him directly to prison — is evident in his obvious assumption that the poetic language of the artist on the witness stand could prevail against the language of the law. After all, society had always applauded his verbal ability to hold a roomful of people in thrall" (15). But Wilde was politically sophisticated in many areas, certainly well aware of the need for discretion if he did not wish to be harassed as a homosexual, and he knew firsthand, from early childhood, the difficulties of an urban, Protestant Irishman with one foot in English and another in Irish Catholic language and culture. Well aware of unconscious forces driving him to do foolish, irrevocable things, Wilde spoke of "feasting with panthers," of "Nemesis" catching him in her net, and of being a "catspaw" between Lord Alfred Douglas and his father. From time to time Wilde admitted that he alone had been responsible for fatally foolish behavior.

Returning to the topic of sexual studies and their connection to politics, Behrendt remarks that feminist and gender criticism, as well as criticism dealing with homosexuality and lesbianism in literature, is political. What varies, she points out, "is the degree to which scholars either acknowledge the political nature of these forms of discourse or openly address the political issues involved." She adds that the "potentially volatile, personal and political nature of sexual subject matter should be acknowledged between author and reader as a matter of moral judiciousness and of moral honesty" (16).

And that is far from being the only problem. "Audience receptivity on the subject of sexuality," due to the capacity of sexuality to disturb and trouble, varies considerably, and an audience remains "essentially quixotic and unpredictable from moment to moment." One often hears the cliché, she adds, that "Freud reduced everything to sex." This is a "hopelessly reductivist" accusation in itself, and Behrendt pins down the reason why with precision: "Implicit in the phrase is the idea that sex is something either low or trivial to which some otherwise elevated matter can be reduced" (17). For most people, "sexuality is the dark and secret self which one dares not assume is like anyone else's dark and secret self, nor dares to attempt to find out." And there are consequences for denying the complexity of our response to writing about sexual matters in literature. Behrendt says to do so is "to deny the matrix of experience in which most of us develop: the Judeo-Christian tradition in which sex and sexuality have become archetypally tainted with fear and anguish because they are associated with the fall of humankind from paradise and from the grace of God." We may understand all of this intellectually, but the hold of these myths on the collective psyche remains quite powerful, one typical, influential result being "the madonna-whore dichotomy which Freud identified" (17).

Her final point in this section is brilliant: "The idea that the study of sexuality may be a questionable (or reductivist) enterprise stems from the association of sex and sexuality with the ultimate reduction of humanity from the grace of god. No study can presume to proceed without acknowledging the magnitude of that issue in shaping the heritage of our attitudes toward the subject of sexuality." Scholarly views, which she goes on to demonstrate in her other chapters, have become "part of the problem, unwittingly, by discouraging fuller assessment of the significance of sexuality in Wilde's aesthetic development." Her goal is to "demonstrate what scholarship has, so far, disregarded — the consistent and dramatic nature of Wilde's sexual preoccupations in literature evident from his earliest published works" (19). This is a highly ambitious and worthy goal, and I think the book should be judged by the degree of difficulty implied by this task, as well as by the author's uneven success in achieving her goal. Assessing the significance of sexuality, apart from identifying its presence in Wilde's works, is a very tall order.

In chapter two, "Sexual Drama in the Early Poetry," Behrendt provides close textual readings of homoerotic themes in Wilde's early poetry. Hers is probably the most thorough study done on this topic. She begins with evaluations of previous approaches to Wilde's poetry, mentioning that early twentieth-century critical attention both to Wilde's works and to his personal life "largely avoided discussions of sexual issues, because reference of any kind necessarily would raise the spectre of Wilde's homosexual behavior." This, many believed, cast a pall on his literary achievement. But Philip Cohen "noted in one of the first studies in recent criticism to consider the reflections of homosexuality in Wilde's writings, [that] Wilde himself extolled the importance of the whole personality in an artist's works" (22).

In chapter three, "Sexuality and Death: The Fate of Wilde's Heterosexual Lovers," Behrendt examines two of Wilde's early plays, *Vera: Or, the Nihilists,* and *The Duchess of Padua,* finding in them the literary influences of Dante and Dostoevsky as well as "the same preoccupation as the major poetry — the concern with the quest for self-knowledge — which reveals the individual torn between instincts and rationality" (64). As in the early poetry, characters in these early plays are often removed from country settings and placed in the city, "where they confront traditions, customs, and belief patterns and ideologies with which they find themselves in deep conflict" (64). These difficulties are what push them "along the path to self-discovery. . . ." Behrendt finds in each case that self-discovery revolves around "sexual involvements which produce anxiety . . . and an untimely death which intervenes ultimately and renders heterosexual passion sexless" (64).

In her close reading of *Vera: Or, the Nihilists,* Behrendt stresses the inner conflicts of the characters — an appropriate emphasis, since inner conflict proved to be a major theme in Wilde's own life, expressed openly in his letters and more subtly in the conflict and contradiction of his paradoxical epigrams. Behrendt points out that even in the title, "Vera," the Latin for "truth" is contrasted with nihilism, which "asserts basically that there is no such thing as truth." Wilde may, she suggests, have also had in mind the Russian meaning of Vera, which is "faith." But more importantly, "the title involves the concept of the divided self . . . the *doppelgänger* — a device central in Russian literature and in the works of Dostoevsky in particular" (65).

Identifying a country versus city motif in *Vera,* Behrendt writes that the "country reveals the individual either in harmony or in conflict with nature as a part of nature's endless cycles of death and rebirth. By contrast, the city is a vision of the world created by human beings which reflects complex and conflicting sets of beliefs, moral codes, and behaviors which form the core of the culture." Vera's transformation occurs in tandem with her move from country to city; she begins as a "simple country girl" and becomes a "big-city nihilist." When she takes the nihilist oath, "to strangle whatever nature is" in her, she rejects both her country origins and her natural self (67). Her natural desires lead her to fall in love with the one man whom her political ideals should force her to reject, the future Czar. Michael, the man who loves Vera, sends her off to assassinate the future Czar, knowing that to do so will in some way destroy her. Behrendt recognizes this move as the beginning of a theme developed throughout Wilde's career, which culminates in an epigram in his final, post-prison poem, *The Ballad of Reading Gaol,* namely that "each man kills the thing he loves" (67).

Ultimately, Behrendt suggests, the "psychic and ideological conflicts in *Vera* reveal Wilde's vision of the relationship between sexuality and death." Vera's conflict, between love for an individual and loyalty to a cause, is one to which Wilde frequently returns in his later plays. Behrendt might have added that Wilde also returned to it in his life, where the lines between loyalty to an individual — his lover, Lord Alfred Douglas — and loyalty to his cause — the rights of the homosexual — blurred, causing the political to become personal. "A patriot put in prison for loving his country loves his country," Wilde said after he had been released from prison, "And a poet in prison for loving boys loves boys" (*Letters,* 705). Behrendt could have developed her argument further, taking into account the relationship of the conflicts between characters in Wilde's plays and the conflicts of his life. After all, Wilde admitted that he had put his genius into his life but only his talent into his works.

Detailing aspects of *Vera* that "establish the play's importance in the development of Wilde's thought," namely that Vera alters her personality "in the service of an idea," Behrendt places this transformation in the context of similar trends in Victorian literature, comparing Wilde's experiments in altering personality in *Vera* and *Dorian Gray* to the late nineteenth century interest in crime and criminal behavior. She remarks that interest in extremes of behavior was stirred up by Jack the Ripper as well as Stevenson's Jekyll and Hyde and Conan Doyle's Sherlock Holmes (70). Wilde, of course, read these writers, and had lunch with Conan Doyle while Doyle was working on *The Sign of Four* and Wilde was working on *The Picture of Dorian Gray.* Behrendt is impressed by Wilde's interest in the "growing popularity" of personality, and the fact that Vera's personality (and, though she does not state it, Dorian Gray's) is altered by an idea, not through some chemical substance, as in *Dr. Jekyll and Mr. Hyde.*

Wilde was, Behrendt believes, influenced by "specifically Russian models in the work of Dostoevsky" when considering models of personality (71). She points to certain patterns in Dostoevsky that may have been emulated by Wilde, for example, that Raskolnikov in *Crime and Punishment* is altered when Sonia Marmeladov reads to him from the Bible, while Dorian is altered by the book given to him by Lord Henry. Wilde's Vera is altered after reading the nihilist creed. The same idea of the transformation of personality through a single text is also used in Wilde's other early drama, *The Duchess of Padua*. In this drama, or melodrama, the heterosexual lovers, Guido and Beatrice, end in a double suicide. Behrendt remarks that "While self-knowledge is possible in Wilde's world view mutual understanding between the sexes is finally impossible" (91).

Chapter four, "Eroticism and the Dialogic Form," begins with a daring claim: "No author's literary *oeuvre* offers a more complex portrayal of sexual subject matter than that of Oscar Wilde." (Hardy? Shakespeare? Ben Jonson?) Still, this is a claim Wilde might have made himself, had he been living in the twentieth century, and like any Wildean truth it has its validity. Behrendt does not expand upon this statement, but instead launches into a discussion of Wilde's "deeply pessimistic view of the attractions and repulsions of heterosexuality" (93).

In her discussion of Wilde's reasons for marrying, Behrendt quotes Richard Ellmann's assessment: "a wife would save him from the moralists, and a rich one from the moneylenders." This is a lighthearted, Wildean view of the difficult situation into which Wilde was cast as a closeted homosexual with considerable ambition to be in the public eye. Behrendt takes Ellmann's remark in a more moralistic vein than it seems to have been intended, suggesting that his "justifiably unflattering assessment implies serious complications for the future of such a marriage." This seems beside the point. She castigates Wilde, insisting that he saw his marriage as "an active disguise . . . involve[ing] the commandeering of another life . . . such a ploy is highly unethical by any standards . . ." (95). As Wilde said, "Morality is simply the attitude we adopt towards people whom we personally dislike" (*CW*, 519). Wilde's desperate need for self-concealment, along with other, lesser known motives, are matters deserving discussion here, but Behrendt ignores them.

She harps on Wilde's "self-centered decision to marry" and "lack of compassion concerning the quality of his wife's life, including her pregnancies" — remarks which seem curiously moralistic rather than helpful in understanding him. That he apparently found his wife's pregnant body repulsive is not surprising, considering his earlier wish to see her as a "grave, slight, violet-eyed little Artemis" (*Letters,* 154), that is, a virgin goddess of the hunt, a boyish sort of a girl, very much like the boyish Sibyl Vane in Dorian Gray. Imagining Constance as a boy may have been the only possible means for him to experience any sexual arousal with her, so that the proof positive of her female sexual identity, evident in her pregnancy, not surprisingly repulsed him. But none of these issues are explored by Behrendt. Instead, she asserts that Ellmann's "portrayal of the affair with [Robert] Ross" — the first man with whom Wilde slept — "is an attempt to portray Wilde . . . as some sort of victim of the homosexual experience. . . . Ellmann seems intent upon restoring a measure of innocence or of naïveté to Wilde's image by suggesting that he fell prey to dark values after the onset of the affair with Ross . . ." (97). I find no support for this view; it seems a willful misreading of Ellmann.

Behrendt goes on to argue that Wilde's "manipulation of the dialogue form," particularly in "The Decay of Lying" (1888) and "The Critic as Artist" (1890), is tantamount to his role on the social scene, because, she asserts, in both cases an older man engages a younger man in conversation in "seemingly Socratic fashion" (100). She criticizes Wilde scholarship for "failing to notice . . . the spiritual seduction of the younger man by the older one, in both dialogues," which she claims "personifies Wilde's premise throughout — that art initiates the perceiver into new realms of experience which are also, in the case of both dialogues, male identified" (105).

There is no evidence to suggest that the main speaker is an older man seducing a younger man. Quite the contrary: sometimes the younger one obviously seduces the older. Wilde took the names of his two sons, Cyril and Vyvyan, for the speakers in "The Decay of Lying," and at the time Cyril was three and Vyvyan two years old. In the dialogue, Vivian (as the name is there spelled) is clearly the leader, and at one point tells Cyril that he would not be admitted to Vivian's club, the Tired Hedonists, because "you are a little too old. We don't admit anybody who is of the usual age" (972). Since Vyvyan was Wilde's younger son, and since he twits Cyril for being too old, it is reasonable to assume that Vyvyan is younger. And in life, Wilde seems by several accounts — Trelawny Backhouse's and Bernard Shaw's — to have been the one seduced by the much younger, but more experienced Lord Alfred Douglas. Behrendt, however, insists: "both dialogues take place between an older and a younger man: Vivian and Cyril respectively in 'The Decay of Lying,' Gilbert and Ernest in 'The Critic as Artist.' Since the older characters are more knowledgeable and worldly, they intellectually dominate Cyril and Earnest" (109). There is evidence that the reverse is true. Wilde wrote a number of epigrams honoring the wisdom of the young, and one of his closest friends, Reginald Turner, who took care of him in his last days, wrote a letter showing how Wilde often felt himself to be seduced by younger men, although he recognized his own seductive powers: "It was [Wilde's] theory that it was always the young who seduce the old . . . One of the most serious conversations I had with Oscar was on that subject when he said that no one had any real influence on anyone else. At that time I ventured strongly to deny that, but when I began to think that he was perhaps rather arguing with himself than trying to convince me I desisted" (Wilde, MST91L/S988, autograph letter signed, 26 August 1935, Reginald Turner to A. J. A. Symons, in William Andrews Clark Memorial Library, Los Angeles, CA).

Behrendt's idea that the dialogues grew out of Wilde's urge to perform live in conversation is a good one, and it is true that the dialogue in his plays — particularly in *The Importance of Being Earnest* — grew out of real conversations, often between himself and Lord Alfred Douglas. There are many other insightful moments in her discussion of the dialogues — for instance, she singles out a passage in "The Critic as Artist" in which Gilbert remarks that egotism "is not without its attractions." She compares this to a passage in Freud, in which Freud suggests that "one person's narcissism has a great attraction for those others who had renounced a part of their own narcissism . . . the charm of a child lies to a great extent in his narcissism" (112–13). There are indeed striking similarities between the perceptions of Wilde and Freud, and much more could be made of them. But Behrendt returns to her argument that in Wilde's dialogues the younger man is converted to the beliefs and values of the older, whereas in reality it is likelier that the reverse is true, or that the ages of the men in the dialogues are not meant to differ significantly.

Chapter five, "The Dandy *Coup de Théâtre:* Homosexual Eros and the London Stage," opens with a psychological acute observation: "Oscar Wilde's literary works as a whole, in the decade from 1880 to 1890, reveal that his central concern is the conflict between biological drives — primarily erotic impulses — and conscious intellectual perceptions in the development of personality" (119). This is again one of his interesting similarities to Freud. After summarizing some of her earlier findings — for instance, that Wilde's view of heterosexual relationships is in his early work pessimistic — Behrendt turns to a discussion of the dandies in his plays, asserting that the "central question for scholarship and plays alike concerns the meaning of the dandy; or, how are we to interpret his words and his actions?" The dandy is deliberately paradoxical, she notes, but then claims that Wilde exploits the nature of the paradox, making it "impossible for the perceiver to know in which half of the paradox truth resides for the dandy" (122). The answer, of course, is both, a fact of which Behrendt should surely be aware, judging by the astute commentary of her earlier chapters.

What is new in Behrendt's argument is her interest in the dandy in relation to homosexual Eros. Discussing in detail the plots of all four comedies, Behrendt wants to show that the dandy is essentially homosexual, which seems unconvincing and is not the most important aspect of the dandy. Because the dandy speaks against marriage does not mean he is always homosexual. Scores of English novels and plays criticize marriage as an institution. But Behrendt hunts out Wilde's criticisms through his dandies, suggesting that criticism of marriage by dandies is tantamount to dandy representations of homosexuality as a better life choice. She quotes Lord Darlington, who tries to seduce Lady Windermere by telling her that he knows she can't live with a man who lies to her. Behrendt points out that these lines "suggest the hypocrisy of marriage, invoke[ing] the image of Wilde's own marriage, which he contrived as a mask for his secretive relationships with men" (138). This Wilde did, but men have other reasons for becoming hypocrites in their marriages. Wilde's outsider status as a homosexual gave him a certain perspective on marriage — perhaps a more disinterested view of the difficulties and necessary hypocrisies of the institution.

Behrendt seems shocked, rather than amused, by Wilde's resolutions of the play's problems: "The play ends on a note of seeming domestic happiness with the young couple reunited. However, the arrangement is based entirely upon false understandings of what has transpired" (140). Behrendt finds it wrong that Lord Windermere continues to believe in his wife's ignorance and naïveté, when in fact she has learned a great deal about the character of the fallen Mrs. Erlynne and has grown to like her. Behrendt finds it pathetic that the Windermeres don't understand each other. That is not pathetic, but comedic; Wilde recognizes the different emotional needs of men and women, jesting that "the proper basis for marriage is a mutual misunderstanding" (CW, 172). This is a realistic, not cynical remark. Behrendt fails to recognize the comedy.

Similar problems abound with Behrendt's analysis of *A Woman of No Importance,* in which she portrays the dandy Lord Illingworth as anti-woman, and as a man who "explicitly suggests that women may never aspire to the ruling order of the dandy" (151). She lays this charge at Lord Illingworth's door because he makes charming, psychologically perceptive, politically incorrect, remarks: "Women are pictures. Men are problems. If you want to know what a woman really means — which, by the way, is always a dangerous thing to do — look at her, don't listen to her." Gerald, his naïve son, then asks, "But haven't women got a refining influence?" and Lord Illingworth replies, "Nothing refines but the intellect." He probably means that because both men and women are sexual creatures, neither possess a refining influence. True, Illingworth also says that "women represent the triumph of matter over mind — just as men represent the triumph of mind over morals" (*CW*, 460), but this is a tongue-in-cheek jest meant to jostle the staid Gerald. We know from Illingworth's behavior that he enjoys the conversation of witty, sophisticated women like Mrs. Allonby, who remain unencumbered by traditional Victorian morality. Such women might themselves be recognized as dandies.

But Mrs. Allonby, who, Behrendt admits, "some scholars consider a female dandy," is in her view "the epitome of Lord Illingworth's description of the tyrannizing, materialistic pettiness of the female sex" (*CW*, 153). Behrendt sees neither humor nor truth in Mrs. Allonby's delightful remarks about the ideal man, whom Mrs. Allonby says "should talk to us as if we were goddesses, and treat us as if we were children. He should refuse all our serious requests and gratify every one of our whims . . ." (*CW*, 447 and Behrendt 153).

In what appear to be shocked tones, Behrendt comments, "Here Wilde uses a woman to suggest that women not only prefer to be regarded as ineffectual children but also consider the 'ideal man' to be one who ensures them that role" (153). Is it really necessary to remonstrate that women as well as men occasionally wish to play the child in the relationship, and that Mrs. Allonby has a particularly charming way of putting this? It is clear from her conversations with Lord Illingworth that they consider each other equals. Her views on the ideal man do not contradict, but rather corroborate this. She and Lord Illingworth freely accept the childlike and childish nature of both sexes, especially in romantic and sexual relationships — which many of the other characters do not. To insist, as Behrendt does, that there is "nothing sympathetic to women or to women's concerns in the play" (152) is to take the position of the moralists whom Wilde spent his career unmasking.

In Behrendt's interpretation, Lord Illingworth's main interest in his son, Gerald, is homosexual — a point of view first uttered by Lytton Strachey, who was joking. But Lord Illingworth has always wanted a son, and expresses a wish to help Gerald as a father and as an older man established in the world and knowledgeable about its ways.

Turning to Wilde's *An Ideal Husband*, Behrendt sees the dandy Lord Goring as a man whose "interference in the affairs of another man creates a bond between them" — a bond which she sees as homosexual, and based upon "contempt for women" (160–61). Taking this position requires losing her sense of humor. She characterizes Mabel Chiltern, the younger sister of the female lead role, as "a minor, selfish, materialistic wit," because she gives the following reason for not wanting to marry a genius, the kind of man she sees her sister as having married: Geniuses, Mabel says, "are always thinking about themselves, when I want them to be thinking about me" (*CW*, 513). This is a lively, perceptive apprehension of the typical narcissism of the truly gifted, and anything but a sign of shallowness on Mabel's part.

In sum, Behrendt sees the dandy as misogynist, not psychologist. But if that were all there were to the dandy, these comedies could not have lasted. They are grounded in love of humanity and acceptance of human foibles.

Finally, Behrendt borrows Mary McCarthy's atypical characterization of *The Importance of Being Earnest* as a "ferocious idyll" — a point of view with which only George Bernard Shaw agreed, presumably because he envied Wilde's talent and success. "The fact that the dandy's humor masks an aggressive manipulation of the listener undoubtedly accounts for the schizophrenic responses of reviewers and critics alike to the play at the time of its premiere as well as in the more recent past" (169–70). It is *not* a fact that the dandy behaves in an aggressively manipulative manner — he teases gently more often than he attacks — and it is not accurate to suggest that most critics react schizophrenically to the play. Most critics say this is Wilde's best comedy and emphasize its lightness, not its aggression.

The final chapter, "Epilogue: Speaking the Unspeakable," makes some interesting — and some inaccurate — observations about the dandy. Behrendt rightly states that the dandies in all four comedies are intellectually superior to the other characters "in matters of self-knowledge," but she is wrong to insist that what sets them apart is their "manipulative insights into the behaviors of others" (179). To call the dandies manipulative misleads by imputing to them a desire to harm others and lead them astray. Instead, they use their influence to change the minds of other characters who are less realistic than they are.

Dandies also, as Behrendt suggests, "assume a role similar to that of the Classical Greek chorus by becoming the audience's guide to the events of the plot" (179). Her final remark, that homosexual Eros is "at the core of Wilde's aesthetics," continues to intrigue, but is never convincingly developed (182).

Julia Prewitt Brown

Julia Prewitt Brown's *Cosmopolitan Criticism: Oscar Wilde's Philosophy of Art,* concerns what she considers Wilde's "most important, but also — especially today when it is in danger of being lost sight of altogether — most elusive legacy, his philosophy of art." In her preface, she states that "virtually everything" written by Wilde after 1888 dealt with a "philosophical problematic" that was "postdualist," and that, like much of nineteenth century philosophy, contained "a political vision, how-ever unsystematic." Continuing a trend of the 1990s, she does justice to Wilde's intellect, remarking that he has been "widely misunderstood and underestimated" (xiii).

In four chapters and an epilogue, Brown finds a significant place for Wilde in western European philosophy, stating, for example, that in some ways he prefigures Theodor Adorno and Walter Benjamin. She explores his idea that the future of art and of civilization depend on "cosmopolitan criticism," pointing out that Wilde was nothing if not "at home in the culture of other nations," but stressing that his contri-bution to philosophical ideas on art was "distinctly Anglo-Irish" (xiv).

Brown begins her book with a useful review of critical assessments of Wilde; she quotes Lionel Trilling's observation that although Wilde's importance as a thinker was steadily growing, it was likely to be over-shadowed by his posturing and martyrdom. That was in 1971. The "high esteem in which Wilde was held as a thinker by W. K. Wimsatt and Lionel Trilling, and more recently by Harold Bloom, has not led to the appreciation of Wilde's critical thinking that one might have ex-pected," Brown writes (xv).

Her ideas are innovative and original. She plays down the English tradition in Wilde and plays up the German and Continental, arguing that Walter Pater's place in the intellectual history she discusses is "relatively minor," and placing Wilde "in the European tradition of thought that stretches from Kant and Schiller, through Kierkegaard and Nietzsche, to the preeminent cosmopolitan artist-critics of this century, Benjamin and Adorno" (xviii). She argues that Wilde's "calculated dodginess" proved important in his attempts to overcome the separa-tion of morality and aesthetics that "governed the thought" of many nineteenth century writers; Wilde was aiming to bring together Hebraism and Hellenism, Apollo and Dionysius, and so forth.

In chapter one, "Wilde's Play-Drive and the Still More Difficult Art of Living," Brown suggests that Wilde "understood intuitively" as a boy "what he would have later learned from reading Friedrich Schiller: the relations between art and life are to be understood primarily in terms of play" (1). Although Brown does not say so, the idea was also important to Freud, who was, like Wilde, indebted to Schiller and Nietzsche; Freud's line of thought in "Creative Writers and Daydreaming" might have enriched her interesting argument. The importance and meaning of play for Wilde are not as fully developed as they might be in this chapter, which nonetheless makes interesting connections between Wilde and other Victorian figures — suggesting, for instance, that Wilde cast "the relationship with [Lord Alfred] Douglas . . . in terms . . . borrowed from Robert Louis Stevenson. In *The Strange Case of Dr. Jekyll and Mr. Hyde* (1886), a work Wilde knew well, it is Jekyll who creates Hyde out of himself . . . Like Hyde, Douglas made greater and greater claims on Wilde's life" (13).

"As Wilde matured, so did this allusive playfulness," Brown writes, "becoming at last the catalyst to his most somber art" (1). Her discussion of Wilde's use of the terms "art" and "life" is placed in the useful context of the dualism of other Victorian prose writers: "It is a mark of Wilde's slipperiness, but also of his sanity, that these key words art and life are simultaneously linked and counterpoised. This equivocation, moreover, is a consequence of Wilde's debt to his predecessors . . . Thomas Carlyle, John Ruskin, John Henry Newman, John Stuart Mill, and Matthew Arnold . . . caught in a dualism that, however different the language in which it is cast, entailed a disabling opposition between an aesthetic principle and an ethical one." Wilde, she seems to imply, felt freer to discard formulae, although he also did not abandon them; "In each of these writers . . . the intermittent qualities of the aesthetic (perception, spirit, spontaneity, inwardness) are set off against those marking the actions and responsibilities of beings who live in the world and who obey the imperative to order the ongoing experiences that Wilde called 'life'" (3).

Brown then makes the point that Wilde is closer to these major Victorians than to Walter Pater, with whose ideas he is often closely associated. But Pater, Brown asserts, had already "completely collapsed the distinction between 'art' and 'life' in the conclusion to the Renaissance, by placing art in the domain of sensations" (3).

This otherwise innovative chapter displays a naïve view of Wilde's sexuality and his — or anyone's — ability to make conscious decisions about sexual tastes. Brown writes that if Robert Sherard, Wilde's close friend, "can be trusted" in his account of Wilde's honeymoon, Wilde's marriage to Constance "was not unsatisfying to him" (11), adding that he wanted to return to his wife after prison. "This suggests that Wilde may have made a conscious choice to exploit a predisposition towards homosexuality," she claims (11). Wilde, in fact, spoke in more detail than the somewhat staid Sherard could stomach about the glories of a "young virgin" giving herself to her husband, but I would not therefore draw the conclusion that Wilde found his heterosexual activities satisfying. He may have been anxious to appear to find them satisfying, or he may have enjoyed the thought of arousing another man, Sherard, by telling him a sexual tale of his wedding night; the latter interpretation is consistent with Wilde's homosexuality.

One of Brown's interesting innovations is to connect Wilde with Kierkegaard, and to suggest that the philosophical alternatives facing Wilde could be found in Kierkegaard's *Either/Or*, specifically in the contrasting aesthetic and ethical philosophies of life described by Kierkegaard. But she draws the conclusion, again naïve, that "If Wilde's personal tragedy has any ultimate meaning, it presumably must be traced in terms of the problematical relation between ethics and aesthetics" (21). Surely there is much more to Wilde's personal tragedy than that. He was not led by conscious decisions, but by what he himself called "Necessity," referring to the Greek goddess Ananke, who drove him mysteriously, that is, unconsciously, toward his fate.

Brown concludes the chapter by quoting Wilde's deathbed quip, in which he said that the wallpaper in his bedroom was killing him and that one or the other of them would have to go. Remarking that "Wilde was an aesthete to the end, but he faced death with the resignation of a moralist" (22), Brown misses the point. He faced death with the wisdom of a humorist, not the resignation of a moralist. Wilde aimed never to be a moralist, though he could not always escape it. He shrewdly observed that "Morality is simply the attitude we adopt towards people whom we personally dislike" (*CW,* 519). Only at his worst, as in the heavy-handed *De Profundis,* was Wilde a moralist, but about that document Brown is curiously optimistic. She perceives it as a culmination of his philosophy, when it was, it seems to me, sad evidence of his mental and physical deterioration.

In chapter two, "Wilde and His Predecessors," Brown discusses cosmopolitanism and its paradoxes, beginning with the definition of a cosmopolitan as one who says, "The cosmos is my polis" (23). This is a good way of approaching Wilde's ambiguities and paradoxes. She writes, "The opposite of the provincial, though not of the patriot, the cosmopolitan may be compared to the nomad, who is at home no-where" (23–24), thus capturing Wilde's lifelong feeling of being at home everywhere, yet nowhere. Brown suggests that the archetypal nomad is Nietzsche, while the archetypal cosmopolitan is Wilde: "Whereas the nomad acknowledges no immediate roots, the cosmo-politan lays down roots everywhere he goes. He makes himself at home, for however brief a stay." Meanwhile, "he has roots, even 'origi-nal' ones, though he is perpetually cut off from them" (24).

Brown then moves to an interesting political speculation: Wilde, who "inherited from his parents an intense awareness of Irish national heritage," did not "embrace a provincial primitivism," but rather "de-colonized himself when he gave himself to the cosmopolitan critical spirit" (25). She points out that he wrote, "criticism which is based on patriotism is always provincial in its result" (25). "The ethnic element," she observes, "is essential to any authentic cosmopolitanism: it is the basis of the cosmopolitan's curious, melancholy, voluntary exile" (25). She explores the development and meaning of cosmopolitanism care-fully, remarking that in theory cosmopolitanism "appears to surrender at the outset all possibility of accounting for anything beyond the indi-vidual, yet in practice, cosmopolitan criticism engages the spirit of na-tionality in understanding above all that the distinctive differences among literatures, architectures, paintings and so on are necessarily bound up with the specific differences among peoples" (30). This is the heart of the chapter, its basic argument, which is built with skill and so-phistication. Wilde's irony "is not the ornament but the essence of cosmopolitanism" (31). His basic ideas stemmed more from Kant than Hegel, she argues, asserting that Wilde's writing "goes back beyond Hegel's vast synthesis of morality and happiness to the critical idealism of Kant." She equates Kant's ideas about the happiness of free rational beings with Wilde's remark in *De Profundis* that "To be entirely free, and at the same time entirely dominated by law is the eternal paradox of human life that we realize every moment" (33).

While the connections to Kant and Continental philosophy are in-triguing and enrich our understanding of Wilde, the discussion of Wilde's relationship to the thought of other Victorians is less successful. The idea that John Henry Cardinal Newman, the Anglican minister who converted to Catholicism in 1845, influenced Wilde not in Ca-tholicism but only in other areas is absurd, and contradicted by Wilde's letters. Why, in any case, the either/or? Brown writes that Wilde's "perennial toying with formal conversion to Catholicism had the air of insolence from beginning to end" (39), as if that made Wilde less serious. She might well have noticed that Wilde was insolent about many things, and serious about them at the same time. Brown also sees an "atrophy of . . . aesthetic sense" in Ruskin's lavish praise of . . . Kate Greenaway . . . it was in these idyllic pictures of small children frolicking that Ruskin's emotional and ethical vision of a better society finally came to rest" (42). Maybe, but that's beside the point. His pedophilia, as evidenced in his passion for Rose La Touche, temporarily obscured his vision — which was admittedly often temporarily obscured — but he went right on seeing through a glass darkly. In her discussion of Wilde and Arnold, Brown's understanding is sharpened by the essential contradictions in Wilde: "The thinker with whom Wilde is most at odds and also perhaps most deeply allied is Matthew Arnold" (47).

Chapter three, "Wilde's Reassociation of Sensibility," begins with the idea that Wilde achieved a "'reassociation of sensibility' at the end of his century when he effectively overcame the strict Victorian opposition between the ethical and the aesthetic . . . not by synthesizing the two, but by demonstrating their interrelatedness while still preserving a distinction between them" (51). This is a ticklish distinction. Hegel's version of synthesis was to combine in order to destroy two opposites, but then to resurrect them as something slightly different — raise the original opposites to a higher power, as it were, using them to provide a new idea. The first example that Brown offers to this demonstration of interrelatedness seems indistinguishable from the Hegelian notion of synthesis. She writes that in part two of "The Critic as Artist," Wilde "begins with what appears to be a contradiction . . . [he] radically separates art and life at the same time [stressing] the importance of an art of life — that is to say, the ideal of human perfectibility" (52). Here the Hegelian synthesis is clear: Art as opposed to Life produces the synthesis "an art of life."

Her own conclusion to this section of the chapter brings the reader back to Hegel, and to Wilde's affinities with Hegel, as demonstrated in his *Oxford Notebooks:* "The most 'subjective' criticism [as the 'record of one's own soul'] . . . becomes the most 'objective,' the freest from the world's influences and standards" (57).

The next section, on Wilde and Nietzsche, offers a fascinating and much-needed tour through Wilde's "uniquely English" response "to a world situation" (57). Wilde and Nietzsche "inherited the same situation in philosophy: what earlier in the century Engels had called the 'despair of reason,' its confessed inability to solve the contradictions with which it is ultimately faced. The flaunting of paradox in each writer . . . is a function of this despair as well as a bid to master it, just as their shared deployment of aphorism may be seen as a sign of resistance to enter any system" (58). Both men remained aesthetes. Their aestheticism "arose out of an engagement with the ancient world, though in neither case was it limited by the presuppositions of scientific linguistics. Wilde identified with classical Greece, Nietzsche with pre-Socratic Hellenism; Wilde's patron God was Apollo, Nietzsche's was Dionysius" (58). Both men found existence bearable only by forging an art out of their own lives.

Brown then states that Wilde's urge to make his life into a work of art owes far less to Pater's conclusion to *The Renaissance* than has been supposed — it is to Nietzsche and other Continental philosophers that Wilde owes much of this intention. Wilde's "self-sacrifice to English law . . . must be seen in the context of his thought. In 'The Soul of Man Under Socialism' he writes of self-sacrifice in Nietzschean terms as a 'survival of savage mutilation' . . . It may be that Wilde's sacrifice, which . . . had for him a renewing moral and philosophical significance, exemplifies Nietzsche's idea" (63).

This chapter includes an unfortunate misquotation: "There is a world of irony in Wilde's oft-quoted remark that he 'lived in fear of being understood'" (66). What Wilde said — in "The Critic as Artist" (*CW*, 1016) — was that he lived in "terror of not being misunderstood." This shows a more complex state of ambivalence. He realized that his endless quips might eventually betray him; as he also said, "nowadays, to be intelligible is to be found out" (*CW*, 390). Brown's comments on this misquotation — that Wilde knew his ideas would be imitated by well-meaning, uneducated people, and that Wilde would not have been surprised by the Nazi's appropriation of Nietzsche — do not therefore follow. Aware that he loved to reveal himself, Wilde's fear of not being misunderstood is not so much a fear of being imitated by fools as it is a fear of self-revelation.

Returning to the idea of Wilde's reassociation of sensibility, Brown remarks that despite its being a notable achievement, it was overshadowed subsequently by "the absolute aestheticism" of Mallarmé and Joris-Karl Huysmans, and then "by the politically motivated repudiation of aestheticism that came into its own in the forties and fifties of the twentieth century" — for instance, by Thomas Mann, who concluded that aesthetic ideology is "absolutely unempowered" to solve problems of the day (67).

The opening of the next chapter, "Wilde's Philosophy of Art," states that publication of Wilde's essay-dialogue, "The Decay of Lying," in January 1889, "marked a decisive turn toward philosophical criticism in Wilde's career" (69). In this work, she writes, Wilde's "earnest wish to advance a new aesthetic gains the ascendancy over the parody of earnestness" (70), but it might be more accurate to say that the way to Wilde's development of a new aesthetic came through his parody of earnestness, and that this parody proved to be part of an essential process, ever-evolving. This is more in line with the idea that Wilde's thought owes much to Hegel's dialectic; Brown, however, is at pains to show Wilde's affinity with Kant, particularly in this chapter.

She states that most serious writers at the end of the nineteenth century, "especially those who, like Wilde, had read Kant, were convinced that there is no eternal or absolute truth accessible to human reason" (70). True, but Kant was not the sole source of this idea. Brown, however, is probably correct to assume that Kant's "antinomies of true reason," in which he "had shown that a proposition can be true from one point of view — religious or teleological — but not from another," would have appealed to Wilde (70). She perceives Wilde as "poised between his aesthetic and moral intentions," as if this were a dilemma for him, whereas it may have been his delighted way of escaping from his real social and sexual dilemmas by projecting the doubt he felt onto philosophical problems. Brown is right to mention that Kant was the philosopher who "decisively introduced the spectator into the concept of aesthetics," and that "we see Kant's influence on Wilde in this emphasis on reception, or creative reception" (72).

The chapter has a good discussion of Wilde as a cosmopolitan artist. "Wilde's achievement as a cosmopolitan artist is no doubt most evident in *Salomé,* in which the influences of Maurice Maeterlinck and the French symbolists are far-reaching and decisive. Derived from Gustave Flaubert's Herodias and composed first in French, this play moves furthest from English tradition, but the first three comedies reveal foreign influences as well" (83). One key influence is Nietzsche, and Brown points — as many critics have done — to similarities between Nietzsche's and Wilde's view of Christian morality as "by and large a symptom of cultural decadence" (84), a morality devoted to self-torture, pain, and sacrifice. According to Brown, Wilde thinks socialism will bring about a new kind of art devoted to pleasure, not martyrdom. She is referring to Wilde's essay, "The Soul of Man Under Socialism." A careful reading of this essay, however, reveals that Wilde felt deeply ambivalent about the suffering and self-sacrifice he claimed to see as a symptom; the idea of indulging himself in activities that would make him suffer had an irresistible attraction that he never understood. This provided the conflict in much of his work, and probably directly inspired a charming short tale about a group of iron filings, arguing among themselves as to whether they should visit the magnet, then being astonished at finding themselves clinging to its side.

Brown goes on to say that Wilde's rejection of moral suffering was part of his indictment of Victorian notions of the good in his plays. She suggests that his comedies preceding *The Importance of Being Earnest* both conceal and reveal a structure of "crisis-resolved-through-sacrifice-intrinsic to it" (85). Quoting Walter Benjamin's remark that "Only in humor can language become critical," she asserts that Wilde mined the language of Victorian melodrama by means of humor, inspiring his audience as well as himself to think critically of it. Not a new point, but well-stated, and Brown's use of Benjamin is helpful. She associates Benjamin's idea that character "is usually placed in an ethical context, fate in a religious one," with events in Wilde's first comedy, *Lady Windermere's Fan,* and comes to the conclusion that in Wilde's comedies "The dandy has no fate because he has no character" (87). This is an intriguing remark, since above all Wilde wished to escape fate, but saw himself as caught in its net.

The following discussion of *The Importance of Being Earnest* employs this formula, not always with an accurate representation of the text: "In a cast of dandies of *The Importance of Being Earnest* . . . no one suffers and no one sacrifices. The nursery-room atmosphere . . . in which the worst sin is the eating of muffins and its biggest threat the arrival of the nanny, Lady Bracknell, takes us into the world of later Victorian nonsense of Edward Lear and Lewis Carroll. . . . In more recent years Monty Python has [sic] recourse to Wilde's comic ideas, especially the idea of 'going too far'" (87). The association of Wilde with Carroll, Lear, and Monty Python is a good one, but Lady Bracknell is no nanny, not in any sense; she is the dowager mother of the play. I don't see Brown's point in casting her as the nanny; literally the nanny is Miss Prism, who refracts the play's problems of identity, and that is no doubt why Wilde gave her that name. (Possibly the comma after Lady Bracknell should have been removed in a final edit of Brown's book.)

Brown goes on to say, quite plausibly, that Wilde in this comedy attacks the idea of social determinism, "that we are built up by the influence of the environment . . . like Pip's covenant with the criminal, Magwitch, in *Great Expectations.* But in *The Importance of Being Ear-*

nest everything, the past above all, can be repaired. Algernon and Jack even go back to their own christenings. Ernest, a character who has never existed, dies and is brought back to life, and no one bats an eye" (88). Brown goes on to say, however, that in the play "the surface of language is presented to us as the only reality and the play *appears* to be celebrating the self-sufficiency of language in itself" (88), an unclear formulation for which there is no evidence. Wilde made it clear that the play concerned much more than language when he said it had "its philosophy . . . That we should treat all the trivial things of life very seriously, and all the serious things of life with sincere and studied triviality" (*More Letters,* 196).

Brown's concluding remarks throw light on G. B. Shaw's and Mary McCarthy's mysterious dislike for the play, and also clarify some of her own ideas about language: having suggested that the play is about learning to bear pleasure as well as pain, something these critics perhaps cannot do, Brown remarks, "To bear pleasure — that is, to suffer it as well as to give it birth — is what the play is about, a burden that has everything to do with language. For Algernon and Jack do not move forward in time toward death, but backward in time toward their own christening, to the paradisiac moment of naming. After this creative moment, after the fall into language, all else becomes empty 'prattle,' in the profound sense in which Kierkegaard uses the word. That *The Importance of Being Earnest* is composed of such prattle is what disturbed Mary McCarthy, who compared it to the suffocating world of Jean-Paul Sartre's *No Exit*" (90–91). With this, Brown stresses the modernity of the play.

More interesting, and more connected to *The Importance of Being Earnest* than Brown states, is her brilliant observation that "the dialogue form" as Wilde uses it in "The Decay of Lying" suggests "that truth itself is contradictoriness" (93). This insight involves much more than language; it involves passions, conflicts, actions, philosophy, perception, the unconscious — much of Freudian and post-Freudian analytic psychology is grounded in this recognition.

Brown's conclusion about Wilde's "philosophical vulnerability on the question of truth," namely that it "may in fact have been the crucial motivating factor in the initiation of a libel suit," ignores the circumstances of Wilde's life that propelled him unwittingly in this direction (93–94); in other words, he was far from rational when he got himself into the lawsuit. He was in a whirl of uncontrollable emotions; he had all the self-control of an already launched missile. To speak of him making a philosophical decision in this situation is unrealistic, especially when he himself spoke of "Nemesis" catching him in her net. He was well aware that he had lost all self-control when he took the fatal steps that led him to his prison sentence and subsequent unhappy remaining years of life.

Brown evades the issue of Wilde's emotional state, insisting that Wilde in his catastrophic plunge into the libel suit had a "will to truth," and that although "such a will may be partly unconscious . . . I have been wary of using the words 'conscious' and 'unconscious,' at least as mutually exclusive terms, preferring to maintain an emphasis on Wilde's whole being, his artistic being" (95). This ignores Wilde's own perception of the separate roles of the unconscious and conscious minds, which are strewn throughout his philosophic dialogues. Here are a couple of samples: "Out of ourselves we can never pass, nor can there be in creation what in the creator was not" (*CW*, 1045). "It is the spectator, and not life, that art really mirrors" (*CW*, 17). These epigrams reveal Wilde's awareness of the ways in which the unconscious mind infiltrates and influences the conscious mind; both can be interpreted as containing the message that no one escapes the unconscious mind. To pass over these perceptions is to ignore an important component of Wilde's philosophy.

Brown's views lead to the overstatement that *De Profundis* is "a culmination of Wilde's philosophic exploration of the vexed relation of art and truth" (95). Wilde wrote out of anguish, illness, and despair. The letter is an epistle with some elegance of thought and phrasing, but it sinks under the weight of Wilde's understandable self-pity. Still, Brown makes some wise remarks about it: "what makes it so moving . . . is the struggle of a soul to will the recurrence of a life down to the last repellent detail in order to affirm it, to achieve a state of mind in which he would prefer nothing more passionately than the repetition of that life just as it has been, in which he would come to see that all events of his past . . . were 'for the best,' and part of 'love of fate' in the spirit of Nietzsche" (101).

In her epilogue, "Cosmopolitan Melancholy," Brown draws an extraordinary conclusion: "To those who would insist that it is impossible, in even a provisional way, to rise above one's prejudices, or to suspend the presuppositions of class, ethnicity, and the like, Wilde would have only one answer: such persons should not be writing criticism" (109). Wilde, in fact, said exactly the opposite: "A critic cannot be fair in the ordinary sense of the word. It is only about things that do not interest one that one can give a really unbiassed opinion, which is no doubt the reason why an unbiassed opinion is always absolutely valueless. The man who sees all sides of a question is a man who sees absolutely nothing at all. Art is a passion, and in matters of art, Thought is inevitable[y] colored by emotion. . . . One should, of course, have no prejudices; but, as a great Frenchman remarked a hundred years ago, it is one's business in such matters to have preferences, and when one has preferences one ceases to be fair. It is only an auctioneer who can equally and impartially admire all schools of art" (*CW*, 1047). The point that class and ethnicity color one's work could hardly be made more strongly.

On balance, however, Brown's is one of the best books on Wilde to have emerged in the 1990s: it takes Wilde's philosophic thought seriously, and demonstrates his relationship to predecessors whose importance has been insufficiently appreciated — particularly Hegel, Kant, and Nietzsche.

Sos Eltis

Sos Eltis's historical study, *Revising Wilde: Society and Subversion in the Plays of Oscar Wilde,* attempts to highlight the radical, specifically the anarchic Wilde in his writings. Eltis suggests that Wilde's dramas have been seen too much as "reproducing the conventions of the popular nineteenth-century dramas on which they were modelled"— an overstated claim, but useful in her attempt to "link the radical Wilde who attacked Victorian society in 'The Soul of Man Under Socialism,' mocked moral seriousness in 'The Decay of Lying,' and outraged conventional sexual and social codes in *The Picture of Dorian Gray,*" with Wilde the playwright, the reputedly careless craftsman (4).

These points have been made before, and made with force by Ellmann, but Eltis adds historical material, especially by looking at different manuscript versions of Wilde's plays. Eltis claims that she wants to recover "the revolutionary Wilde," but at the same time makes a point of saying that she will not deal with his homosexuality. This excludes a major part of what he regarded as his revolutionary feeling. Eltis writes, "In concentrating on certain aspects of Wilde's radicalism — in particular his anarchist, feminist, and socialist sympathies — I have inevitably neglected other topics, most importantly his homosexuality and its influence on his work" (5). This assumes that Wilde's homosexuality, anarchism, feminism, and socialism can be separated, which they cannot.

Of interest is chapter two, "Vera; Or, the Nihilists," concerning Wilde's first play. Eltis has done some nook-and-cranny work, usefully turning up interesting aspects of early versions of the play and its background. She mentions that "Wilde had strong connections with the anarchist movement in France, where avant-garde literature and politics were closely linked" (17), and characterizes Wilde as "in essence . . . a utopian anarchist, arguing that, freed from all restraints, mankind would abandon competition for the pursuit of self-development, and that a natural community of independent individuals would result" (21). This is a good point, which has been made in a more interesting way by Jerusha McCormack, reviewed elsewhere in these pages.

Eltis makes the intriguing point that "Wilde's individualist doctrine also presented many parallels with Taoist philosophy, a philosophy which itself provided one of the earliest bases for anarchist thought" (22). She notes that in 1890 Wilde "enthusiastically reviewed" a translation of the writings of Chuang Tsu, a Taoist disciple of Lao Tsu, who favored "passivity and inactivity." Eltis doesn't probe Wilde's biographic background for reasons why passivity and inactivity might appeal to him, but it is worth studying why a man raised to admire Irish radical heroes became fascinated with passivity and inactivity, for these qualities eventually thrust him into prison when he could not make up his mind to leave London at the crucial moment. Here is one obvious place where not dealing with Wilde's homosexuality seriously affects Eltis's ability to explore his reality and his developing political ideas.

In this chapter Eltis studies the political background of Russian nihilism, investigating the real woman who inspired Wilde's Vera — who may have been one Vera Zassoulich — and noting ways in which, as the manuscript was revised, it became less melodramatic and Vera's role more prominent. "Much of the writing of *Vera* may be melodramatic," she writes, "but the play also contains some delicate touches of humour and irony" (39). This, however, is well known. Less well known is Eltis's point that plays dealing with Russian nihilism were quite common in the 1870s and 1880s, but that Wilde differs in being rather sympathetic to the nihilists and in affording a primary role to a woman as radical. As Eltis points out, "Wilde's portrayal of a woman as the head of a nihilist cell was not only radical, it was also realistic. Nikolai Chernyshevsky's *What Is To Be Done?* records the vital involvement of women in the Russian revolutionary movement, and even British newspapers recognized the equal participation of men and women in the struggle against Russian tyranny" (44).

Part Two: Theater History and Criticism

Kerry Powell

Kerry Powell, in *Oscar Wilde and the Theatre of the 1890s*, uncovers a host of unknown influences — from popular music hall to legitimate theater, including Ibsen — on Wilde's dramatic writing during the 1890s. His research is all the more impressive since many of the texts remain unpublished, existing only in typescripts tucked away in libraries or in worn promptbook copies, if at all. Like the best Wilde scholars, he assumes the paradoxical style of his subject, with one chapter title stressing men with a past, and another the "unmotherly mother."

Powell begins with a new look at the old problem of Wilde's so-called plagiarism, remarking that the "daring thefts of language and incident which characterize Wilde's best plays" are none too apparent in his earliest efforts, but rather in his best plays: "One almost blushes at the echoes of other writers to be found, for instance, in *Lady Windermere's Fan, but in that play Wilde is writing against the grain of his forerunners rather than merely absorbing influence*" [My emphasis]. Powell's next sentence offers the best explanation I have seen for Wilde's so-called plagiarism as a conscious, literary method: "What seems at first shameless borrowings become, after a context, the means to a surprising and individuated dramatic utterance. Paradoxically, therefore, it might be said that Wilde's early plays fail because they are not as dominated by influence as his later successes. The more intimate the embrace of the source, the more Wilde seems able to produce work really his own" (11).

This thesis — that Wilde's originality grew out of his plagiarism — has characteristics common to Wilde's own writing: it is paradoxical, provoking, and realistic. In eight chapters, Powell provides shrewd insights, high points being his discussion of *A Woman of No Importance,* Wilde's least successful comedy, and of his masterpiece, *The Importance of Being Earnest.* Apparently influenced by psychoanalytic theory, Powell speculatively questions reasons for the failure of *A Woman of No Importance*, wondering whether it represents an "unresolved struggle" within Wilde's fragmented personality. *The Importance of Being Earnest* has many sources and resists them all while brilliantly mastering them, Powell suggests, while the sources of *A Woman* are all too visible, undigested, as it were, or not integrated successfully.

Powell's first chapter, "Rewriting the Past," begins by observing that much "of the theatrical landscape of Oscar Wilde's time, including some of its most imposing monuments, remains unmapped" (1). Only a handful of the fifty most popular plays in major London theaters in the 1890s are familiar to most specialists in Victorian literature, since many were either never published or published only as acting chapbooks. Most plays "even prominent ones, disappeared utterly with the final performance" (3).

Many of these plays must have influenced Wilde, and it is this "vanished but essential context of Wilde's theatrical career" (3) that Powell recaptures. As he points out, the "theatrical scene in which so many barely remembered authors played a vital part would have appeared extremely seductive to Wilde" (2). Wilde, in fact, longed to be considered the "English Ibsen," but such recognition, which never came, would not have brought in the cash he urgently needed. Theater held out the prospects of new literary influences as well as quick money-making; "the theatre had become the likeliest place where an ambitious writer could make money" (2). A newspaper, the *Era*, noted that dramatists received ten percent on the gross.

Powell turns next to the curious contradictions in Wilde's creative process. Though Wilde claimed that he remained utterly uninfluenced by other writers ("My works are dominated by myself," he told a reporter, also saying that no one else had in the smallest degree influenced him) the fact was, Powell notes dryly, "that without the spur of influence he could scarcely write a play at all" (4). Actually, Wilde either claimed no influence, or made the influence so obvious that no one could miss it, but this is not a question into which Powell enters.

He covers previous scholarly discussions of Wilde's sources thoroughly, mentioning Harold Bloom's "all too brief" discussion of Wilde as a writer whose "anxiety of influence" was too "unformed" for the "strong poet" who could prevail in the struggle with the literary past, meaning that Wilde seems overwhelmed by his sources. Powell notes a similar train of thought in Isobel Murray (4). He remarks that Bloom's anxiety of influence does not apply to Wilde, because it is not love of a particular writer that inspires Wilde's interest in popular writers of the day, of whom he spoke disdainfully. Wilde knew that writing for the popular stage increased chances that he would lose artistic prestige, but remained well aware that the more the form of his dramas followed the most popular stage dramas, the more money he could make. And "in spite of himself Wilde was energized by popular writing — he liked it when he scorned it, and found his own voice, when he found it at all, in answering the melodramatic clamors and boisterous humor of his rival playwrights" (5–6). In fact, "its vigorous currents overpower him, or threaten to, even in his best work — especially in his best, one is tempted to say" (6).

The example Powell gives is a revelation. A forgotten play called *The Foundling,* popular at just the time Wilde was composing *The Importance of Being Earnest* in the summer of 1894, concerns a 25-year-old orphan who is "regarded askance" by the "formidably conventional" mother of the woman he wants to marry. Like Algernon in Wilde's play, the foundling considers baptism as a way out of his difficulties; like Ernest he wants to know "who I am," and like him also embraces "a maidenly woman of advanced age" under the mistaken impression that she is his mother (6).

But although the words and situations of Wilde's comedy resemble those of *The Foundling,* the spirit differs, Powell demonstrates. In writing *Earnest* Wilde "often took the words directly from the mouths of other people's characters," but his epigrammatic, literary, aristocratic modes of expression were "utterly divorced from the pedestrian language that usually characterized farce." In both statement and expression, "Wilde's play subverts the comedies which from another point of view it imitates." The popular Victorian farces boast heroes who begin by deceiving and disguising their motives, but end by "dutifully enjoining truth, constancy, work, and earnestness." But Wilde's characters do nothing of the kind: "there is no turning back from the life of masquerade and lie, no retreat to the stern embrace of authority." Jack's final line in Wilde's play, that he has "finally realized the Vital Importance of Being Earnest," actually parodies the "contrite moral speeches" of popular comedies like *Charley's Aunt* (1892) and *The Foundling.* Jack becomes earnest by defying earnestness "and the army of Victorian virtues" (6).

Briefly reviewing similar trends of influence in *Salome, A Woman of No Importance,* and *Lady Windermere's Fan,* Powell remarks that Wilde's novel, *The Picture of Dorian Gray,* "had anticipated Wilde's plays in "organizing itself as a countermeasure against certain literary clichés . . ." (8). Wilde's novel borrows the story, imagery, and even names of characters from "a popular subgenre of fiction, rife in the 1880s," that dealt with *doppelgängers* and the supernatural. Powell closes the chapter with a reiteration of his basic, sound thesis, that the "oppressive presence of the source and Wilde's embattled resistance characterize his best plays" (12).

In chapter two, *"Lady Windermere's Fan* and the unmotherly mother,"* Powell writes of this, Wilde's first hit play, that it was immediately seen as "the offspring" of earlier dramas. The popular dramatist Sidney Grundy even claimed that he could not stage a revival of his own play, *The Glass of Fashion* (1883), "because Mr. Oscar Wilde did so, under the title of *Lady Windermere's Fan"* (14).

The basic theme — the fallen woman wishing to regain the love of her daughter — was popular in drama as well as other genres. Powell remarks that *Lady Windermere's Fan* bears a striking resemblance both to Edgar Saltus's novel, *Eden* (1888), and to a now-forgotten play, *Illusion,* by Pierre Leclerq, produced in London in July 1890 (22).

An interesting similarity between *Illusion* and *Lady Windermere's Fan* is that the mother's identity in both plays is withheld from the audience until the fourth act. Originally Wilde planned to inform the audience much sooner, but was persuaded not to, likely by those who had seen *Illusion.*

To explode the morality to which his source plays were wed, Wilde turned to Ibsen. As Powell notes, in *A Doll's House,* "Ibsen had scandalized London theatregoers with a story which ended where more plays about child-abandoning mothers began" (28). Powell suggests that *Lady Windermere's Fan* "belongs in the company of plays by women and by Ibsen and Shaw that give the story of the unconventional, 'undutiful' mother a new telling" (30). But he also remarks that Wilde never completely transcends predecessors in whose plays the mother repents. At the critical moment in Wilde's play, the adventuress, Mrs. Erlynne, advises her daughter to take the conventional route, return to her husband and child, and suffer in silence. "This ambivalence in Wilde's conception of the character . . . perhaps accounts for the markedly different assessments that critics have offered of Mrs. Erlynne," Powell remarks. For him, the play's weakness — and what makes it suffer by comparison to Ibsen and Shaw's plays — "is that for the first three acts it is very nearly drawn into the vortex of the fallen-mother myth it subverts." Powell brilliantly observes that Mrs. Erlynne's name may intentionally echo the title *East Lynne* — "without the 'r' it would be spelled Elynne" — in which Lady Isabel damns herself by inflexible moral rules that she initially denies (31).

In chapter three, *"Salome,* the censor, and the divine Sarah," Powell raises perpetually debated questions concerning "one of the most copiously annotated of all Oscar Wilde's works," namely, "Why did Wilde write the play in French? How could he have gone into the third week of rehearsal when the subject matter appeared certain to arouse the censor and make performance impossible? Is *Salome* a triumph of Wilde's dramatic art or, as one French critic has abruptly put it, 'one of the most famous and one of the worst of his works'?" (33).

Powell's answers are new, interesting, and plausible. He first cites the play's complicated production history, beginning with the difficulty of giving any verdict on the play, since few in the English-speaking world have seen it performed. He then delves into little-known reasons for Wilde's belief that *Salome* would be performed on the English stage, despite the ironclad rule forbidding the dramatization of Scripture. Powell writes that Wilde, "like everyone else in the theatre of the 1890s, knew that the Examiner of Plays permitted works in French to get away with more — much more — than plays written in English. There was the added, and by no means trivial, consideration that Sarah Bernhardt did not speak English" (35). The newspaper the *Era* was as surprised as Wilde that *Salome* was banned by the censor, and wondered why a play that had been "veiled in the decent obscurity of a foreign language" was not allowed to be performed (36).

Salome would not have been the first drama in French to be staged in English "in the decent obscurity of a foreign language." In both religious and sexual matters, the censor applied a much looser standard to plays written in French, and Powell quotes at length from fascinating commentaries in the *Era*. The censor, Pigott, justified his different standards in testimony before a select committee of the House of Commons in 1892, shortly before he banned *Salome,* saying that people "who go to see French plays, played by French companies and written for French purposes know what they are going to see" (37). Wilde knew this, and must have counted on getting by with a play written in French where he could never have submitted the same material in English. But other factors intervened: Pigott had just given testimony to the select committee, which could, had it wished to do so, have endangered his livelihood. The committee did not do so, expressing itself satisfied with his censorship, and saying that such censorship should be extended to performances in music halls. Powell concludes, "it was a strengthened, and probably emboldened, Edward F. S. Pigott who only a few days later looked into the French manuscript of *Salomé* and declared it unfit for performance on an English stage" (40).

Curiously enough, Wilde aided the censor: "Perhaps unconsciously, Wilde scripted his own victimization by authority in the *Salomé* matter," Powell observes. Wilde took no measures to win over the censor. In late May, 1892, "just days before he anathematized *Salomé,* Pigott emphasized that he welcomed 'personal intercourse' with managers and authors 'to avoid unnecessary friction' and remove obstacles which stood in the way of licensing" (34). Wilde might have contacted Pigott privately and negotiated. Pigott liked to talk privately with authors to work out deals, and Wilde had already negotiated with him regarding a play whose authors had travestied him, using his name. He had gone to Pigott to have his name removed. But instead of going to him again about *Salomé*, Powell writes, Wilde "publicly denounced the Examiner as an inept and 'commonplace' official, thus destroying, in all probability, any chance of producing the play in England" (35).

In chapter four, "Unimportant women and men with a past," Powell tackles *A Woman of No Importance*, which he designates "the least successful on stage and with critics" of Wilde's four society comedies (55). Powell suggests several ways in which Wilde reworks the basic conflicts of *Lady Windermere's Fan* in *A Woman of No Importance* — dramatizing the conflicts between puritan and dandy, protesting social inequalities between men and women, and demonstrating concern with a woman's secret. But, he adds, "Wilde's second comedy never really establishes mastery over the well-traveled ground where it trespasses. It does not break free of the domination of earlier dramas to find its own voice or even to harmonize the babble of its many influences" (56).

Like all of Wilde's work, *A Woman of No Importance* owes a great deal to other authors. The basic plot, concerning the illegitimate son who as a young man meets his father for the first time, comes from *Le Fils naturel,* a play by Alexandre Dumas *fils.* Powell writes that in Dumas's play, the son takes a tolerant, not moralistic, attitude toward his mother's shame. This is also the case with Wilde's play — but not at first. Before Gerald learns who his father is, his mother presents him with a hypothetical situation of a young woman, seduced by Lord Illingworth and giving birth to an illegitimate son. Gerald reacts with anything but sympathy: "No nice girl would," says Gerald, blaming the seduced as much as the seducer (act 3, scene 3).

Powell traces connections to French sources of the play — for instance, that the father becomes a man "of no importance" when his money and prestige mean nothing to his son. "Essentially," Powell writes, "*A Woman of No Importance* imports a specialized type of French drama, refurbishing it with an English atmosphere and characters, while repeating what Dumas and others had already done" (58). The play, he concludes, is overwhelmed by its French sources, despite Wilde's claim that he had just given an audience what it wanted by inventing a wicked aristocrat seducing a virtuous maiden. Wittily, Powell adds, "Although Wilde never carried out his threat to become a French citizen after the Lord Chamberlain suppressed *Salome*, he did in effect the next best thing. He wrote another French play — this time, however, in English" (59).

Powell moves on to the consideration of names in *A Woman of No Importance*, finding echoes of Hawthorne: "Lord Illingworth's name bears a provocative — perhaps a taunting — resemblance to Chillingworth's in *The Scarlet Letter*, and Hester Worsley shares her Christian name with the more famous puritan of Hawthorne's novel" (59). Even Mrs. Arbuthnot has a name beginning with A, for adultery. Wilde was, Powell writes, not the first English playwright to appropriate *The Scarlet Letter*. He notes others and their influence, and mentions ideas Wilde borrows from Ibsen that clash with the English tradition of making the fallen woman repent. Wilde's Mrs. Arbuthnot rebels against conventional morality, eventually refusing to marry her seducer, and thus "behaves more as a character in Ibsen than an English drama of the pink-lampshade variety" (67). Wilde did not integrate these two influences in his drama, and it shows. Although Mrs. Arbuthnot is "a defiant and unconventional woman . . . there are moments — critical ones — in which [she] seems as if suddenly possessed by one of the queens of melodrama who preceded her." Powell adds that her "independent views on marriage and maidenhood" are "incompatible . . . with the swooning fit at the end of act III when, Wilde writes, 'She sinks slowly on the ground in shame'" (69).

It could be argued that Wilde strives to reveal an extremely ambivalent mind at work in Mrs. Arbuthnot, and that her inconsistency is part of that interesting profile. In this particular moment of the play, I find her convincing, although many other scenes seem, as Powell suggests, deluged by different and nonintegrated influences.

One other comment of Powell's requires comment. He finds it hard to imagine why a man like Illingworth would take the slightest interest in his dull young son, Arbuthnot. Vanity could easily explain that — the desire to influence and alter a version of oneself — but Lytton Strachey's ideas about Illingworth are most entertaining. Strachey had no difficulty imagining what Illingworth saw in Gerald, assuming that the wicked lord looked forward to buggering his own son.

Finally, Powell concludes, the "Ibsenite conclusion" of the play does not fit the design as a whole" (72).

Chapter five, "Wilde and Ibsen," delves into the Norwegian playwright's influence on Wilde. Powell remarks that although Wilde aspired unsuccessfully to be known as the "English Ibsen," he has usually been strongly contrasted to him.

Powell finds ways to dispose of this view. For instance, he remarks that "it is revealing that [William] Archer, the foremost champion of Ibsen in England, judged Wilde to be London's best playwright even before he had written *The Importance of Being Earnest* and won at least the grudging praise of most critics" (75). Archer proved to be the only critic to connect Salome directly with Ibsen, remarking, "Salomé is an oriental Hedda Gabler" (79). Powell also points out that Wilde was writing his plays "in an atmosphere suffused with Ibsen" (74), whose plays were first performed in London in 1889. English critics loved or hated him; he became "a polarizing force in the English theatre" (75).

Wilde's favorite Ibsen play was *Hedda Gabler*, and Powell finds considerable common ground between them, remarking that both *Hedda Gabler* and *The Importance of Being Earnest* have in common the depiction of a lost literary work as a vanished child (78). Powell compares Ibsen's Lövborg's loss of his manuscript in the gutter, which he calls the loss of "a little child," to Wilde's Miss Prism, who accidentally leaves her manuscript in the bassinet and the baby stowed in her handbag. Then she absentmindedly leaves the handbag, baby enclosed, at the railway station. Wilde's *Salomé*, which seems the most remote from "the middle class drawing rooms of Ibsen," may get some of its power from Ibsen's representations of female sexuality. "There was practically no precedent on the contemporary English stage for Wilde's portrayal of a morbid, sexually frustrated woman of borderline sanity whose only satisfaction comes from causing the death of the man she vainly craves" (78–79). But Ibsen's plays are filled with such women. "Hedda and Salomé — nervous women whose desire turns murderous — represent a total contradiction of the serene purity with which the Victorian male endowed his feminine ideal" (79). And, Powell observes, Ibsenites liked Wilde's *Salomé* very much.

Steeped in Ibsen, Wilde read and re-read Shaw's *The Quintessence of Ibsenism*, where, Powell discovers, Wilde found much "that he could use later — including at least four instances of the phrase, 'ideal husband' which he would employ in 1895 as the title of his most Ibsenite play" (80). Ibsen's play *Pillars of Society* has striking similarities to Wilde's *An Ideal Husband*, Powell finds, something that even William Archer did not recognize. Among other similarities, the most interesting is the hero's confidante in both plays, who, when asked who was harmed by the crime, tells the hero, "Yourself" (83). So stark are the similarities that Powell wonders why Archer, who translated *Pillars of Society* into English, never mentioned them.

Turning to the differences between Wilde and Ibsen, Powell argues that *An Ideal Husband* answers or revises Ibsen, writing a new ending for *Pillars of Society.* "If, as Wilde would say later, he sought to 'out-Kipling Henley' when he composed *The Ballad of Reading Gaol,* with *An Ideal Husband* he tried to 'out-Ibsen Archer' or even surpass Ibsen himself" (84). Ibsen's hero is advised to confess his crime publicly and repent; Wilde's is advised to do nothing of the kind, but to tell only his wife. Few things could be less Ibsenite than Lady Chiltern's concession, in Wilde's *Ideal Husband,* that a "man's life is more important than a woman's," because it has "larger issues, wider scope, greater ambitions." But in the end, Wilde's conclusion "thwarts in more than one way Ibsen's solutions." Wilde's hero, Robert Chiltern, commits a sort of noble crime in its courageous daring — Powell does not use the term Übermensch, but almost implies it — and that is "excuse enough for what Chiltern did and place[s] him beyond the irrelevant morality of women" (86).

In chapter six, "Resisting the Feminist Police," Powell observes that while a major theme of Victorian comedy was the ideal wife — another version of the "Angel in the House" — the dramatic basis of *An Ideal Husband* was the reverse — "Lady Chiltern's demand that her ambitious husband be 'pure' and 'without stain,' her 'ideal'" (89). This is an arresting idea, although Powell's next remark does not amplify it. He states that modern spectators may be surprised to find Robert Chiltern despairing because his wife idealizes him, and wondering why women place men on "monstrous pedestals." I find nothing puzzling, or unusual, in women placing men on pedestals or vice versa. The Victorian ideal of the "Angel in the House" represented a grotesque institutionalization of a natural human mistake, summed up quite well by Oscar Wilde: "when one is in love, one begins by deceiving oneself, and one ends by deceiving others." For *deceiving,* read *idealizing:* that is what lovers do; it is what makes them lovers.

However, Powell correctly suggests that in *An Ideal Husband,* Wilde did something new by presenting a man with a past who struggles with his wife's demand that he be pure. Powell delineates the intellectual and emotional context for ideas about male purity in the 1880s, going into detail about the New Women of the 1890s and their ideas about men. He mentions Carol Christ's observation that the idea of "an ennobled male is inherent in the Victorian belief that women could, in Coventry Patmore's phrase from 'The Angel in the House,' make 'brutes men, and men divine'" (90). The new women writers did not relinquish the idea of female purity, but only insisted that men live up to the same standard. Powell gives a number of instances from contemporary novels, concluding that the "ideal husband" plays of the 1890s are not just fashion, but "belong to a heated debate, carried on in late Victorian literature and journalism, which makes it clear that time-honored ideals of marriage and relations between the sexes were being challenged as never before" (91).

Powell points out, however, that "the very idea of a faultless man seems to strike Wilde as quite unnatural. 'Men become old,' says the delightful Duchess of Berwick in *Lady Windermere's Fan,* 'but they never become good'" (96). While Ibsen's *Pillars of Society* can be seen as "a typical incarnation of the 'ideal husband' myth — presenting the soiled politician redeemed by the police authority of a truly good woman" (99), Wilde's *An Ideal Husband* "denies the new morality" on which most dramas of the "man with a past" ideal were formed. In Wilde's play, the wicked Mrs. Cheveley observes, "Scandals used to lend charm, or at least interest, to a man. Now they crush him." Wilde's play, Powell points out, "begins conventionally enough before turning the tables on an undoubtedly surprised 1890s audience" (101). Wilde's hero, Chiltern, accepts a seat in the Cabinet at the end of the play, "on grounds that the emotional idealism of women should not be allowed to restrain his passion for power" (101) — unlike a character in Pinero and unlike Ibsen's hero.

At least five other plays with an "ideal husband" theme were being staged, or were about to be staged, in 1895, Powell writes, briefly summarizing one of them. Wilde's play stands alone in its different resolution of the problem, but Powell finds fault with the easy influence of Lord Goring, the Wildean dandy in the play, who is, Powell feels, too easily and quickly able to influence Lady Chiltern, the "childless feminist . . . agitator for votes for women" (105). It seems to me that Powell underestimates the degree of her masochism. Wilde recognized it because he was always struggling with his own masochism, of which she was one expression: "I am afraid that women appreciate cruelty, downright cruelty, more than anything else" (*CW,* 86), he wrote in *The Picture of Dorian Gray,* a remark that has often been singled out as an anti-female or feminist statement. Those who do so forget that Wilde arrived at such formulations by looking into his own soul, and that he understood, though he could not control, his own masochism.

In a similar vein, Powell wonders why Wilde's dandy, Lord Goring, "links love and politics so sentimentally . . . preaches such a retrograde sexual ethic as the one he expounds to Lady Chiltern, and . . . ends the play by choosing a domestic life in preference to any other" (105). This is no mystery, and betrays no lack of sophistication on Lord Goring's part. He gives Lady Chiltern, a high-strung, masochistic woman, exactly the sort of advice that will appeal to her need to suffer, but that will also save her marriage, which she wants to save. Lord Goring is "retrograde" in his sexual politics out of sheer sympathy and human interest. Were Lady Chiltern blessed with better self-understanding, and a sense of humor, he might have said, "Oh, come on, leave the man alone." But such advice would have proven fatal, given her desire to suffer — expressed in her pained Puritanism — and her lack of worldliness.

Powell does point out that "instead of converting the lapsed husband to an ideal of the man — a usual outcome in plays of this type, Wilde turns the tables and unconverts the wife just before the curtain drops on the last act" (106). He feels that time has been wasted on the "uncontrolled vacillation" of Chiltern, making Lady Chiltern's reversal implausible. For Powell, it is "awkward and unconvincing" to have her tear up the letter of resignation that she, with her ardent feminist pride, has just written for her husband — but I find this only another believable instance of her aggression: she tears up a part of herself instead of tearing up her husband, and so is satisfied. I find this a sophisticated ending, not a failure; the ending provides some resolution for her controlling desire that he be absolutely pure, her unforgiving demand that he have no flaws.

Powell's final remarks in this chapter are insightful. He writes, "One of the strange features of *An Ideal Husband,* reflective of its historical moment, is that simultaneously it seeks to dismantle and to preserve the double standard as it applies to women." Lady Chiltern, like Lady Windermere, "must develop tolerance," for moral lapses, for lack of perfection. Powell does not say so in as many words, but this implies that these women grow up, ceasing to idealize their husbands as god-like beings the way a young girl idealizes her father. Lady Chiltern, Powell observes, "like her husband, must find the strength of character to be bad" (107).

Powell's next chapter, "The Importance of Being at Terry's," is a brilliant piece of speculative sleuthing. "Although no biographer records it," he tantalizingly remarks, "one day near the end of August or beginning of September 1894 Wilde may have ventured into Terry's Theater in the Strand to see a rollicking three-act farce that would alter the course of his career" (108). By the end of the chapter, nothing seems surer than that Wilde had been to Terry's and enjoyed a now-forgotten three-act farce, *The Foundling*, by W. Lestocq and E. M. Robinson, a play that more than inspired *The Importance of Being Earnest*.

Powell's meticulous coverage of Wilde's literary activities, in relation to the run of *The Foundling*, convincingly reveals the important influence of that play — which survives now only in a few typewritten versions. Wilde never mentions *The Foundling* in published letters or other works, but the comedy opened just at the time he was writing, or was about to write, *The Importance of Being Earnest*, in the late summer of 1894. Just at this time, Wilde wrote an undated letter to George Alexander, actor-manager of the St. James Theater, asking for an advance of £150 on a "slight" comedy "with lots of fun and wit" in it. He wrote *Earnest* in three weeks, and it was "exactly three weeks from the opening night of *The Foundling* to 19 September 1894 — the date stamped on the first typed copy of *Earnest* by Mrs. Marshall's Typing Service, which worked from Wilde's handwritten draft" (109).

Powell discusses the problem of dating Wilde's composition of *Earnest*, which is not recorded; only the date of the first typescript is identified by the stamp of the typing agency. The undated letter in which Wilde states that he was "just finishing a new play . . ." (*Letters*, 364) has been dated August 1894 by Rupert Hart-Davis, but Powell argues that that date is unsupported by evidence. He points out that Wilde, who may well have been in Worthing writing the play by the end of August, could easily have taken the train to London to go to the theater.

Before going into the extraordinary similarities between *The Foundling* and *The Importance of Being Earnest*, Powell discusses the many sources used — and, he says, resisted — by Wilde. One reviewer said *Earnest* "was as full of echoes as Prospero's Isle" (110). The tricks and devices of the play occurred in a number of other plays of the period, and Algernon's "gluttonizing of muffins and cucumber sandwiches" is "reminiscent of the ritual food gags of Victorian farce — from pouring tea in a hat in *Charley's Aunt* to throwing bacon and chops out the window in *Box and Cox*" (110). A number of French farces, Powell writes, anticipate the "Bunburying" motif, with imaginary illnesses attributed to a non-existent invalid so that the hero can get out of undesired social engagements.

Turning then to a point-by-point comparison of *Earnest* and *The Foundling*, Powell mentions the following: both plays include "a domineering aunt" or a "strong matriarch" thwarting a young woman's love for a man named Jack. (In Wilde's play, Lady Bracknell tries to end her daughter Gwendolen's engagement to Jack; in *The Foundling*, the aunt tries to get her niece away from a man named Jack, who is considered inappropriate for similar reasons — lack of family connections.) Both plays include situations in which two women find themselves attached to or engaged to the same man. In both plays, the engaged man does not know who he is. "Confusion about identity was a routine feature of Victorian farce," Powell adds, "but the similarity of *Earnest* with *The Foundling* in this respect may be too close to be explained generically" (111). Powell remains too cautious: the similarities scream from the page. In *Earnest*, Jack Worthing admits, "I have lost both my parents"; in *The Foundling*, Dick Pennell, when asked about his parents, answers, "I've lost them." Interrogated by the matriarch, who wants him to come to the point with more information, Pennell says, "I will . . . I don't know who I am," and Wilde's Jack, in the identical situation, replies, "I don't actually know who I am" (111–12).

Powell goes on to reveal that Jack's and Dick Pennell's reasons for not knowing their identities are nearly the same. Both are foundlings. Further similarities between the two plays abound. The first act of both plays includes a character playing wedding music on the piano. In both plays, young ladies turn out to be the last to know of their engagements.

Wilde also borrows from *The Foundling* the comic use of names, especially the idea of the marital desirability of one name over another. The concept of christening differs, however, in Wilde's much funnier play. In Powell's reading, "the humorous incongruity of the hero's being christened appears only once, and metaphorically at that, in Lestocq and Robson's play. Wilde, by comparison, has Algy and Jack actually make appointments to be christened by Canon Chasuble and introduces baptism as a comic motif in every act of *The Importance of Being Earnest*" (114).

At this point, Powell discusses a key difference between *Earnest* and *The Foundling*, the overarching principle that renders *Earnest* so much more original: "much of *Earnest's* fantastic humor — its quality of having gotten free of trammeling reality — is the result of Wilde's making what are fanciful metaphors in *The Foundling* into actual events in his own farce. Thus Dick Pennell in *The Foundling* never seriously intends to get christened, but Wilde's grown-up babies, Algy and Jack, lay elaborate plans for the ceremony and have every intention of going through with it" (114).

Wilde literalizes another metaphor borrowed from *The Foundling*, that of the similarity between the foundling's story and a sensational novel. While Dick tells his father to listen to "a novel in a nutshell," that is, his life story, in *Earnest*, Miss Prism, the governess, "treats the foundling-hero as a person in a novel — indeed as if he were the three-volume sentimental novel she wrote 'in earlier days'" (114). Powell summarizes the following elements taken from *The Foundling*: the bill collection episode, giving Mama "the slip," the "Baby Boy" finds his mother (after first embracing the wrong woman), and, in an extraordinary similarity, "both plays end with the foundling's discovery that his mother was a woman of rank, lawfully married, and that his father pursued a career in India!" (118).

At this point, Powell gives some of the finest illustrations of his thesis that the more intimately Wilde borrowed from a source, the more original his work became. Wilde loved to turn the ordinary idea inside out, and in writing *Earnest* he "takes up the devices of farce in general, of *The Foundling* in particular, and stands them upside-down" (119). What is "amusing and tangential" in *The Foundling* thus becomes in *Earnest* "improbable but central fact" (119).

The effect of Wilde's reversals of elements in *The Foundling* is revolutionary. Where "a typical farce dissolves into bland conventionality, Wilde's strikes at the root of accepted standards" (120). *The Foundling's* Sophie, discovering that Dick is not really named Dick, assures him that this doesn't matter: "I love you for yourself alone . . ." she tells him. Gwendolen and Cecily in Wilde's *Earnest* do just the opposite. Their lovers must be named Ernest, or marriage is not possible for them. Like most Victorian farces, *The Foundling* ends with all characters whose identities were mixed up being restored to right names and positions, and all who hid their identities apologizing for this wickedness.

Not in Wilde! In *Earnest*, "there is no such decay of lying," Powell quips, using the title of one of Wilde's best-known essay-dialogues, "no decline into the ordered serenity of customary life and conventional view. Instead, the heroes are permanently liberated from their former identities — Jack really is Ernest by the end of the play, and Algernon really is his brother" (120). Nor do they repent their wicked ways.

With these changes, Wilde lambastes the "keystone Victorian ideal of earnestness — with its aura of zealous effort, sincerity, and high seriousness." To be Ernest, Powell interprets, "is to be the 'true liar' who overcomes dreary actuality with charming delusions, pursuing a life of pleasure and beauty without reference to clumsy fact" (121). And therein lies the originality of the play's humor and philosophy.

Powell's final chapter, "Algernon's Other Brothers," is another *tour-de-force,* demonstrating the serious, philosophical wisdom of Wilde in the midst of comedies that have been taken as light or as lacking emotional and intellectual depth. Though Wilde could never have written his own comedies without a "thorough, practical knowledge of what was being done in the lowly theatrical genre of farce in the 1890s," Wilde's plays are entirely different, possessing "an undercurrent of seriousness which was mostly absent among other farces of the day." Powell demolishes the traditional and popular view of *Earnest* as "a wisp of fantasy, void of significance and unconnected even to reality," mentioning Richard Ellmann's view of *Earnest* as "leading toward a ceremonial unmasking, its characters, like their creator, craving to show what they are" (125). Wilde takes serious subjects — identity, death, money, marriage, sociology, economics, and the class system — and attacks the traditional, "earnest" views of these things. Powell quotes Eric Bentley's remark that Wilde's "flippancies repeated, developed, and . . . elaborated almost into a system amount to something in the end — and thereby cease to be flippant" (125).

Identity and crises of identity strike the keynote of many Victorian farces reviewed by Powell in this chapter — a common fin de siècle theme, certainly — and, as he says, the "real answer to Jack's inquiry of Lady Bracknell 'would you kindly inform me who I am?' — is thus more complicated than audiences today can appreciate. His identity cannot be disentangled, any more than his language, from that of the stock hero of late Victorian farce whose holiday frolic leaves the customary verities in turmoil, not least his own sense of self" (133).

In Victorian farces, Powell asserts, there is an "epidemic of mistaken identity" which arises from "a context of repression and revolt. The despotic parent is defied, and with him or her the constellation of authorized values in whose name obedience is exacted." The young people in *Earnest* rebel against "custom itself" when they thwart Lady Bracknell, not just "the stout woman who so brilliantly exacts conformity to it" (131). The modest maidens of Victorian farce are replaced by the aggressive, assertive Gwendolen and Cecily. The serious business of *Earnest* is to critique and to replace Victorian values.

In his epilogue, Powell sums up other qualities that put Wilde's *Earnest* in a class by itself. For instance, in it Wilde "brazenly copies from numerous, if mostly forgotten playwrights, yet surrenders less to his sources than ever before. One does not find in *Earnest* whole acts of indecision, the nearly disastrous hesitations between his own voice and that of another, which disfigure *Lady Windermere's Fan* and *An Ideal Husband"* (141). Powell also provides an answer to the question of why Wilde wrote no dramas after *Earnest*. Acknowledging the truth of the answer usually given, that the harshness of prison life extinguished his artistic powers, Powell reminds us that after prison, Wilde was in exile from the London stage. The conclusion is as sad as it is true: "absent from the turmoil of [the London theatre of the 1890s,] separated by barriers of time and distance, Oscar Wilde was left with nothing to answer, nothing to contend with, and, alas, nothing to say" (143).

Richard Allen Cave

Richard Allen Cave's article, "Power Structuring: the Presentation of Outsider Figures in Wilde's Plays," explores the ways in which Wilde can be seen as a man of the theater, not just a literary playwright. Cave relates that the publication of Wilde's letters "and the recent work of critics such as Kerry Powell and Katherine Worth have shown us the extent to which some roles in Wilde's plays were created with specific players in mind" (38). He observes that Wilde's stage directions, "when interpreted *spatially,* show Wilde devising a number of subtle visual strategies to stimulate and control an audience's imaginative engagement with particular roles" (39). Wilde deployed stage space in relation to his outsider figures, who dominate the action.

Cave discusses "two revealing sketches for stage designs for plays by Wilde," one in Wilde's hand for the last act of *Lady Windermere's Fan,* and the other made during a conversation with him about "a suitable setting for *Salome"* (40). The designs for *Salome,* he notices, are "starkly simple . . . what nowadays we would term 'minimalist.'" Other historical plays of the period were staged in considerably more cluttered settings. "Wilde's suggestions for a possible setting . . . refine the stage-picture down to the basic functional elements required by the action; by so doing he devised a means of consistently drawing an audience's attention to the power relations between the characters that structure the whole action" (41).

Turning to *Lady Windermere's Fan,* Cave focuses on Wilde's placement of a sofa in the last act. The scenery was the same as that required for the first act, but "Wilde was anxious that the disposition of the furniture would not be such as to place Mrs. Erlynne in the same position as that occupied by the Duchess of Berwick in the earlier act, since he wished no lingering memory of how the characters were arranged in the first scene to color an audience's response to the grouping of the actors in the fourth one" (41–42). Cave goes on to argue that the complex psychology of Mrs. Erlynne comes in part from Wilde's "use of stage space" (43). Wilde placed her on the sofa in such a way that she dominates the stage.

The audience's opinion of Mrs. Erlynne's character, Cave suggests, is gradually altered by "a consistently inventive and original use of stage space which continually invents the actress playing her with different manifestations of power" (46). Wilde continued to develop the technique of using space to demand that the audience revise its judgment of a character. Cave goes on to discuss two outsider figures in *An Ideal Husband*, Mrs. Cheveley, the adventuress-blackmailer, and Sir Robert Chiltern, the politician who has broken the law: "The whole play is concerned with ploys to expel Mrs. Cheveley from the stage . . . the stage space becomes, as the plot develops, a correlative for Chiltern's reputation" (47–48). In *The Importance of Being Earnest*, "we never see Lady Bracknell in a space that might be described as her own, not that that prevents her from endeavouring majestically to commandeer any room she enters and impose on it her sense of order and value" (48). Finally, Cave mentions the tableau at the end of *The Importance of Being Earnest*, which he suggests as a resolution of "all possible tensions that are a consequence of intricate power-relations between the characters within the stage space" (49–50).

Joel H. Kaplan

Joel Kaplan, in "Wilde in the Gorbals: Society Drama and Citizens Theatre," discusses a working class slum in Glasgow that existed in Wilde's time, and today "has become the unlikely site for a reappraisal of Wilde's achievement as a society playwright" (214). Kaplan contemplates the staging of Wilde's society dramas at the Glasgow's Citizens Theatre, which was established in the Gorbals in 1945. Focusing on the director/designer Philip Prowse's Wilde cycle of the 1980s — *A Woman of No Importance* (1984), *An Ideal Husband* (1986), and *Lady Windermere's Fan* (1988), Kaplan explores style, audience, and critical response, as well as the question of playing elitist drama at an extremely populist theater.

The Citizens Theatre has had an international reputation since the 1970s, and keeps its prices very low, so that it attracts one of the youngest audiences in Europe — forty-three percent of spectators are under age twenty-one. Philip Prowse's elaborate sculptural sets have been effective there. He has experimented with finding a "stylistic common ground upon which the conventions of genteel society might meet those of moral fable" (216). The first act of *A Woman of No Importance,* for example, "offered spectators a walled garden of brushed gold, with ornamental urns, daffodil banks," and was, according to Irving Wardle, "a pastoral from which nature had been painted out" (216). Other innovations are noted: the wicked Mrs. Cheveley, struggling to remove an incriminating bracelet that she has stolen, "hissed out a clearly audible four letter expletive" and ripped open her bodice, "in effect, crying 'rape' — and striding out past shamefaced master and scandalized man" (219). When the politician being blackmailed, who reconciles with his wife, asks her whether she feels love for him or pity merely, Prowse cuts her answer, "It is love, Robert. Love, and only love."

All this sounds wild, but not Wilde.

Peter Raby

Peter Raby, in "Wilde and European Theatre," remarks that "there is an aura of Englishness about some aspects of Wilde's Hibernian or Celtic plays" (328). Raby reviews recent productions of Wilde's comedies in England, and notes that they are once again "dominant in London's West End" (328). *Salome* was, Raby feels, "Wilde's first great gesture towards the theatre of Europe" (330). Thanks to the English Censor, the play became "a continental work, realizable only in Paris or Germany or Moscow. Written in French, it demonstrates Wilde's instinctive awareness of the potential of a new kind of theatre" (330). Raby feels that the choice of the great French actress, Sarah Bernhardt, for the role of Salome "was astute. What English actress could have taken the part at that point in the development of the English theatre?" He goes on to say that when *Salome* was produced in England, William Archer "suggested that the whole company should have been sent by special train to Berlin before attempting the play" (330).

Raby comments that *Salome* has usually been kept separate from the comedies in critical discussion, and that "the recent production of Wilde's more obviously Ibsen-like plays has [revealed] them as infinitely more subtle, multilayered and ambiguous than they have been usually regarded; less specifically English, more European in their frame of reference" (331). He stresses the connection between Ibsen and Wilde, citing other critics, particularly Kerry Powell, who have recently argued the same point. Not only were a number of the actors involved in

Wilde's comedies also cast in plays by Ibsen, but Wilde also borrowed serious subject matter from him: "This examining and playing with social gesture and convention, and their underlying meanings is, I would argue, what Wilde absorbed from Ibsen. He reveals the inherited Victorian and colonial value system as deeply flawed" (335). Raby argues that Wilde's characters, like Ibsen's, are isolated and often stuck in lives that do not appeal to them, while real life seems to go on elsewhere.

Gerd Rohmann

Gerd Rohmann, in "Re-Discovering Wilde in Travesties by Joyce and Stoppard," argues for two "important rediscoveries of Oscar Wilde in *Ulysses* (1922) and *Travesties* (1974)" (338). It all began with an unpleasant incident after James Joyce directed Wilde's *Importance of Being Earnest* at Zurich on April 29, 1919. Rohmann reports that the actor playing Algernon Moncrieff went into a rage after the performance, insisting that he be paid for the pants he had purchased for the amateur performance. Accusing Joyce of being "a cad and a swindler," he threatened to throw him down the stairs and sue him. Trials followed, Joyce winning and then losing and having to pay Carr's court costs and lawyer's fees, but Joyce took revenge in *Ulysses,* casting Carr as "a soldier of the lowest rank" (341), and making him and those who aided him look like fools. "How deeply the lost lawsuit and uncompensated humiliation hurt Joyce's ego," Rohmann writes, "is proved by the facts that he assumes the beaten Dedalus's role and . . . taking his worst revenge, develops Henry Carr into the worst character in *Ulysses*" (343).

Following Joyce, Tom Stoppard turns Carr into "an old man with a broken remembrance of things past. Wilde's drama . . . is exclusively enacted in Old Carr's memory" (344). Certain scenes, never performed, have shaped his character. Rohmann concludes this interesting tidbit of literary influence with the following remark: "*Ulysses* and *Travesties* cannot be fully understood by the traditional philological approaches to parody and persiflage. . . . The rediscovery of Wilde travestied by Joyce and Stoppard, however, inspires their literary creativity" (346).

Joseph Donohue

Joseph Donohue, in "Distance, Death and Desire in *Salome*," offers the interesting anecdote that after E. F. S. Pigott, the Lord Chamberlain's Examiner of Plays, had officially turned down Wilde's *Salome* on the grounds that biblical characters were prohibited on stage, he wrote to his colleague, Spencer Ponsonby, offering to send the play — which he called "half Biblical, half pornographic" — on for Ponsonby's *private edification & amusement.*" This would seem to illustrate the principle that pornography is defined as whatever gives the censor an erection. Donohue does not pursue Pigott further, but instead follows the rather ill-fated fortunes of *Salome,* mentioning that Robert Ross, Wilde's close friend, referred to the play bitterly as "a household word wherever the English language is not spoken" (119). Donohue goes on to mention the play's "great popularity in Europe, indicated by Walter Ledger's 1909 bibliography of translations into German, Czech, Greek, Italian, Hungarian, Polish, Russian, Spanish, Catalan, Swedish and Yiddish," and its great success as an opera by Richard Strauss.

Meanwhile, Donohue notes, "English literary and dramatic criticism ignored the work even more thoroughly than it did the rest of Wilde's writings" (119). He summarizes various approaches to *Salome,* and to the play's reevaluation that is currently underway, noting that "The mixed tone of wistfulness and bitterness in Wilde's 1892 interview on *Salome* seems only appropriate in view of its subsequent misfortunes" (120). Donohue says, "Salome as dancer, and Salome's dance, together set the keynote for understanding the play. Salome's remarkable psychic distance, her evident preoccupation and her unflinching remorselessness as she negotiates terms with Herod and, later, speaks to the severed head of Jokanaan (John the Baptist) itself, are crucial factors in Wilde's creation of his play and its central character" (121). Donohue does not specify here, but instead discusses what various manuscripts reveal about Wilde's style of composition, noting Wilde's well-known displeasure concerning Aubrey Beardsley's illustrations for the play, which caricatured Wilde in at least four different places. Even so, Wilde "attributed to Beardsley an insider's private knowledge, identifying him as 'the only artist who, besides myself, knows what the dance of the seven veils is, and can see that invisible dance'" (123).

Donohue mentions a diametric opposition between contemporary English and French reviewers of the play, the English mostly hating it and attacking it as derivative, but the French liking it. These early reviews have set the tone for current criticism: "Largely passing over Wilde's own ideas about art and aesthetics as expressed in his *Intentions* and other critical essays, scholarship and criticism on *Salome* have thus remained preoccupied with the plethora of external sources and 'influences' exerted on the author's thinking and writing by previously existing materials . . ." (123–24).

The author then turns to a question that he considers insufficiently assessed, namely the "real extent of Wilde's originality" (124–25). He notices the obvious, for instance, that in Wilde's version of several brief sketches found in Matthew 14:1–12 and Mark 6:14–29, Salome demands Jokanaan's head for her own purposes, rather than acting on the request of her mother. Donohue also notices that in Wilde's setting are "representatives of virtually the entire Mediterranean world . . . a Syrian, a Cappadocian, a Nubian . . . Jews" (125).

Turning to homosexual elements in the play, and the fact that "much commentary has focused on *Salome* as a covert homosexual work," Donohue concludes that there is "no clear line between heterosexual and homosexual concerns in *Salome*" (129). Instead, he feels what is central is "the representation of unquenchably strong desire itself, aside from its specific manifestations in gender and gender relations" (130). "However perverse Salome's desire for Jokanaan's head may be, the immutable strength of that desire itself — so great that it overcomes all the world and life itself — is, fundamentally, what the play is about" (131). This really does not say enough — not enough about reasons Wilde wanted to write about overpowering desire, and not enough about the sources of that overpowering desire. Donohue mentions Salome's strange final speech, in which she says that the mystery of love is greater than the mystery of death, but he makes no attempt to investigate this statement biographically or critically.

He does, however, rightly conclude that *Salome* "deserves renewed consideration as a master work of dramatic authorial self-expression and, simultaneously, a powerful and exemplary piece for the modern theatre: these are the polarities, subjective and objective, of its nature as a work of symbolist art" (137).

William Tydeman and Steven Price

The next study, *Wilde: Salome*, a series of essays on the writing, productions, and varying interpretations of Wilde's *Salome*, is billed by the publisher as the "first book length study of Oscar Wilde's *Salome*," offering a "detailed stage history of this controversial work and its transformation into opera, dance and film." A number of rare illustrations are included, among them the setting for Max Reinhardt's productions — the first after Wilde's death — and for Salvador Dali's designs for the 1949 Covent Garden production by Peter Brooks. Tydeman and Price's *Salome* is part of a series, *Plays in Production*, that also covers thus far Ibsen's *A Doll's House*, Miller's *Death of a Salesman*, and Molière's *Don Juan*. If the Wilde volume is representative, this must be an excellent series. The research is thorough, the writing brisk.

In four chapters and a conclusion, the book covers continental influences on Wilde's writing of the play, European stage productions in the early twentieth century, English stage productions between 1911 and 1990, transformations of the play by the original illustrator Aubrey Beardsley, Richard Strauss's opera, the style of the dance of the seven veils, and film versions of the play.

Mentioning the surprising fact that *Salome* was denied public presentation in Great Britain until 1931, the introduction discusses the impact of Wilde's homosexuality on the controversy surrounding the play and the "cult of overt, self-conscious masculinity" which "dominated the last years of Queen Victoria's reign," contributing to the rejection of the play on moral grounds (1). Commentary ensues on Wilde's attempts to use literary principles evolved by the French *Symbolistes*. The authors remark that Maeterlinck's *The Princesse Maleine* has sometimes been seen as a drama that Wilde attempted to parody in *Salome*. Instead, they argue, "Wilde, by mirroring the Princesse's hesitant, melodic, patterned prose, conjuring up mysterious invisible forces at work on human lives, and capturing Maeterlinck's brooding atmosphere of menace and anguish, was engaging in the sincerest form of flattery" (5).

Chapter one, "Beginnings," explores French influences on Wilde, the history of the play's composition, and the textual history of the play, including some useful information on the location of various manuscripts and some interpretation of that history.

Wilde's treatment of his biblical story, taken from the Gospels, was "preceded by those of Mallarmé, Moreau, Flaubert, Huysmans and Laforgue," the authors mention, adding: "small wonder that as Katherine Worth has observed, 'French airs play all round *Salome*'" (12). Despite the French literary influence and the fact that the play was written in French, its real subject matter "has its roots in Wilde's own academic as well as imaginative preoccupations," so that his choice of a biblical subject with "resonance" from "a collision of conflicting ideologies, Roman, Judaic and Christian," is important, reflecting Wilde's interests as a Classicist and vast knowledge of the Bible (13).

Tydeman and Price discuss three versions of *Salome*, which "all exist in holograph form," that confirm late autumn 1891 as the main period of the play's composition. The first draft is in the Bodmer Library, Geneva; another draft is in the Harry Ransom Research Center at the University of Texas; and a later copy is in the Rosenbach Foundation

Museum, Philadelphia. Accounts dating the play's composition by Rupert Hart-Davis and others are debated, and speculation is raised about Wilde's intentions for the play: "Whether or not Wilde envisaged live stage production for his play from the outset can never be resolved. . . . Certainly Robert Ross's firm assertion that the piece was never meant for stage presentation cannot go unchallenged" (19). No source is given for this surprising assertion, which seems to this reader less than likely.

Chapter two, "Early Stage Productions in Europe," begins with the admission that it would be impossible to cover all early major productions. "Rather than offer a piecemeal guide to as many performances as possible, we have first of all sought to give a detailed account of the earliest attempts to stage the play in France, Germany, England, and Russia." In each country, different styles emerged, "often as a result of the tensions between censorship and the theatrical traditions of the country concerned" (25).

Productions detailed in this chapter are those of the Théâtre de L'Oeuvre, Paris, February 1896; Max Reinhardt's Productions, 1902–04; the London Bijou Theatre, May 1905; the King's Hall, Covent Garden, London, 1906; the Kommissarzhevskaya Theater, St. Petersburg, October 1908; and the Kamerny Theater, Moscow, October 1917.

Particularly interesting is Tydeman and Price's coverage of the audience's reaction to the first public performance of *Salome* staged by Max Reinhardt: they gave the piece "a curious reception. Icy hissing, apparently for the play itself, was followed by friendly applause for the performers and also, it seems, for director and designs" (38). The ambivalence that the play frequently evokes is evident here.

Coverage of reviews suggests an awareness of the role filled by Wilde's sadness in giving rise to this play; the *Berliner Tageblatt* "found in Wilde 'the tired but superior scorn of the decadent,' at whose core 'lies a melancholy longing; melancholy because it is powerless and knows that it will have no fulfillment'" (39). Reviewers also saw Wilde in relation to a new literary age: "now, all at once, his art is bearing new blossoms; he is being translated and people are trying to 'save' him, and he is being played in the theatre. . . . The dead Oscar Wilde remained forgotten, until yesterday afternoon" (40).

While Max Reinhardt's innovative productions had "demonstrated the significance of the symbolist influence," the 1905 London performances at the Bijou Theatre were "stifled by a residual gentility" (40). Unlike Reinhardt's productions, there was no music. Salome, dressed in a toga, danced something deemed weird, Eastern, and "not entrancing." She came across as a "young English lady in the twentieth century," and Herodias was neither older nor less ladylike. Herod fared a bit better, though one reviewer described him as a "caricature of Osric, Slander, [and] Andrew Aguecheek rolled into one" (43).

The next important English production was greatly influenced by an artist friend of Wilde's, who was "the motivating force behind" it, a "pivotal figure in the stage history of the play" (44). Charles Ricketts had been asked by Wilde to design a *Salome* production in Paris, probably with Lugné-Poe, but the plan fell through (45). Tydeman and Price see Ricketts, who worked on designs for *Salome* productions in 1906 and 1919, as one who developed Wilde's ideas and whose experiences with the play reveal interesting differences between British and European traditions of staging. The British stage had too many physical restrictions, while Continental artists had "more generous staging areas" (45). Ricketts was frustrated with the small stage that he was stuck with in 1906, and which he found "ludicrously shallow." All kinds of amateurish problems plagued the production — Salomé's train was lost, she began her dance too soon and it was over too soon, she forgot to cover the head of St. John with a veil — but the audience seems to have liked it anyway.

In 1919, Ricketts presided over a Tokyo production of *Salome* by the Shochiku Theatrical Company. Although he "added touches of oriental detail . . . his final design for *Salome* remained very much in the pattern established in [a] conversation with Wilde over twenty-five years before" (57). Wilde and he had been particularly concerned with colors; Ricketts proposed, for instance, "a black floor, upon which Salome's feet could move like white doves" (46) and a range of bright colors for other characters and backdrop. These seem to have changed in their several conversations, but the basic idea of the black floor set off by bright colors remained.

The various attempts to stage *Salome* in Russia before and during the Russian revolution of 1917 grew out of a flourishing Wilde cult among Russian symbolists, and "no fewer than six Russian translations appeared between 1904 and 1908" since the play could be construed as anti-Church and anti-dogma, a position appealing to the revolutionary spirit of the times (58). Something about the "depiction of the catastrophes awaiting an old, corrupt and collapsing order . . . appealed to the Russian *Zeitgeist.*" In 1907 an attempt to stage *Salome* occurred in Moscow and in 1908, Nikolai Everinov of Saint Petersburg, "the Russian Oscar Wilde" (58), set the play "inside a giant scenic vagina" (60). To evade the censor, no scene with Jokanaan's head on a platter was included, but the Holy Synod, finding the dress rehearsal exceptionally well attended, pronounced the play an "unheard-of blasphemy," and banned it (62).

Chapter three, "*Salome* on the English Stage, 1911–1990," begins with a warning: "The history of *Salome* on the English stage does not allow for a fully coherent narrative." Censorship, amateurism, a scandalous trial in 1918, and a friendlier attitude to the play between 1929–31, are the basic elements (78).

The bizarre atmosphere surrounding the 1918 production has already enticed at least one scholar to write an entire book on the subject: Philip Hoare's *Oscar Wilde's Last Stand*. The gory details, as reported by Tydeman and Price, involve plenty of prudery and paranoia.

The 1918 J. T. Grein production was supposed to support a highly respectable cause: the war effort. But when a certain Noel Pemberton Billing, Independent M. P. for Hertfordshire, saw the advertisement for the play, he seized the opportunity to use the play to show that hidden German influences hampered Britain in the war effort. Grein and the actress to play Salome, Maud Allan, were immediately suspect. Pemberton published his own newspaper, *The Imperialist*, in which he claimed that the Germans were keeping track of 47,000 British men and women who had been corrupted by German agents! Where this exotic number came from no one knows. His assistant editor, one Captain Harold Spencer, had been discharged from the British army with "delusional insanity," and seems to have helped with the story and with renaming the paper *the Vigilante*.

These men wanted blood, and they got it by claiming that a "Wilde cult" drawn from the nefarious 47,000 corrupted British persons was endangering Great Britain in the form of Grein's production of *Salome*. It helped that Grein was foreign, born a Dutchman, and Maud Allan was allegedly a lesbian having an affair with Margot Asquith, wife of the former prime minister. The lunatic Harold Spencer then penned an announcement headed "The Cult of the Clitoris," asserting that if Scotland Yard were to seize the names of the members of "private performances" of Maud Allan's *Salome,* they would "secure names of the first 47,000" (81). Maud Allan and Grein issued a libel writ, and Billing had to appear in court, but then Billing and Spencer were allowed to say anything they liked about the supposed sexual habits of anyone they could think of. This included the Asquiths and the characters in Wilde's *Salome*. Maud Allan was called a "hereditary degenerate" because her brother had been executed for murder. Spencer "contended that any non-medical person who understood the meaning of the title 'The Cult of the Clitoris' must be a pervert and member of the cult" (82). Dr. Serrell Cooke was then trotted in, claiming that *Salome* was such a perverted and sadistic play that it would "induce orgasms" in the "lunatics" in the audience, that Wilde used the imagery of the moon in the play to excite certain types of female erotomaniacs, and that the full effect of Wilde's play would have its effect on these unfortunates if the play were performed on certain days of the month. "In addition to sadism and quasi-lycanthropy, Cooke identified the presence of fetishism, masochism, and incest." Billing claimed that his remarks were not intended to impugn Maud Allan's character, so he got off scot-free (82).

Artists and friends of Wilde were saddened; Robert Ross grumbled that the English enjoyed "kicking Oscar's corpse to make up for the failure of the Fifth Army" (83). Despite all the bad publicity, the production had a fair run, and audience members occasionally had difficulty getting a seat. Tydeman and Price commented: ". . . in an important sense Billing had done justice to the play. Both Maud Allan . . . and the magistrate . . . had asserted that the indecency might have been in the mind of Billing himself" (85–86). Tydeman and Price note Foucault's observation that repressive policing of sexuality was good, in the sense of producing "more and more ways of perceiving and talking about it" (86).

In the following section of the chapter, Tydeman and Price cover productions between 1929 and 1954, starting with what they consider to be "the most important British production yet staged" (86), and the "most challenging and sympathetic treatment of the play yet mounted in Britain" (88). The production took place at the Festival Theatre in Cambridge in 1929, first shown in June as a single performance, and then as a series of performances in November 1931.

The first professional production of *Salome* in London for over twenty years was that of Lindsay Kemp at the Roundhouse in February 1977. "Two aspects of this performance demand particular emphasis: its style, which was a kind of post-modernist 'total theatre,' and its foregrounding of the homosexuality which had almost invariably been treated with extreme caution" (98).

Kemp's production was "an assault on the senses, with deafening drumming, green and blood-red lighting, joss sticks in the hair of the slaves, incense burning in braziers, a live snake and a live dove, smoke, feathers, snatches of Wagner and Mozart, and more besides." As a mime trained by Marcel Marceau and a David Bowie groupie, Kemp had a certain cult status. He aimed to "restore to the theatre the glamour of the Folie Bergères, the danger of the circus, the sexuality of rock 'n' roll and the ritual of Death" (99).

Kemp, who shortened the text significantly, started the play with half an hour of drumbeats before any spoken words, and played Salome himself. Jokanaan had, Tydeman and Price note primly, "a specifically homosexual iconography" (100). The photo reveals a Jokanaan with chains wound around his neck and across his chest, binding his hands behind him, so that the iconography appears to this reader specifically sadomasochistic rather than homosexual. Tydeman and Price add that in Kemp's production Jokanaan's death becomes "an iconographic tableau" in which the prophet "died in a flurry of arrows," adding that this apparent reference to Saint Sebastian "carries a particular significance for gay men," a rather oblique reference to penetration (102).

The rest of the discussion for this section is curiously oblique; Tydeman and Price remark that "in aping the conventions of heterosexual role-play, Kemp's all-male cast was challenging its assumptions." The discussion of what these assumptions are is absent, unless one counts the description of Salome undressing to reveal "a middle-aged man making no pretense at conventional sexual attractiveness. . . . The implication is that this was an unveiling of the self, an honest exposure of the actor's essential being" (102). Is this meant to imply that homosexuals are more honest in unveiling themselves?

The discussion of Kemp's version of the dance is interesting, but also undeveloped. Remarking that they admired the Russian dancer Ida Rubenstein, Tydeman and Price comment, "If it is possible to see the shock of the play as lying in the expression of an unfettered female desire, equally that desire can be condemned as mere vampishness, Salome as archetypal whore. All the more devastating if that desire is now transformed into a mere effect of camp, a desire sanctioned and ultimately possessed by the male." They add that some feminists "have . . . argued against the play on similar grounds," referring to Kate Millett, but in fact Millett does not argue against the play in the work to which they refer, *Sexual Politics*. Nonetheless, Tydeman and Price state, "the shock denouement . . . both celebrates the validity of male homoeroticism and appropriates female sexuality for its own uses" (103). Yes, but what is the point? The significance of gay male "appropriation" of female sexuality (and why not borrowing? Why the rather military "appropriation"?) is not explored.

In chapter four, "Transformations," Tydeman and Price discuss the interesting phenomena that various versions of *Salome* — among them

Aubrey Beardsley's illustrations and Richard Strauss's opera — have achieved a prominence all their own, with several of them seeming to become more important than Wilde's version.

Tydeman and Price comment that while Beardsley's *Salome* "represents one of the finest books of the century," it remains controversial: "its admirers divide into those who believe that in several ways the artist willfully bypassed or misrepresented the poet's self-consciously crafted atmosphere in order both to satirise Wilde's aims and indulge personal imaginative preoccupations without being over-concerned to match them or those of his author, and those who consider that Beardsley subtly captured the true flavour of the work" (115).

A summary of Beardsley criticism follows, particularly that of Linda Gertner Zatlin and of Ewa Kuryluk. Zatlin finds the sexual power struggle in *Salome* to be mirrored in the Beardsley illustrations. Kuryluk examines the anthropological and mythological aspects of the *Salome* story, relating them to the grotesque in art (116).

Opinions differ, say Tydeman and Price, regarding the degree of collaboration between Wilde and Beardsley, but they point out that in "an inscribed copy of *Salome* Wilde was to claim that only Beardsley apart from himself knew the true nature of the Dance of the Seven Veils 'and can see that invisible dance.'" Beardsley's illustration of "The Stomach Dance" is perhaps "its graphic equivalent," they suggest (118). The several caricatures of Wilde that appear in Beardsley's drawing of the moon and in at least two other pictures, of the showman in "Enter Herodias" and of the Tetrarch in "The Eyes of Herod," are seen as going too far by some, and as witty private jokes between Beardsley and Wilde by others. The publisher, John Lane, did not object to male nudes, but did censor penises on a horned hermaphrodite and a naked love god on the title page, and fitted out the male attendant of Herodias with a fig leaf. A masturbatory Salome was vetoed and replaced by a drawing bereft of nudes but including Zola's *Nana*, *The Golden Ass*, and the Marquis de Sade's works on the book shelves drawn in. Beardsley's nude figures are "unlikely to offend today, but some may feel that in introducing coyness and prurient references to a work of frank rather than covert sexuality, Beardsley helped to create an ambiance in which Wilde's play could hardly be assessed fairly" (121).

Another transformation, Richard Strauss's 1905 opera of *Salome*, is then discussed. Tydeman and Price write, "The success Wilde's play enjoyed in Germany when first presented in Hedwig Lachmann's translation at Breslau during 1901 formed the prelude to probably its most exciting and enduring artistic transformation" (122). Strauss was then Germany's leading composer, as well as the conductor of the Berlin Court Opera and Berlin Philharmonic Orchestra. He made some textual alternations, restricting the role of the Cappadocian and de-emphasizing the importance of the moon, but more important, Tydeman and Price argue, "one might wish for rather less ambiguity in the presentation of the heroine." I am not sure that they are right in this objection; Wilde's text implies extreme ambivalence and ambiguity in Salome's love and hatred for Jokanaan, which are never fully separated. Nonetheless, the authors continue, "Despite Strauss's omission of any verbal clues as to Salome's chaste condition, the sensuous quality of the music does very little to confirm it, and occasionally might be felt to contradict it. Through the textual gaps Strauss may have hoped to convince the censor that his princess was a stranger to sexual desire, but the music is hardly in keeping with the composer's vision of Salome as an uncorrupted sixteen-year-old and not 'a cheap seductress'" (124).

Throughout the twentieth century, the actor playing Salome has often sung as well as danced the role, usually removing the final veil, and this is "certainly a feature of at least two performances available on videotape, those of Teresa Stratas in 1974 and Catherine Malfitano in 1990." Maria Ewing sang and danced "into a state of complete nakedness" in 1988 at Covent Garden (130). However, I recall the February 1989 New York Metropolitan Opera version in which the very large Salome, her bulk camouflaged by something resembling a prom dress, was portly enough that the idea of stripping off veils was limited to the symbolism of removing her detachable puff sleeves. That singer's voice was as large as her body, strong enough for the musically demanding role, as wonderful to hear as it was less than inspiring to see during the dance — a typical dilemma of staging *Salome*.

The February 1989 Met Opera production is discussed by Tydeman and Price, who do not mention the dance, but rather the "harsh postmodernist set" of that production. The set was intended "to show correspondences between one fin de siècle and another, striving to convey a sense of impending disaster by having 'limp male corpses' being lowered into a pit early in the action, implying that some kind of cataclysmic plague had engulfed Herod's kingdom." Disasters of our own fin de siècle were thought to be referred to — AIDS and Chernobyl, for example (133).

The next section of the chapter, "The Salome Dancer, 1895–1919," remarks that only in 1895 did dance routines begin to be choreographed, and identifies Loie Fuller (1862–1928) as a pioneer.

Maud Allan's "The Vision of Salome" took its artistic inspiration from Max Reinhardt's production of Wilde's play; Allan saw her as "an innocent girl of fourteen [who is] summoned to dance at the Tetrarch's whim" and seeks advice from her stepmother. Allan did not see her as a *femme fatale,* but rather as childish — an interpretation that seems closely to follow Wilde's text (142–43). Physically, however, Allan was a mature, shapely woman in her thirties. Tydeman and Price remark that "her performance depended on creating sexual arousal and was no doubt designed to do so" (143), rousing critical disagreements from praise to disgust. Allan's notoriety attracted other famous talents to the role — Mata Hari, who only managed to perform the role privately at a party in Rome, given by Prince de San Faustino, and Ida Rubenstein, a Russian Jewish dancer with some ballet training.

After these performances, *Salome* became part of the repertoire of the Ballets Russes during their 1913 Paris season with Tamara Karsarvina in the role (148), but this performance was not considered a success.

The final section of the chapter, "*Salome* on Film," remarks that the British Film Institute's catalogue "lists twenty versions of the *Salome* story, several of which are renditions of the opera, while many others finally have little to do with Wilde" (151). Almost all film versions fail to capture "the symbolic structures of Wilde's play," meaning the repetitions, refrains, and settings (152).

The most interesting of the early films here discussed is Alla Nazimova's 1922 silent film. Before that, there were a few versions in 1908, 1910, and 1918, the last one being "unequivocally a 'vamp' film" (154). Theda Bara, already a cult figure, danced Salome: "Supposedly born in the shadow of the Sphinx, the offspring of a sheik and a princess, she was in fact Theodosia Goodman, daughter of a Cincinnati tailor." Bara's Salome was, according to a contemporary reviewer, "an inhuman fiend, with an insatiable passion for wickedness for its own sake ... even Oscar Wilde's conception of the Princess does not achieve quite the complete heartlessness and abandoned deviltry of the heroine of this film" (156). Having John the Baptist beheaded and kissing his severed head isn't enough for Bara's Salome: she also manages to have David, the High Priest, drowned, tries to poison Herod's wife Mariamne, and then tricks Herod into having his wife executed (157).

Tydeman and Price comment that Bara's Salome, although departing significantly from Wilde's story line, represents as a vamp "in pure

form the misogyny which many have detected as unconscious motivation behind Wilde's fascination with the figure" (157).

Bara herself saw her vamp characterizations as "the vengeance of my
sex upon its exploiters," claiming that she might have the face of a
vampire but the "heart of a 'feminist'" (158). Alternatively, Alla Nazimova, "reputedly a lesbian . . . familiar with the Billing case," had another agenda, and "would have found in Wilde's play a transgressive
sexuality all the more powerful for its inscription within roles all too
easily reduced to heterosexual stereotypes" (159). Nazimova wanted to
question the validity of accepted sexual roles and stereotypes, or to
demonstrate that lesbianism was a valid lifestyle. She sent this message
subtly by using an entirely gay cast, but of course only the *Cognoscenti*
knew that the cast was all-gay.

After William Dieterle's 1953 *Salome*, in which Rita Hayworth, a
saccharine Salome, dances to save John's head, nothing appeared until
1971 when a Danish director, Werner Schroeter, made a film based on
Wilde's text. The following year an Italian, Carmelo Bene, directed a
Salome film with an existential reading of Wilde, glossing the story as a
parable of the "impossibility of martyrdom . . . in a world such as the
present which is no longer barbarian but just stupid. . . . All that is left
is survival" (167). A 1986 version by Claude D'Anna added, among
other things, an emissary of Caesar named Nerva, who accompanies the
sixteen-year-old Salome to the court of Herod and Herodias. Twelve
years before, Herod had killed Salome's father, Philip.

Finally, the most recent film of the *Salome* story is Ken Russell's
1987 film, *Salome's Last Dance*, "reputedly made in three weeks for less
than a million pounds to win a bet." Tydeman and Price have no use
for this production, which they condemn for proposing a "direct and
crudely expressionistic relationship between an artist's life and his
work" (171), a formulation that I find not insulting to Wilde and accurate except for the term "crudely." The authors, however, go so far as
to compare the film to the Billing character assassination of 1918.
Some events in the film are imaginary and some are not; I found much
of the imagined material — for instance, that Wilde sees a private performance of *Salome* in a male brothel — believable. Lord Alfred
Douglas, his lover, is cast as Jokanaan, which seems less believable,
since Douglas was anything but ascetic, and Wilde by most accounts
was the one who was tempted and seduced by him rather than the
other way around. Salome, played by Imogen Millais-Scott, intended to
be a chambermaid at the brothel (Tydeman and Price get her wrong,
insisting that she is a prostitute) was quite realistic as a flunky who

comes to life as an actress, playing Salome as a greedy child-cum-seductress to the hilt. Tydeman and Price condemn "witless bad taste" which, according to them, is "often close to the surface" of Russell's films. So, for instance, when Herod mentions the wind — which directors have often used to suggest the power of hidden forces — the Roman ambassador, "Tigellinus, farts loudly, several times. On receiving John's head, Salome masturbates on top of it" (172). Well, why shouldn't she? Her behavior seems entirely within character, and the fart joke is the sort of thing Wilde would have enjoyed, if one judges by the bad puns in *The Importance of Being Earnest.*

Tydeman and Price's conclusion offers interesting remarks about the obliquity surrounding Wilde and *Salome,* as well as about the changing representations of Salome's sexuality. They credit studies following Richard Ellmann's biography of Wilde for illuminating "problems in the stage presentation of sexuality," and for making it possible to perceive the play as a document allowing "contemporary issues of gender" to be seen. Before the First World War, they remark, "the Salome figure became an embodiment of what anti-feminists viewed as the destructive male-crushing threat posed by a certain type of woman usually designated the *femme fatale*" (175). In the years immediately following Wilde's imprisonment, Salome was generally seen as a predatory castrating vampire type. The single-minded assertiveness of Salome has also been given a politically positive spin; Elaine Showalter, for one, sees her as encapsulating the New Woman, that is, the emancipated woman of the professional class in the 1890s (176).

The authors turn to Kate Millett's account of *Salome* in *Sexual Politics,* because Millett describes Salome as having "an imperious sexual will. . . . Nothing so passive as a vaginal trap, she is an irresistible force and is supposed to betoken an insatiable clitoral demand that has never encountered resistance to its whims before." Tydeman and Price interpret these remarks as sizing up Salome as a "castrating woman," but that is not what Millett says. She offers an essentially Freudian reading here, recognizing the insatiable and impulsive quality of childhood sexuality in Salome, and also perceiving that Salome "is Oscar Wilde too" (177). It is not surprising that Millett took a Freudian view, since her thesis advisor for the document later published as *Sexual Politics* was Steven Marcus, the well-known Freudian critic.

Tydeman and Price criticize Millett for reading Wilde's homosexuality as "something single, unproblematic and knowable" (178), serving up the trendy critics Alan Sinfield and Jonathan Dollimore as counterweights who assert that the concept of homosexuality was only just in the process of being named in the 1890s, and that Wilde "was not generally perceived as homosexual by his contemporaries until his prosecution in 1895" (178). To say that his contemporaries preferred to deny his sexuality, while perceiving, yet not acknowledging the perception, might be more accurate. I discuss Sinfield's work at length elsewhere and so will not comment further on it here.

Tydeman and Price then turn to a topic that is less controversial and therefore requires less jargon — literary influence: "If *Salome* reflected certain aspects of late-Victorian and Edwardian gender politics, its treatment of verbal and nonverbal communication had weighty literary and theatrical implications for W. B. Yeats, who, like Hugo von Hofmannsthal in Austria, suffered a loss of faith in the adequacy of the written word" (179). Yeats and Hofmannsthal both lost faith in words and came to believe that actors and dancers could transcend words; both felt a disgust with the inadequacy of words to convey feeling (179–80). Two of Yeats' plays, *A Full Moon in March* and *The King of the Great Clock Tower* (both 1935), borrow from Wilde's *Salome* "a sexual encounter between a cruel royal personage and an unsubmissive ardent male commoner, albeit one now who dares to woo the indifferent Queen rather than resist her overtures; an act of violent revenge which terminates with the severance of a head; and a ritual dance" (180).

Mentioning a few balletic treatments of *Salome,* in particular a Danish one in 1978 that drew hostile reviews, Tydeman and Price close their book reflecting on a question: "how far is a dancer or choreographer wise to attempt a naturalistic presentation of Salome's performance before Herod?" They comment that "dance as 'self-expression,' dance as an attempt to portray something in terms of literal interpretation, is of comparatively recent origin and may be doomed to fail" (182). They see danger if "the very eroticism may create a sexual frisson which becomes the be-all and end-all of the entire portrayal: the dance should surely represent a high point in the action, not a premature conclusion to the piece." The impact of the work, they reflect, "depends to a large extent on where the emphases are placed in the interaction of the various elements foregrounded in the play." The many opportunities that the drama provides for poets, dancers, lighting designers, designers of sets and costumes, choreographers, composers and musicians "suggest that even in 1891 Wilde may have glimpsed his play's enormous future stage potential" (183).

Works Cited

Behrendt, Patricia Flanagan. 1991. *Oscar Wilde: Eros and Aesthetics*. London: Macmillan.

Brown, Julia Prewitt. 1997. *Cosmopolitan Criticism: Oscar Wilde's Philosophy of Art*. Charlottesville and London: The UP of Virginia.

Cave, Richard Allen. "Power Structuring: the Presentation of Outsider Figures in Wilde's Plays." *Rediscovering Oscar Wilde*. Ed. C. George Sandulescu. Princess Grace Irish Library: 8. Gerrards Cross: Colin Smythe.

Ellmann, Richard. 1988. *Oscar Wilde*. New York: Vintage.

Eltis, Sos. 1996. *Revising Wilde: Society and Subversion in the Plays of Oscar Wilde*. Oxford: Clarendon Press.

Gagnier, Regenia, ed. 1991. *Critical Essays on Oscar Wilde*. New York: G. K. Hall.

Hart-Davis, Rupert, ed. 1962. *The Letters of Oscar Wilde*. New York: Harcourt, Brace and World.

Hoare, Philip. 1997. *Oscar Wilde's Last Stand*. New York: Arcade.

Murray, Isobel. 1994. "Oscar Wilde in His Literary Element: Yet Another Source for Dorian Gray?" *Rediscovering Oscar Wilde*. Ed. C. George Sandulescu. Princess Grace Irish Library: 8. Gerrards Cross: Colin Smythe.

Powell, Kerry. 1990. *Oscar Wilde and the Theatre of the 1890s*. Cambridge: Cambridge UP.

Raby, Peter. 1994. "Wilde and European Theatre." *Rediscovering Oscar Wilde*. Ed. C. George Sandulescu. Princess Grace Irish Library: 8. Gerrards Cross: Colin Smythe.

———, ed. 1997. *The Cambridge Companion to Oscar Wilde*. New York: Cambridge UP.

Rohmann, Gerd. 1994. "Re-Discovering Oscar Wilde in Travesties by Joyce and Stoppard." *Rediscovering Oscar Wilde*. Ed. C. George Sandulescu. Princess Grace Irish Library: 8. Gerrards Cross: Colin Smythe.

Sandulescu, C. George, ed. 1994. *Rediscovering Oscar Wilde*. Princess Grace Irish Library: 8. Gerrards Cross: Colin Smythe.

Tydeman, William and Steven Price. 1996. *Wilde: Salome*. Cambridge: Cambridge UP.

Zhang, Longxi. [1988] 1991. "Oscar Wilde's Critical Legacy." *Critical Essays on Oscar Wilde*. Ed. Regenia Gagnier. New York: G. K. Hall.

2: New Historicism

N EW HISTORICISM WAS inaugurated by the Renaissance scholar Stephen Greenblatt in his introduction to a special issue of the journal *Genre* entitled "The Forms of Power and the Power of Forms in the
Renaissance."[1] In an essay, "Resonance and Wonder," from his 1990
collection, *Learning to Curse: Essays in Early Modern Culture*, Greenblatt remarks that the new historicism "like the Holy Roman Empire,
constantly belies its own name" (164). He then gives the *American
Heritage Dictionary's* three meanings for the term "historicism," and
discusses ways in which his own work goes "resolutely against each of
these positions." Whatever the new historicism is, it excludes the following dictionary definitions seized upon by Greenblatt:

> 1. The belief that processes are at work in history that man can do
> little to alter.
> 2. The theory that the historian must avoid all value judgements in
> his study of past periods or of former cultures.
> 3. Veneration of the past or tradition.

Among Greenblatt's objections to these values of traditional, or "old"
historicism, is its universalism: "New historicism . . . eschews the use of
the term 'man'; interest lies not in the abstract universal but in particular, contingent cases, the selves fashioned and acting according to the
generative rules and conflicts of a given culture" (164). Greenblatt
quotes the objection of a Marxist critic to the new historicism, that new
historicists seize on items that the Marxist considers out of the way and
obscure, among these things, dreams, popular or aristocratic festivals,
denunciations of witchcraft, sexual treatises, reports on disease, birth
and death records. Greenblatt is fascinated to find "concerns like these"
being designated "bizarre" (169).[2]

Since that time, New Historicism has developed into a series of approaches rather than a unified school of thought. Influenced by the
writings of Michel Foucault and Raymond Williams, New Historicists
usually agree with the Foucauldian notion that the author and the living person who write a book should not be equated. The concept of
the author, Foucault claimed, occurred when writers became subject to
punishment for what they had written. "Author" or "Author function"

are therefore, in Foucault's thinking, terms that describe a culture or a society more than they do a person. Using this theory, for example, Oscar Wilde can be read as a text of Victorian culture's homophobia, or a text of English hatred for the Irish, rather than as a personality with a particular inborn human nature that remains constant despite the impact of his culture. New Historicists tend to reject the notion of human nature as an unchanging constant, preferring to believe that many human natures are constructed by many distinct societies. To assert with Aristotle that "fire burns both here and in Persia," implying that people behave similarly everywhere, pegs a critic as an essentialist, and also as a member of the old school of historicism.

A general New Historical trend includes an interest in figures that might once have been designated minor, and might now be deemed marginalized by their culture. A marginalized incident, one that gets pushed to the verge of being forgotten or, alternatively, rejected by a culture, may be interpreted as casting light on secrets or tensions within that culture. For example, during the Oscar Wilde trials, newspapers did not name or describe explicitly his sexual activities. An increased interest in what people ate or how they paid their bills, rather than an attempt to study so-called major intellectual trends in thought or major cultural trends in art, also typifies New Historicism. Yet this remains an incomplete depiction; it is easier to say what New Historicism excludes than to define it precisely: it does not believe in large processes in history that human beings cannot alter; it does not venerate past traditions. Hayden White summed up the New Historicists as follows: "What they have specifically discovered . . . is that there is no such thing as a specifically historical approach to the study of history, but a variety of such approaches, at least as many as there are positions on the ideological spectrum."[3]

Into this category I place an article by Lawrence Danson entitled "Each Man Kills the Thing He Loves: The Impermanence of Personality in Oscar Wilde"; books by Michael Foldy and Lawrence Danson; and an essay collection that examines lesser known features of Wilde's history (*Reading Wilde, Querying Spaces: An Exhibition Commemorating the 100th Anniversary of the Trials of Oscar Wilde*, edited by Carolyn Dever and Marvin J. Taylor). Michael Foldy defines his method in *The Trials of Oscar Wilde: Deviance, Morality, and Late-Victorian Society*, as a "micro-history," insofar as it "examines the complexity of relatively small-scale or 'minor' historical events," which are in fact an index of "larger social and cultural processes which envelop it and of which it is a part" (xi).

Lawrence Danson

Lawrence Danson's study, *Wilde's Intentions*, includes theoretical material that is consistent with New Historicism, particularly Foucault's idea of reading the author as an icon of his culture, rather than emphasizing ways in which the culture made a mark on his personality or ways in which his personality made a mark on the culture.

In "Each Man Kills the Thing He Loves: The Impermanence of Personality in Oscar Wilde," Danson begins with a dramatic moment in *The Picture of Dorian Gray*. The painter Basil Hallward encounters the beautiful young man, Dorian, for the first time, and feels that Dorian's "mere personality" was "so fascinating that, if I allowed it to do so, it would absorb my whole nature, my whole soul, my very art itself" (82).

Danson then raises the interesting question of what "personality" means in this context, "what Basil designates by the word . . . what would it mean to be absorbed by or to escape one . . ." (82). Personality, we are told, is a "Wildean keyword from the time of his earliest reviews and lectures through his writing of *De Profundis*." Wilde's use of the word "suggests that one of the defining problems of early twentieth century literary modernism is already present in Wilde's *fin de siècle* aestheticism" (83). Danson selects quotations from T. S. Eliot, Ezra Pound, and Wilde to show a common thread, the "contradictory notion of a personality that is at once imprisoning and insubstantial" (83), present also in Wilde's precursor Walter Pater.

At times in Wilde's career, Danson finds, "and *The Picture of Dorian Gray* is one such time — the word 'personality' bears the weight of unresolvable contradictions" (85). (But what didn't bear the weight of unresolvable contradictions in Wilde's career? This remark does not distinguish personality from any other aspect of Wilde's life.) Yet Danson states some interesting facts: in the early 1880s, lecturing in America and reviewing in London, "Wilde often used the word in counterpoint to the word 'perfection' in a way to make personality a virtually quantifiable quality, simply half of the equation which equals 'art'" (85). He often contrasted personality with perfection throughout his career.

Danson writes that in some nineteenth century intellectual contexts, there were two extremes in conceptualizing personality — one that he describes as something intangible and continuously evolving, the other "what Maude Ellmann calls 'the unified transcendent consciousness that the nineteenth century had understood as "personality"' (86). He quotes the psychologist Dr. Henry Maudsley in *The Pathology of Mind*

(1879), who wrote that personality is the "physiological unit of organic functions" (86). Maudsley spoke of "something deeper than consciousness [which] constitutes our fundamental personality" (86), a sign that for Coleridge, who wrote in a letter that "we need a new word for something like underconsciousness," and for many other nineteenth-century writers and scientists, including especially Wilde, awareness of an unconscious mind was growing. Danson does not comment on this, however, remarking only that "this is the transcendent, essential, personality which the OED defines as 'the quality, character or fact of being a person as distinct from being a form" (86). Danson has missed the revolutionary moment here, the awareness, not so easily found before the nineteenth century, of a distinct portion of the mind that remains severed from consciousness, and which would be studied and mapped by Freud.

Danson declares that all personalities are distinct from one another, equal, "except that some personalities are more equal than others. The slippage from 'personality' designating mere personhood to 'personality' designating a special person with qualities different in kind or degree from those who" are persons but not personalities, "has happened by the time of Dorian Gray." He speaks of the "commodified" or "media" personality who "depends for its existence upon the perceptions of the less personified consuming others" (87).

Returning to Basil's feeling of being overwhelmed by Dorian's personality, Danson claims that Wilde constructs "a circular system of recognitions." Basil's terror when he meets Dorian face to face "registers the homosexual panic of his self-discovery; yet that discovery can only occur through Basil's recognition of Dorian's personality — a personality which cannot exist in Dorian until Basil has first read it into Dorian by projection from the personality he discovers in himself by reading Dorian" (89). In a complicated way, this traces the ground covered by Wilde in "The Critic as Artist," in which he explores the idea that all criticism projects onto the work of art the experiences and tastes of the critic. Danson quotes Wilde's summary of this idea in the preface to Dorian Gray: "it is the spectator, and not life that art really mirrors." This is in part a recognition of the power of the unconscious mind to form opinions, but Danson never mentions this. In the next paragraph, however, he quotes from Wilde's "Portrait of Mr. W. H.," yet another rendition of the same idea: "Art . . . can never really show us the external world. All that it shows us is our own soul . . ." (90).

In closing, Danson states, "In Wilde's fable, the circle is closed when Dorian in turn finds himself dominated by a personality and filled with a strange idolatry. That dominating personality is his own . . . the personality which kills itself" (92). This is an intriguing observation, not documented — although it certainly could be — by examples from Wilde.

Wilde's Intentions: The Artist in his Criticism, by Lawrence Danson, offers a general introduction to the current popularity and omnipresence of Oscar Wilde; a commentary on Wilde's collection of essays, *Intentions* (published in 1891), and the significance of that title; and essays interpreting each of Wilde's works in that collection.

Danson's introduction begins with a common theme of 1990s Wilde criticism: "still we agree as little about him as when first his ubiquity was the talk of two continents." Like many critics, he enumerates various Wildes: "Whistler's 'amiable irresponsible esurient Oscar': Saint Oscar, the Irish outsider, the queer martyr, the spiritual Oscar, the subversive Oscar; Oscar the canonical, Oscar the impostor, the one and only original, the pasticheur, plagiarist or postmodernist." Wilde's prison letter to Lord Alfred Douglas makes him "for some readers . . . Christlike in wisdom and suffering . . . for others an Ancient Mariner of self-pity" (1).

All this is true, but not new. Neither is Danson's next remark: "All this diversity and disagreement despite the fact that (as I once thought of calling this book) Oscar Wilde Tells All!" The "despite" ignores Wilde's efforts to show that *because* and not *despite* telling all, and *because* truth is constantly evolving, he became many different, conflicting figures, for many people. Because he changed his mind continually about who he was, he also became many different people. One could even say that "despite" efforts to hide behind his exhibitionism, he knew that, as he said, "if one tells the truth, one is sure, sooner or later, to be found out" (*CW*, 1205). He did want to hide some of himself some of the time, and confessed this. In a letter dated late February 1894, he mused on flaunting the Wilde that made the world laugh: "To the world I seem, by intention on my part, a dilettante and dandy merely — it is not wise to show one's heart to the world — and as seriousness of manner is the disguise of the fool, folly in its exquisite modes of triviality and indifference and lack of care is the robe of the wise man. In so vulgar an age as this we all needs masks" (*Letters*, 353).

Characteristic of 1990s criticism, this book largely ignores biography, though it could illuminate much about Wilde's literary and philosophical interests, styles, and desire to shape his own life as if it were a work of art. For instance, Danson remarks, "*Intentions* announces (sometimes by masking) the aggressive fact: in the book we can read

Wilde's intention to secure a powerful position at the centre of the culture whose values he was subverting. . . . With these essays . . . Wilde tried to create the conditions for his own social and literary success . . . to write himself into history by re-writing history" (6). Danson skims the surface of the biographical background giving rise to these ambitions, remarking only that the "Irish son of an Irish patriot would stand at the summit of a newly defined, a revised and perfected, ideal of English culture" (6).

What Irish patriotism meant to Oscar Wilde, however, is not what it meant to his patriotic mother, or to Michael Collins, or to other politically involved men and women. Even where shared political goals exist, patriotism, like most things, includes purely personal elements. In a post-prison letter, Wilde lamented: "A patriot put in prison for loving his country loves his country, and a poet in prison for loving boys loves boys" (*Letters*, 705). This equation of political struggle with the struggle for the rights of the homosexual needs exploration in order to understand Wilde, his writing, and his developing style. Instead, Danson says only this: "Beginnings, middles, and endings are surprisingly elusive in the brief drama of Wilde's career . . ." (2).

Danson's book mixes interesting observations, unclear, jargon-filled or abstract remarks, and dogmatic ideas about what Wilde meant, as though Wilde meant one thing when he usually means several (often intentionally contradictory) things. "The Wildean paradox unsettles the categorical," Danson writes, without getting into specifics. "It performs the Adamic work of naming in a world where all the names have already been used. It asserts the primacy of the speaker over the word, while recognizing that a new, oppositional meaning can only be accomplished by keeping the old meaning in circulation" (10). This is too vague to set Wilde apart from the average megalomaniac. Wilde's methods and motives for "Adamic" naming, or for attempting to redefine the world according to his own personal needs (some of which he neither liked nor understood himself), are not described.

In his essay on *Intentions*, Danson poses the question, "What were Wilde's Intentions?" (13). He remarks that they "had always been suspect" because of the charges of plagiarism leveled against Wilde and later the description of Dorian Gray as "sodomitical." This is beside the point. The public perception of Wilde as a plagiarist or a sodomitical seducer throws no light on his inner world; for that, one must explore his letters, in which he yearns for peace and quiet, as if the role he played as the debonair dandy suited him not at all. He intended above all to understand himself, but could not.

That desire for self-knowledge fueled the most basic of Wilde's intentions, but Danson does not say so. He does remark aptly that "by design, *Intentions* [as a title] brings to mind *Appreciations,* Walter Pater's book published the year before Wilde's and reviewed by Wilde in March 1890" (13). He could say much more about this, particularly since Pater, Wilde's tutor at Oxford, was one of Wilde's heroes and was, Wilde asserted in "The Critic as Artist," one of the essay-dialogues published in *Intentions,* "on the whole, the most perfect master of English prose now creating amongst us" (*CW,* 1017). But no careful exposition of Pater's influence follows. Danson only states that Wilde's character Gilbert, in "The Critic as Artist," brings to mind Pater. Gilbert quotes one of Pater's most famous passages about the Mona Lisa, but it is not immediately clear in Danson's reading that Gilbert is deliberately quoting Pater. Wilde's point — that critics project themselves into their criticism — is omitted. Wilde lets Gilbert pose the question, "Who cares whether Mr. Pater has put into the portrait of Mona Lisa something that Leonardo never dreamed of?. . . . [his criticism makes] the picture more wonderful to us than it really is, and reveals to us a secret of which, in truth, it knows nothing" (*CW,* 1029).

The image of Wilde shaking off the chains of accuracy, and the psychological and critical reality of his remark, the serious point that Pater understands the Mona Lisa because he has projected himself into it, go unnoticed by Danson. Instead, he remarks cynically that Wilde's quoting Pater "is one of his cruder demonstrations of the proposition that 'criticism of the highest kind' . . . treats the work of art simply as a starting point for a new creation. 'The Critic as Artist' takes Pater's work as its 'starting point' so often that it would be tedious to record all its specific echoes of homages, plagiarisms or purposeful distortions" (14). Yes — and yes to much of what follows — Danson's emphasis on Wilde's dialogue with Pater, and Pater as a figure of "unconventional sexuality" as well as a "true artist." But Wilde's essential ideas are lost in this parading of Pater's subtle influence. Pater did not have the idea that he was painting a self-portrait by describing the Mona Lisa. Wilde's recognition of this is a real advance in literary criticism.

Danson often misses Wilde's originality, as when he interprets the following passage from Wilde's "The Critic as Artist":

> . . . he to whom the present is the only thing that is present, knows
> nothing of the age in which he lives. To realise the nineteenth century
> one must realise every century that has preceded it, and that has con-
> tributed to its making. To know anything about oneself, one must
> know all about others. There must be no mood with which one can-

not sympathise, no dead mode of life that one cannot make alive (Danson 16).

Danson attempts to box Wilde into the following meaning:

According to *Intentions,* to be modern is to be *not* of one's age, and to know one's self is to know the 'moods' of otherness. . . . Wilde's definition of modernity as a turning backward, a rejection of the sufficiency of the moment, runs counter to the great Victorian passion for progress. But he has respectable allies in what would otherwise seem a perverse idea. Matthew Arnold . . . had also urged that the 'function of criticism' was to turn away from the activities of the 'present time' and to look instead both outwards, to Europe, and backwards to the touchstone art of older times (16).

These claims are inaccurate. Wilde does not reject the importance of the present. He rejects the idea that the present is "the only thing." He advocates understanding of the ways in which the past has created the present. In a letter of 1886 he remarked, "our most fiery moments of ecstasy are merely shadows of what somewhere else we have felt. . . . I myself would sacrifice anything for a new experience, and I know there is no such thing as a new experience at all" (*Letters,* 185). Wilde had a Freudian and a Hegelian understanding of the forces of the past in creating the present, and of the ways in which the past remains alive in the present of individual persons as well as of entire cultures. Danson's comments fail to recognize this.

Danson does raise some interesting questions, however. "To modern readers, with the blindness . . . of hindsight, one of the most puzzling questions of Wilde's intentions is whether he expected or wanted his sexuality to figure in his public image" (29). Danson speculates about meanings and intentions in Wilde's trials, and about the Marquess of Queensberry's accusation that Wilde was posing as a sodomite. Danson asks, "Why would anyone not guilty want to pose as guilty?" (29) — a question worth answering. Wilde wanted to destroy himself, and he wanted to do so out of some unnamed and undiscovered sense of guilt, which Danson traces to Wilde's homosexuality, but with no particular reason. Wilde's sexuality was not the single defining aspect of his being, although it is the best known. His inner conflicts had many sources, not exclusively or even predominantly the result of his homosexuality. He was torn as a child between his mother's and father's ideals and ways of living — his mother and her wish to be a revolutionary warrior fighting for Ireland, his father's desire to be a solitary scholar. "All women become like their mothers. That is their tragedy. No man does. That's his," Wilde remarked (*CW*, 335). Much more than homo-sexuality underlies the personal unhappiness beneath this remark, but Danson doesn't touch it.

Instead, he forges ahead with a discussion of whether effeminacy and homosexuality were virtually synonymous because of Wilde. "Contrary to his every intention," Danson writes, Wilde "became in the world's eyes not the artist of his own being but the representative of a nature he merely imitated, posing as a sodomite" (35). It was not contrary to Wilde's intentions to become known as one who posed as a sodomite; otherwise, he would have avoided doing so. His plays, with all their humor, include many situations that are blueprints for his eventual disgrace and exposure. That Wilde had many intentions, that he did and did not intend to destroy himself, that he saw a perverse triumph in self-destruction, are topics not entered into here.

The book's second chapter on Wilde's essay-dialogue "The Decay of Lying," one of Wilde's most important and interesting writings, quotes striking insights of Wilde without seeming to notice his psychological and philosophical acumen. He begins with a remark from "The Critic as Artist": "Ah, it is so easy to convert others. It is so difficult to convert oneself. To arrive at what one really believes, one must speak through lips different from one's own. To know the truth one must imagine myriads of falsehoods" (*CW*, 1047). Danson seems not to perceive this as serious, for his only comment concerns the character in the dialogue who utters this remark: "For Gilbert, 'truth' is, since it can be known; but it exists in close rhetorical quarters with 'what one really *believes*' (which is not necessarily synonymous with objective truth), and it — this truth of the mind — cannot be known apart from the imagining of falsehoods" (36). This unclear attempt to restate Wilde's elegant apercu adds little to our understanding of him. Wilde's point, the result of unhappy experience with his own conflicts, is that he would like to be able to convert himself to a new point of view, one that he could accept, and that he finds the only way that he can manage this is by pretending that he is someone else — as he does, for example, when he writes *The Picture of Dorian Gray*. In a letter, he stated that the three main characters in his novel were versions of himself, "Basil Hallward is what I think I am: Lord Henry what the world thinks me: Dorian what I would like to be — in other ages, perhaps" (*Letters*, 352). The "perhaps" reveals Wilde's habitual ambivalence, an inability to convert himself to any one position. As a writer, Wilde tried to quell ambivalence by imagining himself as another person, or as several different persons, and so to put his conflicts outside of himself.

Unfortunately for Wilde, none of the characters whose lips he spoke through enabled him not to doubt every conclusion as soon as he had reached it. He laughs at his conflicts in *The Importance of Being Earnest*, in a bizarre scene in which all the characters speak at once and say exactly the same thing.

Danson never gets beyond restating Wilde's idea that truth comes about through speaking as a "self other than the one which believes — as a mask, or a pose, or a character in one's own dialogue" (36). The implications of this statement for the understanding of fiction-writing are vast. Following Wilde, we can assume, as Freud does, that the characters created by an author represent his or her alternate selves, possibilities that he or she cannot recognize without the mask, namely the illusion that these created figures do not present parts of him or herself. This runs counter to the postmodern notion that the author does not exist — an important consideration, since Wilde is now often perceived as thinking in line with various postmodern ideas.

Wilde's dialogues entered into "a dialogue with a generation of modernists, including not only the Irish Yeats and Joyce, but also Pound and Eliot; Wilde spoke to them, and they replied" (39). Danson focuses on Eliot's description of poetry as "an escape from personality . . . only those who have personality and emotions know what it means to want to escape those things" (38). Eliot captures the reason for a writer's need to create characters here, the torment that forces creation, the need to escape the self that results in the invention of a number of unacknowledged selves. This description is similar to Wilde's remark that "Man is least himself when he talks in his own person. Give him a mask, and he will tell you the truth" (*CW,* 1045). I believe Wilde meant that those parts of the self that are too painful to be acknowledged achieve center stage only in masks, hidden from their creator. This is not, however, Danson's interpretation of the remark. He says Eliot's comment is "an earnest way of saying," as Gilbert says in "The Critic as Artist," that "All bad poetry springs from genuine feeling. To be natural is to be obvious, and to be obvious is to be inartistic" (39). But these remarks of Wilde's do not suggest the same feeling behind Eliot's, or behind Wilde's remarks about masks. In the latter remark about poetry Wilde is making a different point, in fact one similar to Freud's remark in *Creative Writers and Day-Dreaming,* where Freud comments that the artist somehow softens the egoistic nature of his or her daydreams in order to make them appeal to other people. Wilde, like Freud, is commenting that art remains mysterious in some way, and therefore is not "obvious."

Stating that Eliot "is as divided as Wilde about the value of personality" (39), Danson fails to sufficiently explore the point. Wilde was
certainly divided — in the sense of being filled with conflict — about
most things. For Wilde, as for Eliot, personality seems at times evanes-
cent. Danson quotes Wilde's essay "The Portrait of Mr. W. H.," nominally about the mysterious and still unknown man who seems to have
inspired Shakespeare's sonnets: "was there no permanence in personality? Did things come and go through the brain, silently, swiftly, and
without footprints, like shadows through mirrors? Were we at the
mercy of such impressions as Art or Life chose to give us?" (40). Here
Wilde seems to discuss thoughts and feelings as fleeting. Personality, in
the sense of the impact of early experience upon one's beliefs, tastes,
and style of reacting to life situations, was another matter. It was the
fate he tried to run from but instead, like Oedipus, embraced.

Danson appears to acknowledge this in the next paragraph: "The
conflicted notion of an unfixed self-creating personality that is also the
burdening sign of the artist's distinction or doom appears frequently in
Intentions. . . . This conflict informs every aspect of Wilde's work"
(40). The next two sentences, however, do not appear to illustrate this
good point. Danson writes, "In the society plays, culminating in *The
Importance of Being Earnest*," Wilde created a world of characters without depth; the good and bad are exactly the masks they wear and shift.
Alacrity of wit, not depth of personality, distinguishes the admirable
characters from the less admirable" (40).

It is a mistake to view the characters of Wilde's plays as "without
depth." They are paradoxes. Lady Bracknell, dowager of an important
family in *The Importance of Being Earnest*, is a formidable symbol of
power and privilege, adamantly opposed to marriages of unequal rank.
But she cheerfully announces that she was an arriviste who married for
money: "I do not approve of mercenary marriages. When I married
Lord Bracknell I had no fortune of any kind. But I never dreamed for a
moment of allowing that to stand in my way" (*CW*, 374). She is what
she isn't, and yet she is. Algy, her nephew, is "an extremely . . . an os-
tentatiously eligible young man. He has nothing, but looks everything"
(*CW*, 374). These characters certainly possess the alacrity of wit attributed to them by Danson, but they are not, taken altogether, "without
depth," nor is their wit meant by Wilde to substitute for personality.
Instead, he uses these characters to show two sides of social convention
in a continuous dialectical struggle.

Without a serious message, the wit expressed through these characters would not have survived; it would have been considered the stuff

of thousands of farces. Wilde uses their wit to approve of and yet also to deny class distinctions, right from the opening scene. Algernon, the dandy, asks his butler, "Did you hear what I was playing, Lane?" and the butler answers, "I didn't think it polite to listen, sir." Ideally the English butler personifies paradox: he is the perfect servant in the person of the perfect gentleman. Lane's reply demonstrates this, and expresses a condescending criticism behind seeming utmost respect. But no sooner has Wilde hit at the aristocrat than he helps him back to his feet with the remark that accepts the presumption of the aristocrat over the artist. Algy gets back at Lane, announcing, "I don't play accurately — anyone can play accurately — but I play with wonderful expression" (*CW,* 321). Beneath the barbed remark, one can feel Wilde's bitter knowledge that brilliance and wit do not make him the aristocrat he longed to be, and that being an aristocrat does not mean being an artist. These are not shallow remarks, remarks without depth. They represent astute social criticism.

What Danson outlines as the main theme of *The Decay of Lying* — that Wilde wants a world in which we "remake the surfaces" of "our most significant subjective reality," sounds far from the soul-searching Wilde, who in that dialogue wanted to understand nature and art and their relationship — particularly the art he needed to conceal his own nature, and the art humanity needs to endure nature: "Nature is so uncomfortable. Grass is hard and lumpy and damp, and full of dreadful black insects." Art is our "spirited protest, our gallant attempt to teach nature her proper place" (*CW,* 970).

Wilde tackles the relationship between instinct and its social organization and repression. "If we take Nature to mean natural simple instinct as opposed to self-conscious culture, the work produced under this influence is always old fashioned, antiquated, and out of date" (*CW,* 977). Touching on the relationship between civilization and its discontents, Wilde suggests that personality defines perception of nature: "If . . . we regard Nature as the collection of phenomena external to man, people only discover in her what they bring to her. She has no suggestions of her own. Wordsworth went to the lakes, but he was never a lake poet. He found in stones the sermons he had already hidden there" (977–78). In Wilde's view, this can and should work as artistic enhancement: "The justification for a character in a novel is not that other persons are who they are, but that the author is what he is. . . . In Falstaff there is something of Hamlet, in Hamlet there is not a little of Falstaff. The more one analyses people the more all the reasons for analysis disappear. Sooner or later one comes to that dreadful universal thing called human nature" (*CW, 975*). Human nature at its most basic limits exactly what we perceive, shapes it. The accidentals, Wilde says — dress, manner, religious opinions — these are elements of an author's personality that justify who a character is when created by that author.

In this dialogue, Wilde wrestled with the impact of personality or nature, especially in the sense of human nature, upon the creation of art. This has nothing to do with shaping surfaces, the term used by Danson. The liar of the dialogue is one, Danson says, "whose very existence" is "a constant act of self-invention, a protest against mindless nature" (43). But this ignores what Wilde perceived: the liar can never invent himself, or invent anything, apart from what his or her personality — in particular the memories, fantasies and conflicts imposed by early experiences — allows him or her to perceive. The lie exists in the limits to perception set by human experience.

In the course of his discussion, Danson raises interesting questions that would be enriched by exploring biographical dimensions. He asks why Wilde attacks naturalism, "when there were so many points of affinity between Zolaism and Oscarism" (49). In the *Decay of Lying*, Wilde strenuously objects to the kind of realism in Zola's novels, exemplified by the horrible death of the prostitute Nana from smallpox, which is clinically accurate down to the last rotting pustule. Wilde protests that Guy de Maupassant "strips life of the poor few rags that still cover her, and shows us foul sores and festering wounds" (*CW*, 974).

Danson leaps to the conclusion that Zola's final description of Nana's rotting corpse reminds Wilde of the "unspecified sins . . . inscribed in [Dorian Gray's] flesh," and he assumes that Dorian's sin is homosexuality. But in *The Picture of Dorian Gray*, Dorian's face rots in a way that suggests a physical disease rather than a guilty or shameful blot on the soul. Wilde's closest friends, Robert Ross and Robert Sherard among them, believed that he had syphilis, a likelihood accepted by many biographers. It might be worthwhile for Danson to mention that it was not necessarily homosexuality, certainly not homosexuality alone, that rendered Wilde unable to face thoughts of illness and decay with Zola's descriptive enthusiasm. Wilde's fears of syphilis, his preoccupation with stains and blots and illness in his writing, suggest that while thoughts of physical decay tormented him, he could not push them out of his head. Naturally Wilde resented a writer like Zola, whose description of Nana's death must have exacerbated his deepest fears. Because Wilde was the son of a physician, he knew too well the possible developments of the disease. Richard Ellmann, in his masterly biography, concluded that the rotting face of Dorian Gray reveals Wilde's fears of syphilis creeping into his art. In my book, *Oscar Wilde: A Long and Lovely Suicide*, I examine the impact of Wilde's fears of festering syphilitic sores on his developing literary style. Throughout his work, he vacillates between heroically embracing his decay — the decay of Oscar along with the decay of lying — and denying it.

In his third chapter, Danson discusses Wilde's essay *The Truth of Masks*. Highlighting the perpetually changing, self-contradictory nature of Wilde's thought, Danson remarks: "The liar's claim that art refers to nothing but itself and has no relation to brute fact is in stark contrast to the position Wilde had taken in 1883 in his American lecture 'The English Renaissance of Art': 'For the artist . . . there is no escape from the bondage of the earth: there is not even the desire of escape . . . [T]hat work is most instinct with spiritual life which conforms most clearly to the perfect fact of physical life.' It is also in contrast to almost everything in the final essay in *Intentions* except its conclusion" (60). Danson goes on to quote Wilde's conclusion, which is an invitation to change his and the reader's minds about everything that he has said: "Not that I agree with everything I have said in this essay. There is much with which I entirely disagree" (60).

Danson brushes aside Wilde's next remarks about truth in art as that "whose contradictory is also true," remarking that the "calculated mixture of scholarship and cheek is perfect *Intentions*" (60). Wilde's thought here may be condensed, even elliptical, but it is much more than a "calculated mixture of scholarship and cheek," if it can be called that at all. Wilde asks the reader to recall an earlier thought from "The Critic as Artist," namely that art springs from personality, and that it is revealed to personality. The impact each work of art has is different on each viewer. That is one reason why there are no universal truths, why a truth in art is that whose contradictory is also true.

Throughout his writings, Wilde denounces objectivity, which he regards in any case as an impossibility. Thinking dialectically, he arrives at an Hegelian synthesis of Arnold's and Pater's thought, which destroys their original ideas but at the same time rescues and transforms them: "to see the object as in itself it really is not" (*CW*, 1030). In this synthesis he appropriates both Arnold's desire for clear seeing and clear thinking, and Pater's interest in personal experience of the art object, to make it clear that both of these goals can be met only in Wildean art criticism, in which the critic, like the artist, invests his whole soul into his work, deliberately exploiting past experience and prejudice, and in fact, avoiding objectivity.

Danson's commentary on Wilde's comedies, particularly on *Lady Windermere's Fan*, ignores the complexity in the character of Mrs. Erlynne. Danson portrays her as a dandy, who "will be, by choice, unproductive, feelingless, and attractive" (81). He quotes a speech in which she affects to feel this way. But Wilde goes to great pains to reveal that Mrs. Erlynne is tearing her heart out by only *affecting* to be heartless, that her heart is breaking because she is forced for the second time to abandon the daughter she abandoned in infancy. She has returned to London once the daughter is grown for two reasons — to extort money from the daughter's husband and to see the daughter. She finds her love for her daughter unendurable and longs to confess who she is, until she realizes that the daughter could not accept the fallen woman that her mother has become. Out of love for her daughter, she withdraws.

When Danson quotes from the plays, it is usually to make a stereotypical point about gender, or to criticize Wilde for being sexist. In a discussion of *An Ideal Husband*, Danson quotes Lord Goring, the play's debonair dandy, whom he accuses of "disturbingly reinscrib[ing] the most rigidly masculinist idea of gender difference." To incur this condemnation, Lord Goring has only said, "Women are not meant to judge us, but to forgive us when we need forgiveness. Pardon, not punishment, is their mission. . . . A man's life is of more value than a woman's. It has larger issues, wider scope, greater ambitions. A woman's life revolves in curves of emotions. It is upon lines of intellect that a man's life progresses (act 4). Wilde's tone is light; Danson's is heavy, moralistic: "This sexual asymmetry (female curves and male lines), economic disparity ('A man's life is of more value than a woman's') and unequal division of labour (female emotion and male intellect) would be even more offensive than it is were the speaker himself not a figure of social androgyny" (84–85).

Lord Goring's remarks are spoken just when Lady Chiltern, who has idealized her husband, discovers that he has done some insider trading. She can't forgive him, wants him to abandon the career that means everything to him, and imagines that if she succeeds, she will save him from further temptation. She has no idea how much his career means to him. In the nick of time, Lord Goring arrives, assures her that rather than lose her love, her husband "is making for you a terrible sacrifice. We men and woman are not made to accept such sacrifices from each other" (*CW*, 548). Lord Goring apparently perceives what she is blind to, her zeal to punish her husband as well as herself. At first, she doesn't believe Lord Goring, insisting that she and her husband "have both been punished" because she set him up too high, a position from which she now wants to remove him.

In this context — battling a masochism and self-destructiveness unrecognized by the lady — Lord Goring's advice is apt. He realizes that depriving Lady Chiltern of her masochism could destroy both her and her husband, since a preoccupation with punishment seems to be one of her few pleasures. So Lord Goring urges her to say things that belittle her, but she is in the mood to be belittled. Expressing the difference between the sexes as she sees it — and as Wilde sees it at that moment — she satisfies her own need for punishment but does no permanent damage. The lines fed to her by Lord Goring should not be understood as a "rigid, masculinist" prescription, a capsule summary of a late nineteenth century code of behavior for the sexes. They are meant as a ray of light in a difficult situation between two high-strung people, a woman of naïvely high principles, ignorant of the working world and of politics, and her driven, ambitious husband, who loves her severity.

Danson's next chapter covers Wilde's curious praise of a forger and murderer who moonlighted as an artist and a dandy. In "Pen, Pencil, and Poison," Wilde gives "an aesthetic appreciation" of Thomas Griffiths Wainwright, whom Wilde dubbed "not merely a poet and painter, an art-critic, an antiquarian, and a writer of prose, an amateur of beautiful things and a dilettante of things delightful, but also a forger of no mean or ordinary capabilities and as a subtle and secret poisoner almost without rival in this or any age" (CW, 993). This fascinating description of a personality might well be mined for biographical insights into Wilde's literary and personal development. Following Wilde's formulation that man is "least himself when he talks in his own person: give him a mask and he will tell you the truth" (CW, 1045), a critic might ask in what way Wainwright masks or mirrors Wilde, or at least why Wilde found himself so fascinated with Wainwright and wants to write his biography in this essay.

Danson assumes that "the raw material for such a narrative (which would include this essay about the aesthete as criminal) extends from the homoerotic hints in [Wilde's] poem 'Hélas' through the daring self-exposure of 'The Portrait of Mr. W. H'" (87). He concludes that the crimes of Wainwright — forgery and poisoning — remind Wilde of the "crime" of his homosexuality. Forgery, in the sense of creating a false heterosexual identity, could fit with this assumption, but not poisoning, not even in the sense of corrupting young men. A much more obvious kind of poison played a great role in Wilde's life, namely the poisoning of infection from syphilis, which he believed he had contracted at Oxford. With his sexual antics, his many escapades, and even in his marriage, in the period when he mistakenly believed himself to be cured, he believed himself to be a "subtle and secret poisoner" as well. This is one of the hidden texts of Wilde's essay.

In his fifth chapter on Wilde's "The Portrait of Mr. W. H.," Danson asserts that "Like Shakespeare's sonnets, its purported subject, 'The Portrait of Mr. W. H.' offers a key but withholds the heart it might unlock" (102). On the contrary, the essay reveals Wilde's heart to a greater degree than many of his writings. A more vivid depiction of his own urge to die — at least to kill "the thing he loved," his public and professional identity — would not be easy to find. He did and did not believe in the self-destructive course he took when he sued the Marquess of Queensberry, just as his characters in "The Portrait of Mr. W. H." do and do not believe in their theories about Mr. W. H. Like Wilde, they are consumed by ambivalence, which one of them solves through suicide, saying that he dies to prove the seriousness with which he believes in his theory of Mr. W. H.

Danson takes a different tack, asserting that none of the other essay-dialogues in *Intentions* "speak more daringly about his sexual intentions or come closer to giving a name to his numinous sin, and no piece more ingeniously questions the very idea of intentionality by withholding the personality that could intend, or the stability of results which a personality might achieve" (102). True, the subject of Shakespeare's love for the mysterious Mr. W. H. is a tale of homoerotic attraction to the "master-mistress" of Shakespeare's passion, and true, Wilde told the artist Charles Ricketts, who did a bogus portrait of Mr. W. H. for him, that he had been warned "that the subject was too dangerous," as Danson points out (103).

Certainly the essay has as one of its subjects the identity of the homosexual, but a far deeper and more important subject is identity itself, and all the identities that Wilde wanted to assume in his life, including hero and martyr, including artist and scholar and recluse. His mother expected him to become a warrior fighting the British, and told him she would never speak to him again if he left London during his trials, although he would remain "always . . . my son" if he stayed. His father, the dedicated scholar of Irish lore, archaeology, and medicine, set other standards. To separate Wilde's homosexuality and his feelings about his homosexuality from his feelings about the rest of his identity shows a certain tunnel vision. The complications of Wilde's life grew out of ways in which, for example, fighting for the rights of the homosexual merged in Wilde's mind with fighting for the honor of Ireland against the British.

Danson asserts that in "The Portrait of Mr. W. H.," Wilde tried to speak about sexual desire "by withholding the language of his own speaking — always deferring the revelation the language promises, because that revelation, being *in* language, would necessarily falsify the truth" (106). If what Danson means is that Wilde could not find a word for homosexual that was honorific as opposed to clinical or legalistic or morally condemnatory, then it seems to me that wording was never the issue. Wilde appropriated terms as he wished, and as a lord of language he got his meaning across. Inadequate vocabulary and uncertainty about using neologisms were not Wilde's problem. Language was not the issue because language is imprecise. The problem lay in Wilde's attitudes toward his total identity — as an Irishman, an intellectual, a man, a gay man — and on what his role in the world should be.

What the essay actually reveals is Wilde's tormenting ambivalence and self-analytical effort to find some intellectual and moral and emotional stability, so that having chosen an attitude or a course of action in a particular area, he did not immediately doubt his choice and seek the opposite. In "The Portrait of Mr. W. H.," Wilde speaks of being "almost afraid to turn the key that unlocks the mystery of the poet's heart" (*CW*, 1155–56), because he is afraid to see the turmoil of his own heart, or to realize that he experiences feelings of doubt no matter what position he chooses. The final page of the essay points to this conclusion. The narrator sighs, upon discovering that the second of two friends appears to have martyred himself as a result of pursuing a theory about Willie Hughes that can never be proved to anyone's satisfaction: "Martyrdom was to me merely a tragic form of skepticism, an attempt to realise by fire what one had failed to do by faith. No man dies for what he knows to be true. Men die for what they want to be true, for what some terror in their hearts tells them is not true" (*CW*, 1201).

The sixth chapter of Danson's book deals with Wilde's most famous and profound essay-dialogue, "The Critic as Artist," which is, as Danson writes, Wilde's "longest and most ambitious theoretical text, and his most embattled" (128). The chapter begins with a focus on language in isolation. Danson discusses language almost exclusively, apart from any philosophical and psychological ideas expressed by Wilde through language. He begins by quoting Gilbert, one of the two characters in the dialogue, who remarks, "Men are the slaves of words" (127). Wilde, Danson asserts, is the emancipator.

That remains an intriguing idea, especially considering the irony that Wilde longed for freedom from various oppressions, including the oppression of his own thoughts, but the long passage that Danson quotes to support his assertion concerns much more than language. It shows Wilde trying to expand definitions, and in that sense to free language from rigid definition, but in the following passage, Wilde is dealing with ideas primarily, not language:

> [People] rage against materialism, forgetting that there has been no material improvement that has not spiritualized the world, and that there have been few, if any, spiritual awakenings that have not wasted the world's faculties in barren hopes, and fruitless aspirations, and empty or trammelling creeds. What is termed Sin is an essential element of progress. Without it, the world would stagnate, or grow old, or become colourless. By its curiosity, Sin increases the experience of the race. Through its assertion of individualism, it saves us from the monotony of type. In its rejection of the current notions about morality, it is one with the higher ethics (127).

Danson insists that the passage "begins in paradox as 'material' and 'spiritual' change places in the supposedly mechanical shuffling that Wilde's reviewers took to be the essence of his method" (127). The passage does not, however, begin with paradox. It begins with the idea that people see materialism and spiritualism as opposites, failing to realize that material improvements "spiritualize" the world, possibly in the sense that the comforts of civilization provide the leisure for the growth of the life of the mind and spirit.

Wilde wants to make the point that materialism and spiritualism, far from being opposites, work together dialectically. What people call sin or what looks to them like sin is not necessarily what is conventionally meant by the various Christian denominations, but rather is a new idea that may be popularly rejected because it is unfamiliar, but that brings new and valuable things to civilization. Wilde's thinking here is reminiscent of remarks by Shaw, who stated that the reasonable man adapts himself to the world, while the unreasonable man insists that the world adapt to him, and that therefore all progress depends upon the unreasonable man. In any case, Wilde's interest lies not in playing with language or shuffling terms, as Danson states, but in making the case that materialism and spiritualism are deeply dependent upon one another, although most people think that is not the case. Sin was for a variety of reasons on his mind. He wrote plays about sinners, anticipated a day when the public would perceive him as a sinner and a day when his sin would not be viewed as sin at all, when he would himself be vindicated as a hero and a martyr for the cause of gay men, not a miserable sinner.

Interpreting Wilde's dazzling display of erudition — the large number of cultural allusions in the dialogue — as "a power-play, aggrandizing Wilde by making him heir to an ancient and honorable tradition of his own creation" (129), Danson observes Wilde's uses of his immediate tradition, namely that created by Matthew Arnold and revised by Walter Pater and Whistler. As Danson rightly points out, "The technique and allusive dialogue make 'The Critic as Artist' hard to summarize, hard to even follow as a series of logical propositions," but, he observes, Wilde successfully harnesses the "prestige of culturally remarkable individuals" for his own end, namely, "in order to empower the self-credentialled aesthetic critic" (130).

So far so good: Danson describes Wilde's serious ends, his program, his need to "respond to attacks from the aesthetic left, as represented by Whistler" (130). But ultimately Danson's criticism belittles the seriousness of Wilde's thought, by claiming that Wilde is only using "the technique of allusive dialogue" to "claim allies in improbable places" (130). The technique is instead a conscious effort to create a dialectic in which each character, by contradicting the other, arrives at a synthesis that both destroys the original ideas and retains them, transformed, in a new unity. Not recognizing this, Danson claims that Wildean apercus like "the true critic is unfair, insincere, and not rational," and the work of art is "simply a starting point for a new creation" (130), are no more than part of a game that Wilde is playing.

Striking in Danson's criticism is his tendency to perceive Wilde's observations as expressions of playful inaccuracy or insincerity. Wilde's characterization of the true critic as "unfair, insincere, and irrational" arises from his recognition that critics project their own wishes, dreams, and experiences onto the work of art, and that no criticism is possible unless they do so. Wilde knew, and wrote, that so-called objective criticism was worthless because it revealed a critic's indifference. Danson quotes Wilde's most important point, his reversal of Matthew Arnold, "to see the object as in itself it really is not" (130), but dismisses it as insincere and inaccurate.

Quoting Wilde's remark that "It is to criticism that the future belongs," Danson offers no commentary. Instead, he treats Wilde's ideas as mere reactions to hostile criticism of *The Picture of Dorian Gray*. Insisting that the "obvious conclusion" is that the "usual suspect, sodomy," has offended the critics, Danson remarks that this is not the whole story, but that the reviews, "like the novel, are clearly located at the transitional moment when, as Alan Sinfield has pointed out, a modern notion of homosexual identity emerges from a dense nexus of cultural codes" (132). "Obvious" and "Clearly" do not convince. He may be trying to say something simple — that Wilde portrays affection between men with such direct homosexual overtones that critics were offended — but he does not say why. He does not, for instance, suggest that Wilde stirred up in critics homosexual feelings of which they did not wish to become aware — which would be a possible interpretation — but instead resorts to unclear vagaries like "cultural codes."

A worthwhile area of Danson's commentary concerns the reactions of twentieth century critics, Christopher Lasch and Philip Rieff, to Wilde's thinking. Danson observes that more than a century after the publication of Wilde's essay, "the American political scientist Christopher Lasch worries because Wilde's 'religion of art has survived the collapse of the Marxist utopia'" (152). Lasch, Danson points out, uses the word "seductive" to describe Wilde's thinking about socialism, for instance, "In place of self-denial and self-control, [this message] offered the seductive vision of selfhood unconstrained by civic, familiar, or religious obligations" (153). Lasch traces what he sees as the resurgence in the 1980s and 1990s of political ideas that emerged in the student movements of the 1960s and 1970s to the bad influence of ideas Wilde articulated in "The Soul of Man."

So, Danson summarizes, "Lasch compliments Wilde by taking his ideas seriously as a threat to order" (153). (Does Danson not take Wilde's ideas seriously?) Danson goes on in an interesting vein about Lasch being anticipated "in a much more subtle essay by the sociologist Philip Rieff. Rieff in 1970 wrote about what he called the psychiatric fact that 'it is *No,* rather than *Yes,* upon which all culture, and inner development, depends'" (153). Danson does not remark here, although he should, that Rieff takes this idea from the psychoanalyst René Spitz, whose classic work on infant development, *No and Yes,* laid the groundwork for Margaret Mahler and other prominent researchers of infancy. Rieff, Danson asserts, allies Wilde with Marx and Nietzsche in telling men that they need not submit to any power "higher or lower" other than themselves. Maybe, but a close reading of the essay shows that Wilde is, as usual, arguing with himself at this point, trying to convince himself not to submit to lower forces, like various blackmailing companions, or like his extremely mentally disturbed lover, Bosie. The choices Wilde made, and the ways in which he attempts to justify his choices, are embedded in his arguments about socialism.

Rieff's take on Wilde is intriguing for what it reveals about the fear of chaos during the period of student unrest. Danson remarks that Rieff uses "one of Wilde's own tactics, the redefinition of basic terms, to oppose Wilde's sublime anti-authoritarianism" (153). He quotes Rieff as saying that culture is a "deeply installed" authority to which we must submit in order to survive "the assault of sheer possibility," and says that Wilde's claim that the artist can express everything could destroy culture as we know it. Danson sardonically comments, "It didn't happen. Berkeley survived the free speech movement, and authority lives" (154). Not everyone would agree that Berkeley survived intact. But Rieff's idea that Wilde's thinking poses a threat to authority is interesting, and worth exploring. Unfortunately, it gets little commentary from Danson, beyond an apt remark that the threat posed to order by Wilde's ideas in "The Soul of Man" reveals "its continuity with the rest of Wilde's work including *The Importance of Being Earnest.*" What a world of possibilities that sentence opens — chaos is a central theme of *The Importance of Being Earnest,* and one touched on by Wilde in an interesting letter regarding the writing of the play — but it remains a world unexplored. Danson does quote a remark of Rieff's that he considers worthy of Wilde, namely, "When authority becomes external it has ceased to be authoritative." Danson claims that Rieff analyzes what "is really meant" by the "depth of character" that Wilde "famously lacked," going on to quote Rieff concerning Wilde's "grace of opposition to militant truths," which transformed the aesthetic movement from the "dominance of inwardness and towards an externalisation that works against all received forms of character." What Rieff really meant here is not clear, and Danson's notion that Wilde "famously lacked" depth of character is disheartening. In a convoluted sentence, Danson claims that "masks, surface, personality are the gifts of what Wilde strangely calls both socialism and its opposite, individualism" (154).

This is, however, perhaps the only analytic remark of the chapter. Danson moves on to various interests Wilde had in politics, touching on Russian nihilism, Wilde's play *Vera* concerning the nihilists, and some of his poems, reaching no real conclusion. The last two pages of the chapter — and of the entire book — include some textual commentary, again riddled with a certain contempt for Wilde: "The in-your-face first sentence of 'The Soul of Man Under Socialism' begins the essay's work of linguistic renovation." Danson quotes this first sentence, which asserts that socialism would relieve us from "that sordid necessity of living for others," and then dismisses Wilde's thought with: "What is called altruism is in fact sentimental self-martyrdom, like that of the Happy Prince, a futile if understandable response to finding ourselves 'surrounded by hideous poverty' . . ."(164). If that is true, it is beside the point. The sources of Wilde's "sentimental self-martyrdom" and the paths he took personally and politically, the ways in which they fueled some of his wittiest and most original thoughts, are ignored by Danson. In the final paragraph, he reminds us that he told us at the start that Wilde "largely failed in his project of renaming the world in order to make himself" (166). But what has Danson got to tell us about the meaning of the failure, since he has bothered to write a book about Wilde? Nothing. He wants to "pay tribute to the greatness" of Wilde's "failure." I would have praised Wilde's success.

Michael Foldy

Michael Foldy's earnest, scholarly study, *The Trials of Oscar Wilde: Deviance, Morality, and Late-Victorian Society*, attempts to understand the trials of Oscar Wilde as a barometer of late Victorian attitudes toward deviancy. In his introduction, Foldy writes, "This exploration has been motivated by a desire to identify and explain precisely what it was about Wilde that seemed to threaten and outrage a late Victorian society that, much like our own, was exposed routinely to shocking public scandals, especially sex scandals, many of which involved notable persons" (xi).

This formulation seems naïve since the question can easily be answered. Wilde's open, casual display of sexual interest in other men frightened and angered many Victorians. It thrust into their consciousnesses awareness of emotions that they had succeeded in repressing until Wilde burst on the scene. Those who struggled, indeed strained, to hide sexual feelings for their own sex from themselves, hated Wilde. Making them aware of hidden sexualities, he increased their conflicts. Some feared same-sex love because they ignorantly associated men who love men with pedophiles, murderers, and committers of incest. These ordinary people who preferred not to know about sex remained, as Wilde remarks in *An Ideal Husband*, men "who every day do something of the same kind themselves. Men who, each one of them, have worse secrets in their own lives . . . That is the reason they are so pleased to find out other people's secrets. It distracts public attention from their own" (*CW*, 504). Attacking Wilde proved an effective way for these people to reinstate their repressions. This association was encouraged by popular ideas about degeneracy, which was then a concept taken seriously by criminologists like Max Nordau and Cesare Lombroso. Few dared to challenge the concept, an exception being G. B.

Shaw, who wrote a satirical piece entitled, " A Degenerate's-Eye View of Degeneracy."

Foldy's unstated assumption — that the heterosexual scandals the late Victorians seemed to enjoy discussing were equal to the Wilde scandal — fails to consider the difference between the two types of scandals. The Wilde scandal threatened to undo the repressions of late Victorians, who found it unbearable that they might resemble Oscar Wilde or have in common with him certain sexual desires. These Victorians did their best to suppress, and often succeeded in repressing, sexual feelings they considered to be either wicked or abnormal, in particular any such feelings for members of their own sex. This need to avoid perceiving or being associated with homosexual feeling was completely different from — in fact, the opposite of — the thrill of the scandals involving heterosexuals, "many of which involved notable persons," according to Foldy (xi). Heterosexual scandals lessened the guilt of self-identified heterosexual Victorians, for if an admired celebrity was having an affair, it might not be so bad, so sinful, after all.

Foldy says, "When I first encountered the trials, it was difficult for me to understand why the public's reaction to Wilde was so hostile, and moreover, why it remained so for several generations after his death" (xi). This statement ignores the basic difference between one kind of sexual scandal and another for the late Victorians, and reflects a lack of understanding of the psychoanalytic theory that he claims to employ for large parts of his study. His work, he writes, "has been inspired and informed by the methods and ideas of many thinkers representing a variety of disciplines, among them: the cultural anthropology of Clifford Geertz and Mary Douglas; the hermeneutics of Hans-Georg Gadamer; the social theory of Emile Durkheim, Georg Simmel, Daniel Bell, and Pierre Bordieu; the history of science and medicine of George Canguilhem and Michel Foucault; the psychoanalytic self-psychology of Heinz Kohut; the reception theories of Wolfgang Iser and Georges Poulet; and the critical/social theories of Fredric Jameson, Susan Sontag, Guy Debord, Jean Baudrillard, and Mikhail Bakhtin" (xii). All of these thinkers have been influenced by Freud, some quite profoundly, but Kohut and Foucault in particular. To begin a study heavily influenced by psychoanalytic thinkers with an incomplete discussion of the importance of the unconscious is therefore a hindrance.

The problem begins with Foldy's remarks on memory: "Surely [the] process of erasing Wilde from the cultural memory began with the trials, but how had it happened, and why did it happen as it did?" (xi) This statement suffers — as does the rest of the book — from an incomplete definition of memory, that is, a psychoanalytic definition incorporating the unconscious. This is an unfortunate deficit, given Foldy's main intentions for the book. "Ultimately," he writes, "this book represents a dual effort: to reconstruct Wilde as the social and cultural symbol he became in 1895, and to reconstruct the popular *mentalité*, or consciousness, that perceived the symbol" (xi). For a study of this kind, consciousness and *mentalité* make no sense without an understanding of their relationship to the unconscious.

Despite such flaws in methodology, however, the historical thrust of the book raises interesting questions. The book is a "micro-history," Foldy writes, endeavoring to "represent the trials within the context of the different forces and trends that were moving British politics and society, and of the views, values, and attitudes that were expressed by Wilde's contemporaries" (xi). Insofar as it illuminates these things, the book is worth reading.

In an introduction and six chapters, the book covers the history of the Queensberry libel trials, Wilde's trials, and the press coverage of both trials, before moving on to three chapters whose titles announce their highly theoretical orientation: "The Cultural Climate of the Trials: Heterosexism and Homophobia as Historical Constructs"; "The Pathology of Pleasure and the Eschatology of Immanence: Theorizing Wilde's Identity and Desire"; and "'Social Purity' and Social Pollution: Wilde and the National Health." Foldy describes the last three chapters as "the heart of the study." His summary of chapter four exemplifies an inadequate understanding of the mechanisms of the unconscious, in combination with essentially sound historical ideas (albeit clothed in abstraction and jargon) — a common factor throughout the book. I have therefore quoted a portion of it: "In this chapter, I discuss 'heterosexism' and 'homophobia' as dynamic and transitive historical phenomena which are culturally specific and socially constructed. I argue that the mechanisms of restraint and the structures of repression, which represent the reification of 'heterosexism' in virtually every modern society, comprised a very powerful (if very discreet) social presence within English society before the trials, and that this presence became even more powerful, and even more obvious, as a direct result of the Wilde trials" (xiv).

A look at the chapter confirms my initial impression that the term repression, which appears frequently in the chapter, is not understood by Foldy. Repression, as Freud and other psychoanalytic writers defined it, means the retention of a thought or a wish in the unconscious mind by unconscious mental energies pushing the idea deep into the mind and pulling it even deeper. The wish remains unperceived by the person who has repressed it because these unconscious forces have succeeded in preventing it from rising to consciousness. If such wishes are forced to the surface — as when Oscar Wilde behaved romantically toward Lord Alfred Douglas in full view of the other patrons of the fashionable Café Berkeley — the defenses that made their repression necessary for the reduction of pain, that is conflict, in the individual are threatened, typically with dire results: such an individual, forced to face the rejected contents of his or her mind, can become extremely angry, irrational, and violent. At the Café Berkeley, those who saw Wilde and his lover could not, on one occasion, look away from a love scene that made them uncomfortable, because Lord Alfred Douglas wanted so much to be seen that he fired a pistol at the ceiling.

Foldy reveals a limited awareness of this situation when he writes that in the context of the Wilde trials, the term "homophobia" means "an individual intrapsychic phenomenon which describes 'irrational' feelings of 'fear and hatred' toward other individuals who espouse same-sex desire and/or engage in sexual practices with members of the same gender, which I will hereafter refer to as 'same-sex passion'" (67). Had he then gone on to describe the content of the irrationality — rage and hatred caused by the threatening feelings forced into the unconscious, feelings then vented against their source in the outside world, in this case Wilde — the chapter may have been more interesting. Instead, he offers an assertion in which the term repression — though not complete comprehension of it — appears: "heterosexist ideas, and to a lesser extent homophobic ideas — as well as the mechanisms of restraint and structures of repression which represent the reification of heterosexism — have been ingrained in our consciousness and embedded so deeply within our existing cultures that heterosexist ideas, mechanisms, and structures are simply taken for granted" (68).

Foldy compares "homophobia" with "heterosexism," defining "heterosexism" as the "advocacy, rationalization, and institutionalization of the idea of 'compulsory heterosexuality' within a specific group, society, and/or culture" (67). Although such a thing as "compulsory heterosexuality" — a term coined by Adrienne Rich — certainly exists, it is not here defined (except implicitly, as a malevolent force). The concept of repression, which elucidates the enforcement of compulsory heterosexuality in many societies, is not integrated into Foldy's discussion. Where self-identified heterosexuals greatly outnumber homosexuals, and where same-sex desire is feared because it is repressed, compulsory heterosexuality holds sway. Foldy gets closest to acknowledging the importance of unconscious feelings and repression when he says that "heterosexism" represents "the collective expression of the inarticulate fears and narcissistic rage of homophobic individuals" (67). While this may seem descriptively accurate, it does not explain the source of the rage, which derives from the loosening of repressions.

It might be interesting to approach "heterosexism" as an ideology — that is, to explore the reasons that various societies have subtly or directly advocated heterosexuality and frowned upon or condemned homosexuality — but it does not seem possible to do so from an exclusively historical, cultural, or sociological stance without recourse to Freud's theories and those of his followers. For instance, the advocacy of heterosexuality that began under the Emperor Julian in Roman times reflected the empire's need for soldiers, and the discouragement of homosexuality derived in part from the practical need to discourage nonreproductive relationships. But this practical need does not explain other reasons for heterosexism, or for the narcissistic rage that Foldy correctly identifies as one of its chief components.

Other parts of the book — the more historical, less theoretic sections — prove interesting and highly relevant to the Wilde scholar. Chapter one, "The Queensberry Libel Trial," offers a lucid, detailed account of the trial of the Marquess of Queensberry in April 1895 for libeling Oscar Wilde. For the most part this is a very familiar story, told here with great clarity and precision. The most original section of the chapter, entitled, "Queensberry, Rosebery, and the Outcome of the Trials," deals with Lord Queensberry's apparent possession of evidence against high-up government officials, including Lord Rosebery, the Prime Minister: "The evidence itself, of unknown form and content, was suspected of containing information confirming a 'homosexual' link between Rosebery and Queensberry's eldest son, Francis Archibald Douglas, Viscount Drumlanrig" (22). After Drumlanrig died under mysterious circumstances, allegedly shooting himself by accident, Queensberry began his active persecution of Wilde, trying to disrupt the opening night of *The Importance of Being Earnest* and hounding him at every turn.

Foldy summarizes the arguments of Richard Ellmann and H. Montgomery Hyde regarding Lord Queensberry's anger at Wilde, which they believe was caused by the shock of Drumlanrig's death: "I believe Ellmann is correct in arguing that Queensberry was at the center of the government's 'plot' against Wilde, but not for the reasons that he provides. The letter introducing the names of Rosebery and Gladstone into evidence had nothing to do with Queensberry's accusations against Wilde, but rather with Queensberry's anger over a perceived Rosebery-Gladstone-Royal insult handed to [him] through [his] other son [Drumlanrig]" (23–24). Edward Carson, the attorney for Queensberry's defense, argued that the letters had to do with Lord Drumlanrig being made a member of the House of Lords, an event enraging his jealous father, who had not been so honored.

Foldy believes "the heart of the matter," namely "evidence asserting Queensberry's influence over Rosebery," is circumstantial, but was deeply felt by Rosebery, and had "a deleterious effect on both Rosebery and, through him, on the Liberal Party" (24). Queensberry, Foldy continues, exploited leverage against Rosebery to keep the name of his son, Lord Alfred, out of the Wilde trials. "Curiously, the period of the Wilde trials and the hypothetical pressure from Queensberry coincides with a 'breakdown' in Rosebery's health from late February until the end of May." The nervous collapse has been attributed to an influenza epidemic, and also to the effect of Rosebery's nephew's death, but Foldy thinks otherwise: Queensberry may have been "putting pressure on Rosebery, exactly how and in what way we cannot be sure, but most likely by threatening public exposure of the alleged incriminating evidence" (25).

The evidence presented by Foldy suggests that Rosebery's troubles were indeed essentially the result of severe psychological stress. Information from the journal of a close friend of Rosebery's states that Rosebery could sleep only two hours per night just before Wilde's trial. He also experienced disorientation, obvious to all around him, during the time that Wilde was out on bail (26–27).

The chapter also discusses Rosebery's possible homosexuality (a term that Foldy frequently places within quotation marks, like the term "fact," following a theory popularized by Foucault that the concept of the homosexual person did not exist in the same way during Oscar Wilde's lifetime.) Foldy suggests that if Drumlanrig, Lord Alfred's dead brother, and Rosebery had been lovers, Rosebery must have been in severe mourning during the time of the Wilde trials.

Chapter two, "Wilde's Criminal Trials," covers ground already firmly trod by Ellmann, Hyde, and others, but is clear and well-written. Foldy describes Wilde's arrest, transferal to prison, and the course of the two trials.

Chapter three, "The Reception of the Trials in the Press," includes some interesting historical background on the readership of Victorian newspapers in the eighteen-sixties and eighteen-seventies, creating the framework for editorials about Wilde in the eighteen-nineties. Some of those editorials are quoted at length. They make fascinating reading, confirming a degree of rage against Wilde that would seem incomprehensible, were it not for his role in undoing certain repressions. As a result, some came to hate him — enough to hope that he would kill himself, according to one of the editorials. Foldy does not analyze the degree of rage with any reference to repression. Instead he discusses the sex scandals that intrigued the late Victorians. All but one involve heterosexuals, and the one that does not is the Cleveland Street homosexual brothel, which allegedly involved royalty — "the eldest son of the heir to the throne" (50).

Chapter five begins with a section entitled "Wilde's Ontological Aesthetic of Dissent," an unnecessarily complicated heading. "The key to understanding Wilde's identity (as he himself conceived it) can be found in an offhanded remark during the Queensberry libel trial as he was being cross-examined." Wilde is asked about a letter, which he describes as "beautiful." When the prosecutor asks what he thinks of the letter "apart from art," Wilde retorts that he "cannot answer any questions apart from Art" (97).

Using this remark as a springboard, Foldy discusses the "aesthetic contents of Wilde's remarks before the Court," adding that these as well as the aesthetic content of Wilde's sexuality "have never before been developed in any systematic way, [and] it will be a primary goal of this chapter to do so" (98). Foldy explores the ingredients of Wilde's aesthetic, considering one of them to be Wilde's "philosophy or world view" (98) in which Wilde declared himself an antinomian. Foldy perceives both a Christian attitude and a "camp" sensibility in this declared antinomianism. In Christian theology an antinomian is "one who believes that faith alone, and not necessarily obedience to existing moral laws, is necessary for salvation" (99). In camp sensibility, an antinomian is one desiring "to subvert the existing status quo" (99), Foldy writes. To these notions of Wilde's self-declared "antinomianism," Wilde adds the various psychoanalytic definitions of antinomianism as a form of narcissism in a laundry list. There is more summary of theory — from Gadamer to Heinz Kohut to Freud to Susan Sontag — than there is thought about Oscar Wilde and his cryptic assertion that he was a "born antinomian."

The final chapter begins with a quotation from W. T. Stead's journal, *The Review of Reviews*, widely known and respected in the last decade of the nineteenth century. Commenting on the outcome of the Wilde trials, Stead wrote an inflammatory paragraph that shows the degree of deep offense that even a well-educated, liberal journalist took to

Wilde (a fact whose significance is not commented upon by Foldy). Stead wrote that Wilde's conviction and sentencing "has forced upon the attention of the public the existence of a vice of which the most of us happily know nothing" (128). This captures the effect of Wilde perfectly: by compelling people to see his sexual desires, he disturbed their repressions, unleashing their rage against him. Stead's use of the word "forced" is significant. He resented, as did many, being driven to see a kind of sexuality that he did not want to see.

This revolutionary daring, which was experienced by Wilde's contemporaries as "forcing," has turned out to be a good thing, because enlightened attitudes have developed toward many formerly condemned sexualities. That, however, is another story. The tragedy for Wilde was that he probably never took seriously the depth of the repressions he so lightheartedly disturbed, since he had already found the path to sexual freedom himself. For such a man, it was easy to forget that others remained deeply uncomfortable thinking about most forms of sexuality, especially homosexuality.

Referring to Stead's remarks, Foldy says that a sexual double standard existed; "if Wilde had ruined the lives of half a dozen young girls instead of indulging in indecent familiarities with young men, he would never have been prosecuted" (130–31). This is explained as Stead's desire to protect women from unscrupulous men, but it is also another indication of Victorian attitudes toward heterosexual sex scandals — namely, that they were less likely to disturb repressions. Self-identified heterosexual males might enjoy the fantasy of corrupting young women, but they remained deeply disturbed by the idea of sexual activities with men.

The chapter goes into detail about Stead's ideas regarding "Social Purity," defined by Foldy as "an umbrella term which describes the loose associations of a multitude of relatively small but very outspoken reform movements, or groups, in the 1880s and 1890s" (132). Evangelical Christianity and feminism were chief influences.

After a discussion of the various purposes of groups within the Social Purity Movement, Foldy suggests that W. T. Stead's remarks about Wilde "and his ostensible threat to the nation must be understood within the context of the goals and ideology of that movement" (135). The language used to describe the movement is technical and dry. Essentially, Foldy suggests that social purity movements were efforts to create a more satisfying culture when the culture was undergoing a number of stresses, or when people saw their culture as inadequate (Foldy here relies on theories of the anthropologist Anthony F. C.

Wallace). Wallace's theories, as presented here, do not distinguish one culture from another, for what culture has not been dissatisfied with itself and tried to revitalize itself? Degrees of dissatisfaction vary, but there has never been a cultural nirvana. In the case of the fin de siècle, however, Foldy is arguing that public fears of "degeneration" and "decadence" — catch-all alarmist terms — as well as the "threat to traditional Christian values represented by the increasing secularization of society," contributed to a "national psychological climate of anxiety, stress, and disfunction" (137). Again, this may be true, but it does not in itself distinguish the late Victorians from any other population facing the end of a century.

In summing up the specific threat of Wilde, which society needed to purge in order to feel pure again, Foldy writes: "Wilde's image was invested with much more than just a deviant sexuality. Rather, he represented a frightening constellation of threats which conflated all these disparate elements and associations: he represented foreign vice, foreign art, and indirectly, the legacy of foreign rulers; he represented the useless, lawless, effeminate, and sexually debauched upper classes; he represented an elite and effete form of art, and an atheistic and anarchistic aesthetic; finally, and tragically, he represented the abuse of privilege and the misuse of talent" (149). All this is true, but the extreme vilification of Wilde seems unlikely to have been based on these things alone. It had to have come from the tampering with repression, against which people felt driven to defend themselves. Without invoking the concept of Freud's unconscious specifically, Jerusha McCormack has also implied that Wilde was hated for provoking people by trying to undo their repressions. In "The Wilde Irishman: Oscar as Aesthete and Anarchist," she suggests that Wilde as a dandy "represents the transactions by which the powerless, the nobodies, assume power and importance . . . What the dandy performs is a kind of psychic jujitsu — he 'throws people' by using the force of their attitude to defeat them. In effect, by means of his performance, the dandy gets his audience to share his contempt for itself" (*Wilde the Irishman*, 89). This effectively sums up Wilde's ability to get the audience to face sexualities for which they had contempt, forcing them to see in themselves the potential for experiencing these sexualities, or the actuality of having experienced them.

In his epilogue, Foldy discusses Wilde's celebrity status, arguing that such status "is in great part based on either public ignorance or the willful denial of the many facts of a person's life, facts that, once they emerge in the context of a criminal trial, invariably contradict the image that has been publicly constructed" — and by "constructed," Foldy apparently means also publicly accepted — "the image in which the public wants to believe, and which the public idealizes" (151).

This is and is not true. As I have stressed earlier, the public may idealize a self-identified male heterosexual celebrity even, or especially after, he is accused or found guilty of sexual "crimes." Foldy's book contains an impressive amount of historical research about the period, a digest of contemporary theory about Wilde and about Victorian attitudes toward homosexuality, and a good summary of incidents of Wilde's trials. The book does not, however, offer much in the way of a new understanding of Wilde.

Carolyn Dever and Marvin J. Taylor, eds.

Reading Wilde, Querying Spaces: An Exhibition Commemorating the 100th Anniversary of the Trials of Oscar Wilde, is a slim volume — 92 pages, including references. It consists of nine essays, approximately ten pages each, by graduate students in the Victorian Studies Group at New York University. Written to commemorate the centenary of the Wilde trials, the essays make use of the extensive holdings of the Fales Collection of English and American Fiction at New York University, according to the editors, Carolyn Dever of the Department of English and Marvin J. Taylor of the Fales Library.

Marvin Taylor has achieved a certain notoriety as a character in Moises Kaufman's highly successful play about Wilde's trials, *Gross Indecencies,* which at the time this book was written, was enjoying an extensive run in New York. In his play, Kaufman includes a scene between Taylor and himself, in which Taylor's longwinded and occasionally jargon-filled answers to the playwright's straightforward questions about the Wilde trials are occasions for audience amusement. For example, Kaufman asks Taylor "what happens" in Wilde's trial, and Taylor answers, "Well, what happens in the trial is he comes head on up against legal discourse, and perhaps I would even say legal-medical discourse. And he begins to lose to this sort of patriarchal medical discourse that makes him appear to be a homosexual, as opposed to . . . hum . . . someone who has desire for other men." Kaufman asks incredulously, "Are you saying that Wilde didn't really think of himself as 'homosexual'?" and gets anything but a direct answer. "Did Wilde consider himself a kind of person?" Taylor begins. "See, this is what I think is important about the Wilde trials, too, hum. . . . It is after the Wilde trials that people begin identifying themselves as a specific type of person based on their attraction to people of the same sex. See, it created the modern homosexual as a social subject. Whether Wilde himself thought he was that type of person . . . hum . . . there's nothing in what I know of Greek and Latin literature that says that the Greeks and Romans thought of themselves as homosexuals. So there's nothing necessarily that Wilde would have read that would have made him construct his identity as a homosexual . . ." (Kaufman 76).

In other words, Kaufman's Taylor offers Foucauldian formulations about the concept of the homosexual person not having existed in Victorian times, which are risible in the context of the play. Although the term "gay" did not exist in quite the modern sense, it did in fact exist (as Eric Partridge's dictionary of slang, and no doubt other sources, reveal) and it then covered more ground. Any kind of sexuality that was not conventionally acceptable could in the late nineteenth century be referred to as "gay." For instance, Frank Harris, a friend and biographer of Wilde, refers to a heterosexual female prostitute whom he visits as a "gay" woman. This suggests that, contrary to Foucault's and other scholars' views, there was in the nineteenth century such a thing as a particular type of person defining him or herself by a particular type of sexuality.

It is certainly a mark of the 1990s that these essays are written by graduate students. Like the other collections of essays reviewed in these pages, they vary in quality. The best, containing the most original research and thought, along with interesting excerpts from previously unpublished letters between Wilde and friends concerned with publishing his last poem, "The Ballad of Reading Gaol," is Anjali Gallup-Diaz's "The Author, His Friends, and The Ballad of Reading Gaol: Epistolary Acts." The other essays that are most worth reading, because of their clarity as well as the research, are concerned with historic and literary points — Frederick Roden's "The Scarlet Woman," concerning Wilde's interest in Roman Catholicism; Chatham Ewing's "American Wildes," concerning perceptions of Wilde on his American tour in 1882–83; and Timothy L. Carens's "Restyling the Secret of the Opium Den." But all the essays are of some interest.

The first essay, Sarah Blake's "The Tired Chameleon: A Study in Hues," is concerned with the one-issue student publication at Oxford, "The Chameleon," that celebrated homosexual love and published the then-notorious sonnet, "Two Loves." The sonnet contains a dialogue between two figures representing heterosexual and homosexual love, the latter introducing himself by the phrase made famous during Wilde's trials, namely the "love that dare not speak its name." Blake offers first, however, a description of the Fales exhibition that parades jargon, not clear thinking: "Each of the display cases examines a space — sexual, physical, intellectual, literary — which Wilde que(e)ries, demanding a rereading, perhaps even a 'right' misreading" (3). It is worth pointing out that students do not write like this without having been taught to do so. Wilde's remarks in "The Critic as Artist" about the necessity of the critic "intensifying" his own personality in order to "interpret the personality and work of others" (*CW,* 1003) has been ignored by at least the last generation of influential teachers. These students' personalities do not show behind the jargon; they have, for the most part, not dared to be original, although their work reveals that they are smart enough to be so.

Blake's subtitle, "A Study in Hues," takes Wilde's Shakespeare essay, "The Portrait of Mr. W. H.," as a "primer" for "the Wildean reading programme," and "an allegory of reading" (5). In the essay, Wilde advances the idea that Shakespeare's mysterious Mr. W. H., to whom he dedicated the sonnets, was a man named Willie Hughes. Blake's idea is not clearly developed, although it is transmitted in an interesting shorthand. She suggests that by the end of Wilde's essay, when the identity of Willie Hughes is continually disputed, "we, as readers" are left with the "implied question" of whether we believe in Willie Hughes. "Answering yes would place us alongside the other men who believe, able to see that art is endlessly revised and created anew, changed to the hue of the chameleon who changes to it, or who reads within it" (5).

Francesco Coppa's essay, "I Seem to Recognize a Device that Has Done Duty in Bygone Plays: Oscar Wilde and the Theatre of Epigram," begins with the assertion that "Oscar Wilde's primary literary genius was as an epigrammist." Asserting that Wilde's plays "are structured like epigrams," he makes the point that epigrams "illustrate their author's mastery of discourses" (13). Certainly — but the discourse that Wilde had really mastered was the dialogue, especially the dialogue with himself, and the epigrams growing out of those dialogues might be profitably regarded as Wilde's armed truces with himself, as compromise formations. This is not a point that Coppa makes, however.

His points are nonetheless interesting. Noting that Wilde's epigrammatic language is identified with him, and that Henry James accused all the characters in Wilde's comedy *Lady Windermere's Fan* of talking "equally strained Oscar," Coppa comments that even though Wilde's characters tend to sound like him, "epigrams are structured in such a way that it is possible for them to come from the mouths of many different characters" (13). One of his final points is also good, namely that Wilde's characters "speak in epigrams, but their identities are also epigrammatic." Much could be made of this point, and it is a lost opportunity that it is not further explored, but in any case, Coppa has focused on the epigram in a new way.

The third essay, Frederick S. Roden's "The Scarlet Woman," focuses on two important forces in Wilde's life, "the Hellenic, or the aesthetic world of classical Greece, and the Roman Catholic Church." As Roden points out, classical Greece "evokes the memory of a society of antiquity whose literature and philosophy were at that time being re-examined in university culture," while Catholicism was a "vital religious institution with a culture as well as a controversy all its own" (21). He points out that Wilde was attracted to the "difference, the otherness of the Church," and convincingly connects this to Wilde's understanding of himself as different because homosexual. Roden points out that many of Wilde's early poems are concerned with religious themes, which are particularly Roman Catholic.

The paper is filled with detailed and interesting observations, including a comment on a Victorian caricature of Wilde called "The Bard of Beauty," in which lilies "meticulously grow from the ground where his feet touch. The picture is similar to many of Christ on the cross, from the foot of which lilies grow. The illustration shows angels fluttering about him as if he were ethereal. Curiously, an object which resembles a pickle is sketched in the corner of the picture. A similar if not identical image representing domesticity is to be found in religious art" (24). Roden goes on to say that this image — which typically represents the mundane and mortal — is "especially amusing when considering the fondness for cucumber sandwiches in *The Importance of Being Earnest* and its suggested association with furtive male sexual behavior" (24). Roden makes the interesting point that possibly "the common occurrence of the 'perverse' that Victorian Protestants found in the medieval and Roman Catholic, and that was so attractive to Wilde, might help to explain this otherwise rather peculiar connection" (24–25).

In the following essay, "Wilde at Oxford/Oxford Gone Wilde," Peter Chapin argues that Wilde "laid the intellectual foundations of his later work" at Oxford (27), and also discusses social and personal changes arising out of two great intellectual influences on Wilde, Walter Pater and John Ruskin. Mentioning that John Wordsworth, the great nephew of the poet, was a junior colleague of Pater's, Chapin tells the story of Wordsworth objecting to the morality of Pater's *Renais-*

sance, and, through a series of events, young Wordsworth getting a promotion that normally would have gone to Pater. Chapin reports that Benjamin Jowett, the powerful master of Balliol, had discovered Pater's homoerotic love for an undergraduate, William Money Hardinge, whom Wilde later knew while working on Ruskin's ill-fated road project.

Chapin details "the most significant controversy" during Wilde's years at Oxford, the competition for the Slade Professorship of Poetry, a post that Matthew Arnold had held a decade before Symonds and Pater sought it. Symonds withdrew from competition, Chapin recounts, after attacks appeared branding him as a homosexual, attacks which implicated aestheticism and Hellenism as effeminate and immoral (30). Chapin discusses Wilde's poem, "Hélas," which echoes "Hellas" and probably, in the opening line, deliberately echoes Pater's use of the verb "drift" in the latter's conclusion to the *Renaissance.* Wilde's poem is, following Pater, "organized around an opposition between Greek seriousness and Christian asceticism" (32).

In the next essay, "American Wildes," Chatham Ewing discusses Wilde's American tour of 1882–83. Hired to promote the Gilbert and Sullivan operetta, *Patience,* Wilde, according to Ewing, wanted to "spread abroad a portrait of his own and his fellow aesthetes' resistance" to the popularization of Aestheticism in *Patience* (35). Ewing speaks of Wilde's need to "solve the riddle of harmonizing aestheticism and broad publicity" (35), which may be an overstatement. His letters suggest considerable enjoyment in his popularizing of the movement. While lecturing to miners in Colorado, he spoke of Benvenuto Cellini, about whom they grew quite enthusiastic, enough to ask Wilde why he hadn't brought the great man with him to America. When Wilde explained that Cellini was dead, the miners, greatly to his amusement, asked "Who shot him?"

Ewing suggests that Wilde's playful photography shoot at Sarony and attendance at a performance of *Patience* helped establish his image for the American public. He makes the interesting point that the Sarony photos are "terrifically overdetermined artifacts," that in one of them Wilde appears to be a male "Odalisque," after the Delacroix painting (39). I know of no other critic who has made this observation. Ewing also points out that Wilde takes pains to advance the idea of America as a reflection of Aestheticism in his lectures.

The following essay by Lisa A. Golmitz, "The Artist's Studio," offers a familiar history of the aesthetics movement, with one good summing-up: "Aestheticism, a word derived from the Greek meaning 'one

who perceives,' was a movement that privileged perception over creation" (43). She mentions the amorality of the movement and its identification with homosexuals.

Allison Pease's essay, "Oscar Wilde Plays on Two Stages: The Club
and the Home," concerns Wilde's attitude toward the middle class and
its morality, which are, she points out, "precisely the class that is missing from *The Picture of Dorian Gray.*" It is when the actress Sybil
Vane's story "begins to follow the path of a bourgeois comedy in her
engagement to Dorian Gray," she shrewdly observes, "that Wilde sees
fit to kill her" (3). Pease argues that the home and the club are respectively symbols of Victorian male and female ideals. The ideal man was
the gentleman in his club, the ideal woman the middle-class angel in
the house. "It is interesting to note that, while for Ruskin womanhood
is equal to the home, for Wilde, woman is, in most contexts, a symbol
of the middle class" (55). Wilde, she claims, "altered the space" of the
club as well as the home: "The 'House Beautiful' shifted the focus away
from domestic relationships within the home toward the projection of
an image that had a sensual impact on its visitors" (55). Wilde's home
was the site of decadent dinner parties, not the usual middle class fare.

The following article, Timothy L. Carens's "Restyling the Secret of
the Opium Den," compares Wilde's opium den scenes in *The Picture of
Dorian Gray* to that of other Victorian writers, particularly Dickens and
Conan Doyle, noting that "[r]ecent analyses of opium den narratives,
which flourished in the last decades of the nineteenth century, cite
Wilde's version as a typical example of the genre" (65). Carens sets out,
entertainingly and accurately, to demonstrate that Wilde proved innovative, not typical, in his opium den scenes. While Wilde is a "careful
student of some conventions" (69), the ones he omits "are significant"
(70). Detailed descriptions of opium preparation and smoking are ignored by him. Wilde "privileges secrecy over exposure in his plot," lav-
ishing attention "on the veiling and unveiling of the secret vice," but
showing little interest in opium smoking per se (72). Carens concludes
that while most opium den narratives "attempt to thrill the reader with
stories of adventurous forays into inaccessible neighborhoods and secret
lairs" that are presented as "facts," Wilde remains indifferent to fact,
"redirecting attention from an ability to capture reality to an ability to
refashion it." The focus is not on the "daring and accuracy" of the narrative but on the "language of the writer" who has "consciously built
between the reader and the opium den an 'impenetrable barrier of
beautiful style'" (74).

In the final essay, "The Author, His Friends, and The Ballad of Reading Gaol: Epistolary Acts," Angeli Gallup-Diaz examines six unpublished letters from Robert Ross to Leonard Smithers (pornographer and publisher of Wilde's final poem, "The Ballad of Reading Gaol") in late autumn and winter 1897. Robert Ross, Wilde's devoted friend and literary executor, was as Gallup-Diaz points out "responsible for the recirculation and reprinting of Wilde's works after Wilde's death in 1900" (77).

The Ross-Smithers letters "tell a short dramatic tale of how the 'after-Reading' market for Wilde was negotiated," Gallup-Diaz writes (77). The drama also involves another letter in the Fales collection from Robert Sherard, Wilde's friend and first biographer, to Carlos Blacker. During Wilde's exile years, the friendship with Blacker, a friend of Wilde's wife as well as Wilde, was strained. Wilde's promotion of Aestheticism, with the idea that the object of living was to "become a work of art," led to the challenge of marketing Wilde without using his name, since Wilde, as a result of his imprisonment, was virtually taboo.

The Gallup-Diaz essay concerns details about the writing and publishing of "The Ballad of Reading Gaol" — including attempts to censor some of Wilde's prison descriptions, and his disgruntled revising of lines thought to be libelous — as well as information about the ways in which Wilde's name was eased back onto his public manuscripts. The content of Robert Ross's letters show that Ross is "at pains to alleviate as much as possible the burden of 'success' that attends a man who is overcommodified by his own name" (79). The name Wilde would not, Ross believed, sell copies of any of Wilde's works.

But that was to change. In May of 1899, "a sixth impression of a thousand copies" of "The Ballad of Reading Gaol" appeared. Ross, who in October 1897 had written in one of the Fales collection letters that Wilde's name "must always be mentioned if not printed in inverted commas," was proved correct. In the seventh printing, which followed in June, the publisher, Smithers, suggested "that Wilde insert his own name next to C.3.3. [his convict number that had been printed in lieu of his name]." Gallup-Diaz adds, "And so [Oscar Wilde] is finally printed on the title page, enclosed in brackets: a semiotic device close enough to inverted commas to prove Ross's prediction correct" (89).

The article contains amusing, gossipy, previously unpublished trifles concerning Wilde's and Ross's lives as gay men, as well as a shrewd assessment of Robert Ross's worth as Wilde's literary executor: "In carefully staging Wilde's works for the public, Ross effects a valediction worthy of the nineteenth century's greatest aesthete. Wilde emerges as

an artist, who has regained the right to hold a mirror up to society"
(89).

Notes

[1] Stephen Greenblatt, Introduction, *Genre*. See vol. 15. (1982): 1–2.

[2] Stephen Greenblatt, *Learning to Curse*. (New York: Routledge, 1990): 164–69.

[3] Hayden White, "New Historicism: A Comment." *The New Historicism*. Ed. Harold Veeser. (London: Routledge, 1989): 302.

Works Cited

Danson, Lawrence. 1994. "Each Man Kills the Thing He Loves: The Impermanence of Personality in Oscar Wilde." *Rediscovering Oscar Wilde*. Ed. C. George Sandulescu. Princess Grace Irish Library: 8. Gerrards Cross: Colin Smythe.

———. 1997. *Wilde's Intentions: The Artist in his Criticism*. Oxford: Clarendon Press.

Dever, Carolyn and Marvin J. Taylor, eds. 1995. *Reading Wilde, Querying Spaces: An Exhibition Commemorating the 100th Anniversary of the Trials of Oscar Wilde*. New York: Fales Library, New York U.

Foldy, Michael. 1997. *The Trials of Oscar Wilde: Deviance, Morality, and Late Victorian Society*. New Haven: Yale UP.

Greenblatt, Stephen Jay. 1982. Introduction to "The Forms of Power and the Power of Forms in the Renaissance." *Genre* 15: 1–2.

———. 1990. *Learning to Curse: Essays in Early Modern Culture*. New York: Routledge.

Kaufman, Moises. 1999. *Gross Indecency: The Three Trials of Oscar Wilde*. New York: Dramatists Play Service.

McCormack, Jerusha. 1998. *Wilde The Irishman*. New Haven: Yale UP.

Sandulescu, C. George, ed. 1994. *Rediscovering Oscar Wilde*. Princess Grace Irish Library: 8. Gerrards Cross: Colin Smythe.

White, Hayden. 1989. "New Historicism: A Comment." *The New Historicism*. Ed. Harold Veeser. London: Routledge.

3: Gay, Queer, and Gender Criticism

THE GAY AND QUEER criticism in this chapter belongs to various schools, all having in common a moral impulse opposing homophobia and a desire to explore the cultural and political influences on the formation of gender roles and gender identity. Writers in this section attempt to understand Wilde's ideas about his sexuality, and the impact of his sexuality upon his and our culture.

Jonathan Dollimore

Jonathan Dollimore, in "Different Desires: Subjectivity and Transgression in Wilde and Gide," tells the story of André Gide's fateful 1895 meeting with Wilde in Algiers, when Gide was still hiding his same-sex desires from himself, and Wilde proved eager to welcome him out of the closet. Wilde was, Dollimore remarks, "intent on undermining the younger man's self-identity, rooted as it was in a Protestant ethic and high bourgeois moral rigour and repression," a conformity, Dollimore suggests, "to which Wilde was, notoriously, opposed" (48). Gide's first reaction — to run away from meeting Wilde, and then to run back to see him — precipitated a major change in his life and writing. Dollimore speculates that Wilde wanted to "re-enact" in Gide "the creative liberation" that Wilde's own "exploration of transgressive desire" had produced nine years earlier, in 1886, when Wilde reportedly experienced his first same-sex encounter with Robert Ross. "But first," Dollimore asserts, "Wilde had to undermine that law-full sense of self which kept Gide transfixed within the law. So Wilde tried to decenter or demoralize Gide — 'demoralize' in the sense of liberate from moral constraint rather than to dispirit; or, rather, to dispirit precisely in the sense of to liberate from a morality anchored in the very notion of spirit" (49). This seems a longwinded way of saying that Wilde wanted to loosen up the strait-laced young Gide.

Dollimore describes how Wilde procured a young Arab musician for Gide, and Gide wrote that he had five orgasms that night. At "this suitably climactic moment," writes Dollimore, "we postpone further consideration of Gide and turn to the anti-essentialist, transgressive aesthetic which Wilde was advocating . . ." (50), namely Wilde's advocacy of socialism. Dollimore's rhetoric is like cold water splashed on hot lovers. The scene doesn't warm up. The connection between the liberation of Gide, and Wilde's advocacy of a particular socialism, based on individualism and on reconstructing society so that poverty will become impossible, is not made clear.

Camille A. Paglia

Paglia begins "Oscar Wilde and the English Epicene" as follows: "Oscar Wilde is the premier documenter of a sexual persona which I call the Androgyne of Manners . . . The Androgyne of Manners inhabits the world of the drawing room and creates that world wherever it goes, through manner and mode of speech." This intriguing premise could use considerable follow-up; it might, for example have been interesting to speculate why Alec Guinness in drag proved to be such a successful Lady Bracknell. It is not enough to say that, in general, "Sleekness in a male is usually a hermaphroditic motive," and to add that Leslie Howard, Rex Harrison, Cary Grant, David Niven, Michael Wilding, and Fred Astaire all seem to have this sleek, "hermaphroditic" quality (94). Paglia's assertions beg the question: what is the meaning of androgyny for Wilde and his world?

It is not the case in Wilde's world, as Paglia claims, that "The salon is an abstract circle in which male and female, like mathematical ciphers, are equal and interchangeable; personality becomes a sexually undifferentiated formal mask." Although wit is sometimes equally the province of men and women, Wilde's men and women, even or especially the wits, fall into distinct, some might say sexually stereotyped roles. Their witty comments underscore these roles. A good example is the conversation in chapter seventeen of *The Picture of Dorian Gray,* between Lord Henry Wotton and a character described as "the pretty Duchess of Monmouth," who has red lips and "white hands" that "move daintily" among the teacups. She teases Lord Henry by calling him "Prince Paradox," and when he refuses the title, she counters, "Royalties may not abdicate." He sighs, stating that she wishes him "to defend my throne," and by way of defense offers "the truths of tomorrow," but she says she prefers "the mistakes of today." So far they have quite a flirtation going (Wilde having described her husband as a "jaded-looking man of sixty"), and then Lord Henry says, "You disarm me, Gladys," provoking her to say, "Of your shield, Harry: not of your spear" (146–47). The sex roles are indeed well defined among these wits.

Paglia stereotypes sex roles: she speaks of the "male feminine in his careless, lounging passivity, the female masculine in her brilliant, aggressive wit" — as if passivity were generally accepted as a feminine trait and aggression as a masculine one. There is no particular justification given for this; it seems accepted as a convention.

She makes an intriguing assertion for which she provides no evidence, namely that Lewis Carroll influenced Wilde. Paglia quotes several of Carroll's absurd utterances, for example Alice's conversation with the Red Queen, in which Alice offers to cut the Red Queen a slice of a leg of mutton, and the Red Queen takes "cut" in the social sense and declines with "it isn't etiquette to cut anyone you've been introduced to."

An obvious affinity exists between some of Carroll's and some of Wilde's absurdities, but affinity is not necessarily influence. Both writers laugh the laughter of despair, laughter in the face of terrible conflicts: Wilde jokes exclusively about things that in real life tormented him, problems he could never transcend; Carroll, likewise. But Paglia makes none of the necessary connections. Her final summary is, however, arresting: the "Wildean epicene unites the great English dramatic theme of aristocracy with Late Romantic Estheticism and Decadence" (107). The overall impression Paglia's essay leaves, however, is of a maelstrom of undigested, but original, ideas. Her last thought — that works of "epicene wit," a category in which she places Wilde — are dominated particularly by "scandal and gossip," and that there is little of this in Lewis Carroll because the Alice books have no sexual "free energy," ignores the sexual energy of Carroll's fairly obvious pedophilia in his photographs of Alice Liddell, and the not so thickly disguised sexual energy of many scenes in the Alice books. Alice's conversation with the Red Queen, whose favorite hobby is an obvious symbol of castration, is an example: "Off with his head!" she screams.

Christopher Craft

Christopher Craft, in "Alias Bunbury: Desire and Termination in *The Importance of Being Earnest*," begins with a quotation from W. H. Auden. Auden remarks that he wishes he did not know all he knows about Wilde's life when he reads *The Importance of Being Earnest*: "when John Worthing talks of going Bunburying, [I wish] I did not immediately visualize Alfred Taylor's establishment" — that is, the male prostitute whose house Wilde visited (119). Craft then remarks, "As a character 'always somewhere else at present,' as a figure thus *sans figure,* Bunbury had been devised by Wilde to inhabit the erotic inter-stices of the double bind here represented by Auden's *volonté d'oublier,* his drive to forget" (119).

It is not so clear that Auden wants to forget Wilde is homosexual and enjoyed the purchased pleasures of rent boys — Craft seems to take Auden's meaning as such — as it is obvious that Auden wishes he did not know about either the self-destructive indiscretions of Wilde or about Wilde's miserable fate. Auden implies this when he adds that when he finishes reading the play, he imagines a "nightmare panto-mime scene" in which "at the touch of a magician's wand . . . the country house in a never-never Hertfordshire turns into the Old Bailey, the features of Lady Bracknell into those of Mr. Justice Wills."

Craft's article makes the case that the never-seen Bunbury character is an "empty signifier," apparently meaning a sign by which Wilde re-fers to homosexuality without naming it. "Strictly speaking," Craft writes, "Ernest cannot admit or acknowledge the erotic force of the gay male body, which must therefore be staged as an atopic body, a body constitutively 'somewhere else at present.' Hence, the flickering pres-ent-absence of the play's homosexual desire, as the materiality of the flesh is retracted into the sumptuousness of the signifier, whether in the 'labial phonemics' of Bunbury, all asmack with death and kisses, or in the duplicitous precincts of the plays most proper and improper name, Ernest . . ." (120). This sentence goes on for four more lines, but they do not help to make it clearer.

Craft makes an interesting biographical point, namely that Charles Parker, a sometime valet and prostitute patronized by Wilde, is proba-bly invoked in the names "Parker and Gribsby," solicitors who appear in a scene (deleted from the play) to arrest Algy for expenses incurred at the Savoy Hotel (125). Craft mentions also that the word "Earnest" contains a frequently overlooked pun on Urning, the term devised by Karl Heinrich Ulrichs to refer to gay sex. Craft's comment on this, as on so much, is not clear, but is meant to be amusing: "The *Urning,* to put it wildly, would hide in Earnest, thereby pun-burying and Bun-burying at the same time. . . . 'Everything,' Derrida says, 'comes down to the ear you hear me with'" (131).

In his unnecessarily complicated conclusion, Craft attempts to con-nect Bunbury with the hero's name, Ernest John: "The interchange-ability of these two terms (in exile Wilde even referred to *Earnest* as *Bunbury)* suggests an irreducible isomorphism between the technically unspeakable homoerotics of interminable Bunburyism and the struc-tural bifurcation of the nominally heterosexual male subject . . ." (133),

which apparently means only that the heterosexual identity of the hero
Ernest conceals some homosexual buns.

Ed Cohen

Ed Cohen, in "Writing Gone Wilde: Homoerotic Desire in the Closet
of Representation," opens with a theatrical, witty description of the
1895 Wilde sex scandal, mentioning the "good family romance" of the
outraged father of Wilde's lover — Queensberry — and the homosexual world of Wilde, depicted as sucking "the lifeblood of morality"
from the "tender body" of Lord Alfred Douglas. This lively opening is
nearly identical to the opening of Cohen's 1993 book, *Talk On The
Wilde Side* (see below). The argument following — that the term "homosexual" was emerging as a new category with new ideologies for
"organizing male experience" along with other types — "the adolescent, the criminal, the delinquent" — is advanced with slightly greater
clarity than it is in the book. Cohen writes, "The shift in the conception of male same-sex eroticism from certain proscribed *acts* . . . to
certain kinds of *actors* was part of an overall transformation in class and
sex-gender ideologies" (69). "Bourgeois hegemony in Victorian Britain
was consolidated as part of a process of organizing "sex" and "class"
into "an effective unity," Cohen writes, with "the homosexual" being
"crystallized as a distinct subset of male experience only in relation to
prescribed embodiments of 'manliness'" (69).

Cohen turns then to Eve Kosofsky Sedgwick's explorations of
"maleness" in English literature in her book, *Between Men: English Literature and Male Homosocial Desire*. Eager to apply her ideas to Wilde,
he summarizes her theory as follows: "she suggests that we must situate
both the production and the consumption of literary representations
depicting male interactions (whether overtly sexualized or not) within a
larger social formation that circulates ideologies defining differences in
power across sex and class" (70).

This definition — the idea that the society and culture circulate
particular ideologies about sexuality — needs specificity, but none is
offered. Cohen merely goes on to assert that Wilde's "texts . . . embody
an especially contradictory nexus of class and sexual positionings" (70).
He does not illustrate these contradictions, but instead mentions
Wilde's family and education at Oxford, and then writes that Wilde
"consciously constructed and marketed himself as a liminal figure
within British class relations, straddling the lines between nobility, aristocracy, middle class, and — in his sexual encounters — working

class" (70). It is not clear what is meant by "constructed and marketed" here. If Cohen means that Wilde set out consciously to sell himself as someone who wanted to be perceived as on the edges of society, that is incorrect. Wilde wanted to sell himself as different personalities at different times — as an aristocrat, or as a celebrity, or as a professor of aesthetics, or as an arrogant wit. He wanted to be noticed, and sometimes felt driven to be noticed even, or especially, when he knew it would be dangerous to be noticed — for instance, when picking up male prostitutes. The curious problem of Wilde is that although he knew his dangerous behavior made him an outsider, and although he did not want, at least consciously, to be an outsider or a criminal, he did things that made it impossible for his society to see him in any other way.

Cohen does not approach these complexities.

We next turn to Cohen's book, *Talk on the Wilde Side: Toward a Genealogy of a Discourse on Male Sexualities.* The cultural and political definitions of the term "homosexual" that grew up around Oscar Wilde, the ways in which he came to be a controversial symbol, are a fascinating area of study, but unfortunately tend to inspire some of the worst writing in academia. The title of Cohen's book, as well as remarks in his acknowledgments and prologue, promise an investigation of the three trials of Oscar Wilde, a method used to discern the ways in which people now understand and talk about male sexualities. Cohen's quest is spurred by personal concerns: his book began when he was recovering from a "life-threatening illness" that made him want to write about "something that 'touched' me." What touches him is what "viscerally" he had "excluded from my academic life . . . my identity as a gay man. . . . not only did I not know what it meant to experience 'my identity as a gay man' . . . but I was becoming increasingly less sure about what it meant to 'have' such an 'identity' at all" (ix). This is the remark of one who feels lost, uncertain of everything because he feels uncertain about who he is and who he should be. Presenting his book as a quest to understand and validate his sexual identity by exploring the life of a brilliant, tragic figure who has come to epitomize that sexual identity, Cohen tackles a potentially lively and moving subject. But the closer he gets to approaching this stated topic, the further his prose gets from coherence.

Ed Cohen is capable of writing lucid, flowing prose:

> During the late spring of 1895, the trials of Oscar Wilde erupted from the pages of almost every London newspaper — and indeed

from the pages of almost every newspaper throughout Europe and North America. With a cast of characters that included one of London's most renowned and remarkable playwrights; a famously eccentric member of the British aristocracy; his son, a beautiful and effete young lord; a band of legal luminaries, including the highest ranking barrister in the nation; and a chorus of working-class men of tender age and questionable morals, it is hardly surprising that the sex scandal both captivated public interest and boosted newspaper sales (1).

Why then would he choose to write most of his book like this?

By playing upon these indexical connotations of Wilde's commoditized self-image, the newspaper headlines testify that the semiotic shift from proper name to cultural category is predicated on the unarticulated nexus of difference (or "ideology") that overdetermines "Oscar" as a meaningful signifier (136).

Or, take another random sample from a discussion about AIDS, perceived, as Cohen puts it, as a "naturally" "homosexual" disease in "the American social imaginary":

Hence, the significance of this contemporary reinvestment in a disease model of sexuality must be understood both as a way of making sense of the fear and uncertainty occasioned by an emerging epidemic and as a way of remapping the shifting boundaries of gender and sexuality that were destabilized by the politicized (sexual) practices of the feminist and lesbian/gay movements (13).

The first quotation is descriptive rather than analytical, but the other two passages — the analytic writing — contain the most unclear prose: "remapping the shifting boundaries," "destabilized," and "politicized" are code words. They never get decoded; their significance does not become clear. What argument, what message, lies beneath this pile of Latinate abstraction? I delved deeper into Cohen's prose in search of an answer.

Asserting that the "binary pairing homosexual/heterosexual continues to define the poles between which male gender identities are plotted" (10), he claims that since the nineteenth century the term homosexual has had negative connotations, unlike the terms gay and lesbian: "Homosexuality . . . continues to bear within it the mark of absence — the absence of power, of success, indeed, of all the ideological markers that masculine privilege engenders within a patriarchally organized, capitalist world system" (11).

Intent on proving that the term "homosexual" is always used today to imply that heterosexual is better ("popular deployment of 'homosexuality' today continues to reassert the normative potential of 'pro-creative heterosexuality' along with the corresponding normative gen-der expectations" [11]) Cohen turns to journalistic depictions of the AIDS epidemic. He quotes a passage from a *New York Times* science reporter, Gina Kolata, which he characterizes as an attempt to "draw a *cordon sanitaire* around the 'normal' heterosexual population." He ap-parently wants to demonstrate that Kolata typifies a trend in the media, portraying gay men as the main or only source of one of the worst plagues known to humanity. Cohen quotes from Kolata's report on the Fifth International AIDS conference in June 1991 in the *New York Times*, in which she writes:

> In this country, it is still uncertain whether there is an independent AIDS epidemic among heterosexuals. Although the AIDS virus spreads heterosexually and the total of heterosexual AIDS cases is ris-ing steadily, such cases still appear linked to the infected pool of intra-venous drug abusers, meaning that the epidemic has not yet taken on a life of its own among heterosexuals who do not use drugs.

It is clear that Cohen interprets this piece of writing as a negative view of gay men, but it is not clear why. He writes:

> The terms of this description clearly demonstrate the ways the popular representations of AIDS are invested in defining the boundaries of the 'epidemic' by sexually specifying the 'types' of individuals who mani-fest HIV related illnesses. In so doing, they mask the semantic work involved in producing such conceptual demarcations and instead make such categorical distinctions seem intrinsic to the 'natural history' of the disease. In the *New York Times* article, this naturalizing occurs in the slippage between Kolata's use of the adverb 'heterosexually' as a metonym for the unnamed sexual practices through which AIDS 'spreads,' the adjective 'heterosexual' as a designation for a particular group of people who have been diagnosed as 'having' AIDS, and the noun 'heterosexuals' as a signifier for the majority population of 'this country' which may or may not be manifesting 'an independent AIDS epidemic.' That the distinctness of the 'heterosexual' is asserted here through its many grammatical guises suggests that embedded in this way of imagining and representing the complex constellation of so-matic events, relationships and meanings we call 'AIDS' is a corollary interest in drawing (sexual) boundaries between kinds of people (12).

Notable in this piece of writing is the use of the term "boundaries" and its cognates — "demarcations, categorical distinctions," which ap-pear four times in the passage, preceded by "cordon sanitaire," another boundary suggesting a preoccupation with walling off or restricting something. An idea? A finding? Hoping for enlightenment, I sent Cohen's commentary to the *New York Times* reporter he quotes, Gina Kolata. In an e-mail dated April 6, 1998, she wrote:

> I had not seen Ed Cohen's book and, to be honest, I cannot understand what his point is. I think that what I wrote is crystal clear. It also is an accurate description of where the HIV epidemic is smoldering. Does Cohen want me to describe sexual practices in graphic detail? Or does he think that there is no difference in sexual practices between heterosexuals and homosexuals?"

I think it likely that in her question she approaches the topic that provokes Cohen's ire. He believes that "popular," that is journalistic accounts about AIDS, have an ax to grind ("are invested in," he writes), creating sexual "types" of individuals. He puts quotation marks around the word "types," as though different kinds of people did not exist — as though there were not some people whose sexual tastes run primarily to the opposite sex, and some to their own. He objects to "unnamed" sexual practices in Kolata's piece, although by designating them heterosexual or homosexual she has in fact named them. It is the naming to which he seems to object. It would go beyond the purview of this book to speculate why that should be, but it is too bad that a book that begins with such an exciting and valid ambition, tracing the meaning of such an emotionally charged word as "homosexual," founders precisely at the point where that word's meaning should be explored.

Cohen's book is divided into two sections, "Against the Norm," and "Pressing Issues." Each of these has of three chapters. There is also a prologue entitled "A Funny Thing Happened on the Way to the Trials; or, Why I Digress," and an epilogue, "What's in a Name?" that concerns again the term "homosexual" as one emerging "during the second half of the nineteenth century." At that time, Cohen believes, it became "inseparable from and literally incomprehensible without its 'normal' twin, 'the heterosexual'" (211). Cohen's objection to this pairing is not elucidated.

The first section includes the following the chapter titles: "Embodying the Englishman: A Theoretical Fiction"; "Taking Sex in Hand: Inscribing Masturbation and the Construction of Normative Masculinity"; and "Marking Social Dis-Ease: Normalizing Male 'Continence' and the (Re) Criminalization of Male Sexuality." In the second section, the chapter titles are "Legislating the Norm: From 'Sodomy' to 'Gross Indecency'"; "Typing Wilde: Construing the 'Desire to be a Person Inclined to the Commission of the Gravest of All Offenses'"; and "Disposing the Body: 'Gross Indecency' and the Remapping of Male Sexuality." The contents of these chapters are no clearer than their titles. I will, however, touch on themes that emerge at the beginning and end of the book.

In Cohen's prologue, one of the more readable, interesting sections of his book, he tells the story of how he became interested in the trials of Oscar Wilde. The trials, as he astutely points out, "coincidentally appeared to constitute the three acts of a modern tragedy, giving a 'natural' aesthetic shape to the already tantalizing events," especially following as they did on the heels of Wilde's "highly popular West End hits," which "paled in comparison" (1). Cohen relates that he first read H. Montgomery Hyde's *The Trials of Oscar Wilde* in a graduate seminar, and notes that the Hyde edition "presents itself as 'verbatim transcripts with an introduction.'" Cohen continues that he "naively flew off to London to find the documents upon which Hyde had based his "complete transcription of all three trials" (3), only to find a researcher's nightmare: "something was awry. Not only did there not seem to be any transcripts available from any of the proceedings, but many of the other documents relating to the cases were also missing. And when I frantically started to question why this overwhelming absence existed, since it threatened to sink my project before it had embarked, one very helpful official at the Public Records Office told me, in a most soothing voice designed, I'm sure, to defuse my increasingly visible hysteria: 'Don't worry sir. It's not necessarily suspicious'" (4). Panicking, Cohen wrote to H. Montgomery Hyde, who wrote back saying, "I did not use any transcripts of the trials in my book and in fact relied on press reports in addition to *Oscar Wilde: Three Times Tried,* published anonymously by Stuart Mason (Christopher Millard)" (4). This volume, Cohen notes, was also based on press reports and personal reminiscences.

So far, Cohen's reader has been provided with a real find: it is indeed significant that the source that researchers have relied on for decades, Hyde's *Three Trials*, is not, as was previously thought, based on actual court transcripts but on newspaper reports. Many have noted this, but fewer thought about it. Cohen has considered the subject deeply. Unfortunately, what he has to say about his find lacks the clarity of his entertaining tale of groping through archives for non-existent documents. He reports that he then went to the British Museum's "newspaper dungeon in Collingdale" to look at the "hundreds and hundreds of columns of tiny newsprint devoted to depicting Wilde's passage through the chambers of the Old Bailey" (4).

What follows next is the closest thing to a thesis that Cohen's book possesses. The more Cohen read, he relates, "the more I realized that far from providing me with 'factual' accounts of these complex legal proceedings, as Hyde and others had heretofore assumed, these texts were themselves highly mediated stories whose narrative structures organized and gave meaningful shapes to the events they purported to accurately represent" (4). So far, so good, but these "narrative structures" remain abstractions in Cohen's account. The bias of each particular newspaper is not clearly discussed; this will be elaborated on later. Cohen claims — in Italics, too — that *at no point did the newspapers describe or even explicitly refer to the sexual charges made against Wilde.* He wonders "how it was that everyone could seem to know what it was that Wilde was accused of without it ever having to be positively stated" (5).

"It" was, however, positively stated. As H. Montgomery Hyde points out, Wilde stood accused "of offences against section 11 of the Criminal Law Amendment Act, 1885," and section 11 specifically prohibited "indecency" between male persons in public or in private. "Indecency" connotes what Woody Allen got across when he was asked if sex were dirty and answered, "It is, if you're doing it right." The English law of 1885 made it clear that even in private, men were not supposed to give each other orgasms, but according to long held English custom and tradition, the law did not spell that out in so many words, relying instead on the word "indecency" to convey that meaning, among others.

Incidentally, Hyde's account is not indirect, and sexual acts are named or described. For example, part of the testimony concerns stains on the sheets in Wilde's hotel room that the prosecution wanted to prove had been caused by anal penetration. Wilde's lawyer, Hyde reports, "was obliged to deal with this aspect of the case. . . . There was a perfectly innocent explanation for the stains on the sheets, he suggested. His client had been suffering from attacks of diarrhoea at the time" (Hyde 254). Other testimony concerns kissing and fondling. So the court, the spectators, and the papers, had a clear idea of what was meant by "indecent."

What the law meant in practice differed, as many laws do, from what the law meant on the books. What the law meant in practice was that neither the authorities nor the public wanted to become aware of sexual behavior between men. Women were not included in the section

11 ban on "indecent" behavior, allegedly because when Queen Victoria was asked whether they should be, she reportedly sniffed, "Ladies don't do such things." In practice, gay men who kept their private lives concealed were seldom arrested; only those who went very public, like Wilde — who held hands with Lord Alfred Douglas in the Café Berkeley, a very fashionable watering hole — or who were unlucky, or incautious enough, to become the prey of blackmailers, ended up in court. Lord Alfred Douglas fired a pistol at the ceiling of the Café Berkeley because he felt irked that he and Wilde had not been sufficiently noticed. After that, the lovers were "discovered" by the discreet crowd who had been longing to ignore them.

The idea that Wilde's crimes are not *named* in the press is the issue on which Cohen's book stands or falls. Mountains are made out of the "indecency" molehill. He claims that:

> much as I reveled in and was piqued by Hyde's many retellings, my training in literary and social theory led me to be somewhat skeptical about the impact that Hyde's now canonical rendering has had upon the story . . . because the issues at play in the case seemed to me quite central to how contemporary male sexualities have been (re)produced and (re)presented throughout the century . . . I wondered if there wasn't another way of shaping the story that could avoid Hyde's characterological orientation while illuminating what I imagined to be the large social and political stakes (3).

By "Hyde's characterological orientation," Cohen means Hyde's old-fashioned idea that Wilde's "abnormal sexual drive" led Wilde to forsake "normal sexual intercourse," until Wilde "made the fatal mistake of extending the range of his homosexual acquaints to a different social class than his own" (2–3).

Of course, Hyde's view is outdated. The idea that homosexuality is abnormal has finally been discarded by most of the intellectual establishment, even by the American Psychoanalytic and American Psychiatric associations. Hyde's idea that Wilde's range of partners included lower class men fails to explain his arrest and imprisonment. It was demonstrably Wilde's recklessness, his insistence on being seen and known as a man who enjoyed the sexual favors of other men, that got him arrested. Had he met men "of a different social class" secretly, like the vast majority of British homosexual men of his time, he would never have ended up in prison.

Unfortunately, Cohen's reinterpretation offers nothing better than Hyde's hackneyed and passé view. Concluding remarks in Cohen's epilogue elaborate on his earlier assertion that the conditions under which the "homo/hetero pairing emerged" in nineteenth-century Britain has resulted in an attempt to "fix" the "incommensurate dispositions we have come to know as 'class,' 'sex,' 'age,' 'gender,' 'race,' and 'nationality'" (212). Maybe, maybe not. He does not explain the idea enough to justify it. He continues: "I believe that by historically positioning 'male homosexuality' within the field of male subjectivity per se, we may come to a better understanding of the exclusionary — if not aggressively repressive and violent — effects that the castigation of sexual and emotional intimacies between men has engendered. Indeed, such a relational understanding may enable us to explore more concretely why many men tacitly accept, as well as actively engage in, manifestly hateful and bloody attacks on 'other' men to whom such intimacies can be attributed . . ." (212).

This seems a complicated way of saying that open-mindedness on the part of men in general would help to decrease violence against homosexuals. Cohen's jargon avoids the obvious, namely that men who assault homosexuals feel threatened not by the homosexual behavior they perceive, but by the suspicion that they themselves might have occasionally experienced homosexual feelings they cannot accept and want to forget. Freud's idea of repression explains a great deal of homophobia, since he understood human sexuality as innately bisexual, on a continuum from homosexual to heterosexual, with the possibility of either preference being openly felt or repressed.

Cohen's interpretation of bias on the part of various newspapers seems forced and does not convince. For example, in chapter six, "Dis-Posing the Body," he asserts that "As soon as Wilde himself became the subject of legal scrutiny, it was very clear that it was his body — and metonymically the constitution of the male body — that was at stake in the production of public meanings engendered by the case. Since . . . the trials in which Wilde stood accused of 'acts of gross indecency' were not organized around the interpretation of written texts, but rather were focused on determining the legal status of particular somatic relations, the disposition of Wilde's body became the key to understanding the meaning of these 'crimes'" (181–82).

Cohen's meaning of Wilde's body and "metonymically the constitution of the male body" being "at stake" in the "production of meanings" of the court remains murky for many pages. Examples meant to illustrate his claim, concerning Wilde's physical appearance, finally appear. Cohen quotes from newspaper reports intended to demonstrate the strain of the trial on Wilde. The *Evening News*, for instance, states, "Wilde looked worse this morning than ever previously during this terrible period of his history. His hair was unkempt and his face pale." A few days later, the same paper reported that "Anxiety and suspense told their tale, and in the first moment as [Wilde] stood moistening his parched lips, he looked more haggard and troubled than before" (193–94).

Cohen interprets these and similar sympathetic portraits of Wilde's suffering as follows: "Since [the newspapers] could not explicitly narrate the stories of the 'acts of gross indecency' for which Wilde was actually being tried, [they] instead displaced the significance of these unarticulated acts onto the body of the supposed actor. Indeed, by the time of his conviction, the repeated representation of Wilde's physical being was so imbued with the significance of these 'criminal behaviors' that it itself became almost a character in the journalistic stories of the trial . . . in these reports the significance of such images [of the haggard Wilde, for instance] was . . . overdetermined in so far as it made Wilde's body into a hieroglyph of the crime he had committed" (195–207).

This idea that the newspaper accounts of Wilde's unhappy, pale, haggard face were intended as a code for the message that Wilde was a degenerate and therefore looked bad does not convince. What is most impressive about the newspaper descriptions is their sympathy toward Wilde. They emphasize his suffering, while not failing to report on his crimes as graphically as the times would allow. The papers informed the public of kissing, fondling, and fecal stains on sheets. This is surely not less than the public awareness in the O. J. Simpson trial of bloody gloves and wife-battering. Why is Cohen so intent on proving that the papers wanted to present an unsympathetic view of Wilde? The answer would fall beyond the purview of this book. Suffice to say that a view of the papers as even slightly sympathetic to Wilde's predicament, or a view of the language of the trial as fairly direct, not censored, could not deliver what Cohen's cover copy promises, namely, to take up "bourgeois discussions on 'manliness' as they appeared in various political, pedagogical, religious, medical, legal, and literary writings" in order to demonstrate "how this discourse constructed a 'proper' Englishman, and how crucially male gender was made to be a natural consequence of male sex."

Alan Sinfield

Alan Sinfield's *The Wilde Century: Effeminacy, Oscar Wilde and the Queer Moment*, is part of Columbia University Press's *Between Men/Between Women* series, announced on the frontispiece as "a forum for current lesbian and gay scholarship in the humanities and social sciences. . . . Established to contribute to an increased understanding of lesbians, bisexuals, and gay men, the series also aims to provide through that understanding a wider comprehension of culture in general." The book is quite uneven, ranging from indigestible gobbets of theory to sensible historical analysis.

Sinfield's book, like Ed Cohen's, on whose theories it builds, takes up the fascinating topic of ways in which aspects of gender, like effeminacy or same-sex attraction, are — or are not — perceived in different times. As in Cohen's book, Wilde is the means for exploring what Sinfield believes are radical changes in the perception of gender attributes that occurred as a result of Wilde's phenomenal rise and fall: "our stereotypical notion of male homosexuality derives from Wilde, and our ideas about him" (vii). Unfortunately, Sinfield's book has many of the same problems as Cohen's, namely unclear, jargon-laden writing, use of highly charged politicized words like "queer" without much guidance from Sinfield about the importance of the term, and faulty reasoning. The use of the word "queer" remains controversial. Ed Cohen devotes more than a page to uncertainty about whether it should be reclaimed by the gay community. Sinfield should have devoted more clarification to his own use of the term from the outset.

Sinfield theorizes that the contemporary idea of the "queer" man arose through the Oscar Wilde trials. Before Wilde's trial and imprisonment, he argues, effeminacy, frequently considered a traditional component of queer identity, was not usually considered a sign of homosexuality. "Queer identity," however, is not defined until two pages before the end of the book, where Sinfield writes,

> I have used the word historically as the one in currency during the heyday of the Wildean model. In the 1970s, 'gay' was established as a way of moving on from all that. However, a key difficulty for any oppressed group is that you don't control your own language . . . lately 'gay' has been used continually in the UK gutter press alongside their words ('poof' and so on), [that is, insulting terms] and thereby is contaminated with many of their resonances . . . The aggression and ambition in the readoption of 'queer' are directly proportionate to the degree to which its use proposes to overturn the historic, hostile meaning . . . 'Queer' says, defiantly, that we don't care what they call us. Also it keeps faith with generations of people, before us, who lived their oppression and resistance in its initial terms (204).

The book is divided into eight chapters and a preface that sets out a primary question and Sinfield's approach to it, namely:

how did [Wilde] get away with . . . going around looking and talking
the way he did, and putting such characters on the stage [as seemed
camp or queer in the modern Gay sense]. And the answer must be:
they didn't see queerness in the way we have come to see it. Our interpretation is retroactive; in fact, Wilde and his writings look queer
because our stereotypical notion of male homosexuality derives from
Wilde, and our ideas about him (vii, preface).

Again, even though every educated reader possesses some sense of the
term queer used by groups like Queer Nation, and knows that "queer"
is a term that was originally used as an insult but has been appropriated
as a badge of rebellion by the group originally tormented by its use, it
would be helpful to get much more explanation of the meaning of
"looking queer" and what that meant in the 1890s as well as today.
Even among groups who appropriate the term "queer" for political reasons, considerable disagreement exists about its significance.

Chapter one, "Queer Thinking," begins with the idea that homosexuality was "not manifest" from Wilde's effeminate style, on the
grounds that one as sophisticated as Frank Harris or one as personally
hostile to Wilde as Lord Alfred Douglas's father did not at first believe
the tales of Wilde's same-sex encounters. Sinfield's immediate assumption is that effeminacy did not betoken homosexual activities in those
days. Does this not beg the question of whether people were then
driven to deny homosexuality, and effeminacy as its sign, more than
they do today, because it was deeply threatening? Sinfield does not take
up this possibility. Instead, he asserts that "the trials helped to produce
a major shift in perceptions of the scope of same-sex passion" (3). He
remarks that Ed Cohen has "shown how newspaper reports of the trials
avoided specifying Wilde's alleged crimes — they were regarded as too
horrible to be named" (3). This is not entirely true, and tends in any
case to weaken Sinfield's argument. That the word "sodomite" was
considered too horrible to be printed argues not necessarily that the
public remained unaware of its meaning, but rather that it longed to
forget, to repress, what Wilde had forced them to perceive, what the
public had in fact long perceived but preferred to deny or to ignore.
Omitting a few specificities, or substituting graphic descriptions with
words like "indecency," was about as successful in reinstating their repressions as Phaedra when she forbade the name of Hippolytus to be
spoken: she only thought about him more and more, until she was
driven again to pursue him. Passions cannot be stamped out; the repressed invariably returns.

Sinfield does mention that after an 1871 trial involving a homosexual couple for cross-dressing, the offenders were released, apparently because, in Neil Bartlett's reasoning, "the court was wilfully blind" (7). Exactly. The human capacity for denial does not change; it is probably just that different times and different cultures deny different things. For a variety of reasons, many people no longer deny their perceptions of same-sex attraction in the ways that they did in England a century ago.

But Sinfield insists: "My argument about the emergence of a queer identity around Wilde is constructionist: it holds that sexualities (heterosexual and homosexual) are not essential, but constructed within an array of prevailing social possibilities" (11). In other words, fire does not burn both here and in Persia, as Aristotle suggested, but is constructed: there exists no homosexuality without the word, there is no homosexual person without the concept of homosexual person, there are only acts of same-sex passion. Sinfield declares this without elaboration as though it were self-evident.

In chapter two, "Uses of Effeminacy," Sinfield advances his theory of the social construction of effeminacy, offering as an example a poem of 1905 called "The Female Boy":

> What in the world is the use of a creature
> All flabbily bent on avoiding the Pitch
> Who wanders about, with a sob in each feature
> Devising a headache, inventing a stitch?
> There surely would be a quick end to my joy
> If possessed of that monster — a feminine boy.

Sinfield offers the idea that the effeminate boy is despised as girlish, not as homosexual. But what does "girlish" mean here? The poem's second line, in which the boy is "flabbily bent" suggests the lack of an erection, and this lack appears in the context of the poem to be equated with girlishness. Only the essential differences created by biology make the equation possible: girls don't have penises. Sexual organs are not "constructed" by language or culture. The readiness of the feminine boy to be penetrated, his coy impotence, are the features defining his girlishness and the girlish role enjoyed by men who enjoy penetration by other men, and who are therefore known as homosexual.

Chapter three, "Manly Sentiments," begins with the idea that "in the nineteenth century, there was a new insistence that men be manly — together with a demand that women be domestic." These movements were "fraught with anxieties," Sinfield writes, the kind of anxieties that "cluster so persistently" around "gender constructs in our culture" (52). These assertions remain unspecified, abstract; they are presented as if they were self-evident.

Sinfield moves on to the topic of sentiment and sentimentalism, which he vaguely endows with gender: in a nutshell, effeminacy connoted "leisure-class uselessness" and aspirations toward refinement and taste. "Fine living and fine feeling seemed to belong together," and to be brought together under the watchword "sentiment," meaning "both judgement and feeling," and "hence constituted perhaps the most ambitious claim to combine what were regarded as masculine and feminine properties until the 'new man' of today." Manliness produced wealth and femininity "might show how to consume it elegantly" (53). Sinfield offers little in the way of specific examples, apart from a mention of the Earl of Shaftesbury's announcement in his *Characteristics of Men, Manners, Opinions, Times* (1714) of a desire to soften the manners of the landed gentleman, "but not to the point of inducing so much softness or effeminacy as unfits him to bear poverty, crosses or adversity" (53).

Sentimentalism is discussed as a problematic concept that sometimes implies feminine feeling, but this does not appeal to Sinfield, who offers the *non sequitur* that "imagining the feminine as a source of pure feeling did not, of course, produce feminism" (54). His general comment on sentimental novels of the eighteenth century and their impact on the culture of manliness in the nineteenth century, particularly on the complicated figure of the dandy, is filled with what is at the present writing (2000) high fashion critical cliché: "Masculine philandering colonizes and exploits feminine sentiment — yet at the cost of appearing ridiculous or indecent. This unstable formation could not become the dominant recipe for manliness, but some of it fed into the seductive/disreputable upper-class dandy" (54).

Turning to the nineteenth century, Sinfield becomes more interesting, discussing Alfred, Lord Tennyson's long poem, *In Memoriam* (1850), a love poem thinly disguised as an elegy to a close male friend who drowned, in which Tennyson compares himself to a maiden waiting for her fiancé. "What is striking," Sinfield rightly remarks, "is that Tennyson believed he could write in such a manner without fear of a damaging same-sex implication being drawn. This shows the extent to which an element of feminine feeling might still be legitimate" (58). The classical models of the ancient Greeks and their attitudes toward homosexuality had been acceptable in the poetry of the early nineteenth century, but by the time the poem was published, the *London*

Times complained about the "sweet" and "feminine" tone of the piece. Years later, in 1889 after the Cleveland Street scandal and the Labouchère Amendment, both of which significantly frightened closeted homosexual men, Tennyson "took pains," Sinfield notes, to distance himself from anything that could be construed an effeminate interest in Arthur. "The Victorians were preoccupied with the proper limits of middle-class manliness" (60).

Novels in which manly comradeship seems poised on the edge of turning into sexual passion are discussed, fear of homosexuality being the obvious issue, but Sinfield writes that "We should not expect to unearth any single cause for the Victorian demand for manliness. The key was the assumption that women belonged at home while men should go out into the world" (62). Sinfield's next remark alludes to Victorian fears about homosexuality: "the very institutions [that is, boys' boarding schools] that were supposed to protect men from effeminacy were the ones where same-sex practices flourished" (65). It has long been known that a hyper-masculine or "macho" appearance often conceals fears about masculinity that may be related to homosexuality.

Sinfield suggests that the dandy figure "from Beau Brummell (1788–1840) through to Wilde" represented a rebellion against "manly middle-class authority" by "displaying idleness, moral scepticism and effeminacy" (69). Proceeding to examples drawn from Wilde's comedies, Jack and Algernon of *The Importance of Being Earnest* and Lord Goring of *An Ideal Husband,* Sinfield claims that in both plays women bring out leisure-class frivolity, that is, effeminacy, in their men, and his point is that this effeminacy is not homosexual but heterosexual: these men are all "heterosexual philanderers" (70–71).

This does not tell the whole story. If Wilde's dandies are attempting to be perceived as heterosexual philanderers, it is just as likely that he, as well as any contemporary of his with life experience, perceived them to be closeted homosexuals attempting to cover their tracks by making a show of pursuing women. Another explanation for the effeminacy or limpness of the dandy exists: such men are thought to be so exhausted by sexual conquest that they are made effeminate, in the sense of not being able to summon up an erection after all their hard work in bed. This is the old idea of Mars being unarmed by Venus, disabled by love, an idea that could justify turning away from women to a homosexual who felt conflicted about his sexuality on the grounds that women are dangerous. In any case, Wilde hints constantly at homosexual activity beneath the everyday life of his apparently heterosexual dandies — they live double lives, joke about "bimetallism," which is meant to suggest bisexuality, and they have engraved silver cigarette cases just like the kind that Wilde himself gave to young men, to give a very few examples.

Sinfield argues that the dandy figure "served Wilde's project because he had a secure cross-sex image, yet might anticipate, on occasion and in the main implicitly, an emergent same-sex identity. . . . Wilde is exploiting the capacity of the image of the dandy to commute, without explicit commitment, between diverse sexualities" (73). The idea that Wilde had a "secure cross-sex image," if it means that Wilde felt confident and unconflicted about ambiguities in his sexual orientation, is frequently contradicted by Wilde, whose letters during his years at Oxford reveal considerable *angst* regarding his sexuality and how much of it he should share or reveal. It is difficult to imagine any gay man of intelligence and feeling in the nineteenth century feeling happy and confident about his sexuality, since he would never be able to show it openly without incurring the terrible consequences that Wilde endured in his trials and imprisonment.

Nonetheless, Sinfield proceeds to a point that becomes the linchpin of the book's major argument about effeminacy not being considered homosexual or "queer" in nineteenth-century Britain: "Because of, rather than despite, the ambiguity of [the character Lord Illingworth's representation as a dandy], the image of the queer emerged around and through the figure of Wilde" (74). The apparent dénouement — coming at the end of a section — is the following: "The really significant intrusion of the dandy, in the figure of Wilde, was his last, for it marked his transformation into the queer. 'The dandy as effeminate seducer (or rather seducee) could be swallowed by the writers of the "nineties,"' Moers remarks, 'but not the dandy as homosexual'" (75). The point here seems to have been made before, and it is not clear what Sinfield wants to add to the well-trod ground covered in far more elegant and intelligent prose by the late Ellen Moers.

The final section of this chapter, headed "Catholics, anarchists, Jews, women," generalizes that when any one of these named groups were criticized, they were labeled "effeminate" (75). Sinfield comments that whenever an empire wanted to dominate a people, it liked to declare them effeminate, in the sense of being inclined by nature to submit. He then gives examples drawn from Charles Kingsley (1851) of Protestant hostility to Anglo-Catholicism, stigmatizing Catholics as effeminate; from W. F. Barry's 1887 novel *The New Antigone* of Anarchists as effeminate; from Otto Weininger's *Sex and Character* of Jews as effeminate. It is an old Freudian story that the penis can be associated with big guns, and that those thought to have neither a penis nor a big gun are more easily trampled upon — they are "effeminate."

Chapter four, "Aestheticism and Decadence," begins with a section labeled "Sweetness and Light" that discusses the age-old association of artistic interest and ability with homosexuals. Here again Sinfield's argument depends on repetition, not reason: "Aestheticism became a component in the image of the queer as it emerged, but it is a mistake simply to read this attitude back before the Wilde trials" (84). More trite anachronisms follow in the wake of the idea that something about the aesthetic is feminine — for instance: "Very many poets and novelists have been women, despite the attempts of academic English to write them out of the story, and a hint of effeminacy lurks around many male writers" (85).

Sinfield inadvertently disproves his own argument now and then, choosing examples to show the irrelevance of homoeroticism that instead reveal its relevance. For instance, he remarks that commentators have "proposed some same-sex allusion" in Gilbert and Sullivan's operetta *Patience* — which Wilde was hired by the impresario Richard D'oyly Carte to popularize in the States — and quotes the following lines:

Then a sentimental passion of a vegetable fashion must
    excite your languid spleen,
An attachment à la Plato for a bashful young potato, or a
    not-too-French French bean.

Incredibly, Sinfield ignores the obvious allusion to homosexuality in the line "attachment *à la* Plato," insisting that there is "no reason . . . to associate same-sex passion with vegetables; the lines surely say that one might love a vegetable and it would have to be in a platonic — non-sexual, non-meaty, bloodless — way" (92). This potato is "bashful," however, meaning sexually shy and ready to be seduced. Stating that the lines are "narcissistic, not homoerotic," Sinfield cannot help undermining even this distinction by pointing out that Freud's association of narcissism and homoeroticism "is still some years ahead" — implying that this is a valid association. In any case, Freud only followed the ancient Greeks and Shakespeare.

In the chapter's final section, "Picturing Dorian Gray," Sinfield advocates the idea that Wilde's novel "invokes the queer image, to some readers at least, *despite at no point representing it*" (103; Sinfield's ital-

ics). He tries to make the point that Basil Hallward, the artist in love
with Dorian Gray, is not a dandy or a "queer," but is involved in same-
sex passions, and that Dorian Gray is rumored to have corrupted
women as well as boys, and that therefore it is "tricky to get any fix on
Dorian Gray's vices" (102). It may be tricky to ignore the obvious, but
Sinfield tries hard: "Same-sex passion seems always on the point of getting said in the novel; its omission, indeed, seems significant" (104).
This ignores the reality that had Wilde written his seductive dandy,
Lord Henry, an explicit proposition for Dorian, and included an un-
mistakably sexual gesture, the novel could only have gone underground
as a secret text for closeted gay men. Wilde wanted to go mainstream,
to sneak his sexuality into the public domain and only ultimately, as a
last grand gesture culminating in his courtroom speech about the
"Love that dare not speak its name," to shout it from the rooftops. He
did say in a letter that he found the artistic life to be "a long and lovely
suicide," and that he was "not sorry that it was so" (*Letters,* 185).

Chapter six, "Class Relations," concerns itself with "the emergence
of a queer stereotype," but now the term "queer" has gone back to
meaning "homosexual" in general again. Sinfield mentions the memoirs of Beverley Nichols and Robert Graves, in which homosexual
practices are indulged in but denied. Nichols has an older friend who is
a baronet, and whom Nichols's father likes for that reason, until the
baronet gives the young Beverley a copy of *The Picture of Dorian Gray,*
at which point Beverley's father spits on the book and tears out the
pages with his teeth. This violently strong hatred of homosexuals suggests a need to deny a part of the self that was threatening to become
conscious. Had the father not had any homosexual longings, or had he
experienced homosexual longings that he felt happy about experiencing, he would not have behaved so violently (130).

My point is that the concept of the unconscious is missing from
Sinfield's argument, as is the concept of a cultural homosocialism and
homosexuality induced by specifically British versions of institutions
like the boarding school, the navy, the church, and the prison. In upper
class Britain of a century ago, homosexual feelings were stirred up by
the educational style of confining boys to all-boy schools. Robert
Graves, Sinfield himself observes, makes the point that when girls are
not available, small boys are the next best thing, because they are
"small, weak, and stand in need of protection," just like girls (131).
But again, the main point here is that a whole society created men with
strong homosexual longings, who for myriad reasons strove to relin-

quish that homosexuality, and often did so by the unconscious defense mechanism of repression.

Sinfield, however, confines his discussion to class, not the functions of the mind. He piles on anecdotes from memoirs and novels in which some form of homosexual behavior is expressed, mentioning, for example, John Galsworthy's *The Island Pharisees,* in which two young Etonians appear at the opera in evening dress, looking, Galsworthy says, like "a couple of Oscar Wildes." This, Sinfield crows, "is Oscar Wilde queerness," but nothing new has been said about the term "queer," which means homosexual sometimes and at other times a particular type of homosexual (the kind who likes prostitutes), and at still other times it means the kind of homosexual who asserts loudly that he doesn't care what the hostile straight community thinks.

An understanding of unconscious mental function might help here, particularly because Wilde appears to have played on the unconscious homosexuality of the British, trying to force their hidden longings to become conscious. He did so at the cost of his freedom and ultimately his life. Their fury — exemplified in the judge's disgusted denunciation of Wilde and expressed desire to be able to hand down a more severe sentence — had the terrible force of a reaction against an unleashed repression. It was as though Wilde wanted to tell the British, "Look, I know many of you feel as I do, sexually attracted to men, or at least somewhat so, and I think you should all be as conscious of it as I am." That was the real reason Wilde went to prison. Had he crept around, quietly enjoying homosexual encounters in such a way that no one saw him, then he would have been left alone.

The penultimate chapter, "Freud and the Cross-Sex Grid," accuses Freudians of being anti-homosexual. Some are — Sinfield quotes several of them at length — in the sense of regarding homosexuality as a sickness to be cured, though this is no longer the position of the American Psychoanalytic Association, which has in recent years openly declared itself to be supportive of homosexuals and no longer considers homosexuality an illness.

The chapter title, "the Cross-Sex Grid," refers to the terms masculinity and femininity and Freudian notions of them. Sinfield accuses Freud of being "unwilling to relinquish" these concepts "however illogical he finds them to be." What he quotes to support the idea that Freud finds the terms "illogical" shows only that Freud finds the terms inadequate to cover all the complexities of human sexuality, but the best we have thus far: "psycho-analysis cannot elucidate the intrinsic nature of what in conventional or in biological phraseology is termed 'masculine' and 'feminine': it simply takes over the two concepts and makes them the foundation of its work" (163).

Sinfield's chapter is based on this willful misreading of Freud, and on the assumption that masculine and feminine are always misleading terms, if only because what the terms mean always remains somewhat elusive. The assumption that certain behaviors are always associated with biological masculinity and femininity, though these behaviors vary from species to species and within one species, does not appear to interest Sinfield, who wants to blame the terms for modern misunderstandings of homosexuality or of "queerness." He writes, "Feminine and masculine are cultural constructs, obviously with the primary function of sustaining the current pattern of heterosexual relations" (169).

He gets this idea — and it is a popular one, not all his own — from Jean Laplanche, who claims that Freud has "no proper conception of what activity and passivity are" (169). He claims that Freud was "taken in" by "ideology," specifically by the notion that receiving the penis in intercourse was "passive" while inserting it was "active." No one with an imagination could deny that receiving the penis can be very active indeed, or that insertion can be quite passive. Freud, knowing this, interested himself in fantasy, specifically the fantasy or fantasies typically associated with insertion and reception of the penis. Often, he observed, masochistic and passive fantasies were enjoyed by women receiving a penis, no matter how active those women were during sexual intercourse. It is also possible for sadistic and aggressive fantasies to accompany the insertion of the penis. Freud was well aware that the terms "active" and "passive" could not be correlated to masculinity or femininity exclusively, but because of the biological reality of masculine and feminine genitalia, believed that the concepts were too important to give up — even though they could not adequately describe much of human sexuality.

Sinfield, wed to the idea of indicting the terms masculine and feminine for privileging heterosexuality over homosexuality, asks, "Who is active, who is passive, in fellatio?" (170). He might have acknowledged Freud's position — that the answer to this question depends on the fantasies of the parties involved.

Let's take the case of Oscar Wilde. Sinfield doesn't, although Wilde is the topic of the book, and surely Wilde's thinking on the subject of fellatio ought to interest us, especially in connection with a culturally influenced concept like effeminacy. Wilde did not write about fellatio directly, but we know that he practiced it because his lover, Lord Alfred, said that Wilde liked to suck him, but that Wilde stopped this because Lord Alfred let him know he did not like it. We know that Lord Alfred's whim was Wilde's command, that Wilde willingly enslaved himself to him, that Wilde felt himself to be compelled by Lord Alfred to do things that otherwise he would not have done — like sue Lord Alfred's father for libel. We know that Wilde saw himself as the "catspaw" between Lord Alfred and his father, and we know that Wilde identified himself with an ancient Roman catamite, Sporus.

In other words, Wilde experienced himself as passive, in the sense of not taking action against Lord Alfred's destructive whims, or rather in the sense of liking to submit to Lord Alfred's whims, and we know that no matter how tormented Wilde felt about his "passive" role, he did what he could to retain it. Wilde, in fact, remained active in many ways; one could even say that he actively sought his own downfall by pursuing Lord Alfred, but within the relationship he wanted to feel as though he were being led by the nose. He therefore had a strong desire to be led, and took pleasure in being led, even though he did not always recognize this pleasure — in other words, it was an unconscious pleasure.

The point is that for one man, Wilde, performing fellatio on his lover meant submitting to his lover, while for another man, or for a woman, it might mean something different altogether.

The final chapter, "Subcultural Strategies," has almost nothing about Oscar Wilde in it, though lip service is paid to the notion of the "Wildean model of the queer" no longer "simply dominant" (191). (Was it ever?) In any case, this model has never been sufficiently defined.

Joseph Bristow

Joseph Bristow, in "'A Complex Multiform Creature': Wilde's Sexual Identities," argues than Wilde can "at last be applauded for what he assuredly was: a gay man who paid a terribly high price in being publicly shamed for his physical intimacy enjoyed in private with other males" (196). While the burgeoning gay and lesbian studies of Wilde have greatly reduced the previous generations' tendencies to ignore Wilde's sexual life, or to treat it as a "course of some embarrassment, if not prurience, in university seminars" (195), as Bristow rightly says, Wilde was assuredly *not* sent to prison for sex enjoyed in private. He was paying a price for sex enjoyed in public, or for advertising in public that he was planning to have sex with other men.

Bristow remarks on the effects of the current critical generations' open mind about sexuality and homosexuality on Wilde studies. Just when it seemed that we could talk openly about Wilde's homosexuality, he observes, "sound objections" have been raised "against critical methods that would reduce each and every moment of suggestive obliquity in Wilde's writings to an undeniable instance of homophile intensity" (196). The objections have been raised not by homophobic critics, Bristow emphasizes, but by scholars committed to investigating "how a category such as 'homosexuality' came into being in the first place, and why it might not readily apply to the life and works of Wilde" (196).

After an entertaining review of a witty and scholarly article by Christopher Craft about the many meanings encoded in the term "bunburying" (including "pun-burying"), used in *The Importance of Being Earnest* to refer to the double lives of the young men, Algernon and Jack, Bristow asks what "might be amiss" about "this dazzling analysis." The answer, he insists, "lies in the ways such an interpretation could be accused of molding Wilde's drama into a play with a fully developed homosexual undercurrent, one that would comply with our post-Stonewall comprehension of not only what it might mean to be *homosexual,* but also what it means to be *gay*" (198). Bristow then covers familiar ground, well traversed by Michel Foucault and other scholars regarding the classification of sexuality, who argue that the concept of the homosexual as a type of human being did not exist "until the closing decades of the nineteenth century." Sodomy was until then known as "a sexual act, not a style of sexual being" (198), Foucault has written.

In Wilde's time, a number of homosexual activists and medical researchers had come to use the term "invert" to describe a homosexual person, by which they meant a male mind in a female body or vice versa, and Bristow claims that "the very idea" that Wilde was "in any respect 'inverted' came as something of a shock to him" (199). The letter that Bristow quotes, however, suggests anything but that the category in which he might be medically or psychologically placed was what upset him. Wilde wrote: "My life cannot be patched up. Neither to myself, nor others, am I any longer a joy. I am now simply a pauper of a rather low order: the fact that I am also a pathological problem . . . I am tabulated, and come under the law of *averages! Quantum mutatis!*" (*Letters*, 695). What torments Wilde here is not being classified in general, but cast down from high estate to nothing, a mere pauper, and not even an unusual one, but one that German scientists had been tabulating. Wilde said that the worst thing in the world was not being talked about, and when he got out of prison, uttering his name was *Verboten* in polite society. He was very much not being talked about — he was gone. The English were doing their best to forget about him, and he felt lost and lonely. This is not the same as being upset about his sexual classification by German scientists, which, under happier circumstances, sitting in the Café Berkeley enjoying the best champagne, for instance, would have interested and perhaps amused him.

Bristow goes on to say that Wilde, "until the time of his prison sentence, had no perception of himself as either a 'homosexual' or an 'invert,' even though these almost interchangeable labels were gaining credibility within scientific circles in the mid-1890s" (199). Wilde's letters certainly contradict this point of view. To select one — of many — examples, in 1894 he wrote to George Ives, a prominent author and criminologist who was also homosexual. According to Rupert Hart-Davis's notes on Wilde's letters, Ives had told Wilde of being "attacked in the *Review of Reviews* for an article in the *Humanitarian,* in which he had expressed disappointment that Grant Allen's essay 'The New Hedonism' shied off the problem of homosexuality." Ives was attacked for writing "in praise of unnatural vice" and of idealizing Sodom and Gomorrah. Wilde answered, "When the prurient and the impotent attack you, be sure you are right" (*Letters,* 375). To say that such a thinker as Wilde defended homosexual acts without having himself in mind seems meaningless in this context.

Bristow, nevertheless, goes on to quote Alan Sinfield and Ed Cohen, scholars who make hairsplitting distinctions between the "defiantly effeminate" and the "modern homosexual." He also quotes Eve Kosofsky Sedgwick's work, which argues against the "unquestioning acceptance of the 'inverted' Wilde" (203). She states that Wilde's "own eros . . . was most closely tuned to the note of the [Classical, Dorian, philhellenic] pederastic love in process of being superseded . . . by the homo/hetero imposition" (203). In other words, she feels that Wilde's ideas about homosexuality are greatly influenced by Plato's *Symposium,* in which guidelines are set up to gradually deflect the homosexual partnership from physical to spiritual attraction. An excellent undergraduate classicist, Wilde was well versed in Plato, but to say that he grounded his personal rules about his sexual behavior, or perception of his sexuality, in Plato mainly, is not accurate. He was nothing if not extremely eclectic, as his letters make clear.

Bristow goes on to explore a "handful of significant episodes that force us to reassess Wilde's representation of dissident desires" (204).

He explains that through a reading of Wilde's "Portrait of Mr. W. H.," he will show "why the reading of 'homosexuality' is by necessity thwarted" by that text (204). He claims that the framework of this work — various Classical and Renaissance ideas about male friendship, including Ficino's translation of Plato and Montaigne's — actually "confounds every scrap of evidence that might be rallied to specify the 'friendship' it is clearly championing" (206). He then exhaustively reviews the *Portrait*, an essay-novella concerning young men who obviously eschew heterosexuality, arguing about evidence concerning the identity of Shakespeare's Mr. W. H., and willing to commit suicide to assert the validity of their theory. At the same time, Bristow summarizes several modern interpretations of it, including Lawrence Danson's claim that Wilde deferred naming his same-sex desire as a political act, and Alan Sinfield's rejection of this view on the grounds that since the modern concept of the homosexual person did not exist, Wilde could not have been discovering "a queer precursor" in Mr. W. H.

I find the theory of the supposed great difference between contemporary and late nineteenth-century conceptions of the homosexual unconvincing. Wilde referred to his hired male partners as "renters," and today boys for hire, "rough trade," continue to be known as "rentboys," since what they earn or what they extort pays for rent. Renters were real human beings who thought of themselves as homosexual, even if they used other terms to designate their type of person.

Final sections on *The Picture of Dorian Gray* and Wilde's comedy belabor the point, finishing with the idea that even if there is what modern readers call a 'homosexual subtext' in *The Importance of Being Earnest*, "that is not to claim that [any so-called "Bunburyist"] was ever at any point the 'homosexual' that Wilde, in our confused modern age, was for decades thought to embody" (215).

The argument strikes me as a curious avoidance of Wilde's clear understanding of himself as a homosexual person, not as a man who occasionally committed homosexual acts. Examples from his letters and his famous courtroom speech on the *Love that Dare not Speak Its Name* are too numerous to quote.

Works Cited

Bristow, Joseph. 1997. "'A Complex Multiform Creature': Wilde's Sexual Identities." *The Cambridge Companion to Oscar Wilde.* Ed. Peter Raby. New York: Cambridge UP.

Cohen, Ed. 1991. "Writing Gone Wilde: Homoerotic Desire in the Closet of Representation." *Critical Essays on Oscar Wilde.* Ed. Regenia Gagnier. New York: G. K. Hall.

———. 1993. *Talk on the Wilde Side: Toward a Genealogy of a Discourse on Male Sexualities.* New York: Routledge.

Craft, Christopher. 1991. "Alias Bunbury: Desire and Termination in *The Importance of Being Earnest.*" *Critical Essays on Oscar Wilde.* Ed. Regenia Gagnier. New York: G. K. Hall.

Dollimore, Jonathan. 1991. "Different Desires: Subjectivity and Transgression in Wilde and Gide." *Critical Essays on Oscar Wilde.* Ed. Regenia Gagnier. New York: G. K. Hall.

Gagnier, Regenia, ed. 1991. *Critical Essays on Oscar Wilde.* New York: G. K. Hall.

Hart-Davis, Rupert, ed. 1962. *The Letters of Oscar Wilde.* New York: Harcourt, Brace and World.

———, ed. 1985. *More Letters of Oscar Wilde.* New York: Vanguard Press.

Hyde, H. Montgomery, ed. 1962. *The Trials of Oscar Wilde.* New York: Dover.

Paglia, Camille A. 1991. "Oscar Wilde and the English Epicene." *Critical Essays on Oscar Wilde.* Ed. Regenia Gagnier. New York: G. K. Hall.

Sinfield, Alan. 1994. *The Wilde Century: Effeminacy, Oscar Wilde and the Queer Moment.* New York: Columbia UP.

4: Reader Response Criticism

REApER-RESPONSE CRITICISM has never been a unified school of thought, but rather a disparate series of voices that join in their rejection of the New Critic's ideal of studying the work of literature exclusively, ignoring its effect on the reader. William K. Wimsatt and Monroe Beardsley advanced the New Critical ideal in their essay, "The Affective Fallacy," and Reader Response critics depart from this principle, shifting their focus to the reactions of readers or audiences.

The idea of analyzing the reader's response to a text dates back to Aristotle and Plato, but has been developed by French structuralists, who see the perceiver as the maker of reality; by semioticians, and by a few American critics, especially Kenneth Burke, Louise Rosenblatt, and Walker Gibson. The problem of establishing what we mean by "the reader" is an interesting one that has never been definitively enunciated by any one school. Occasionally the author of a reader-response text simply labels his or her opinions as those of the "reader." I found this to be the case, for example, with Stanley Fish's essays on seventeenth-century prose in his book, *Self-Consuming Artifacts*. There, certain writers are invariably depicted as trying to trick or fool the reader, and the reader is seen as confused and bewildered. I was not the reader Fish had in mind, since I never felt that these writers wanted to trick or fool me as a reader.

In the excerpt below, Michael Patrick Gillespie attempts to write Reader-Response criticism about Oscar Wilde. I found the book as a whole unsuccessful, but useful, because its failures can usually be traced to a typical problem of 1990s Wilde criticism, namely the avoidance of Wilde's personality in the traditional and psychological sense of the term, and an apparent belief that it is possible to read and understand Wilde's writing without knowing anything about his personality.

Michael Patrick Gillespie

Michael Gillespie's book, *Oscar Wilde and the Poetics of Ambiguity*, is described on the dust jacket as the "first critical approach to Wilde's canon based on reader-response theory," in which Gillespie "synthesizes over a century of criticism, highlighting specific elements while deliberately ignoring others." Reader-response theory as employed here does not describe and analyze the responses of various Wilde readers. Rather, it asserts the importance of the "impact of [Wilde's] consciousness on the act of reading" without considering Wilde as a person or as an author, and without interpreting his works. Gillespie is clear on this point, asserting that readers do not come "to a clear comprehension of Wilde's writing by using a simplistic doctrine of authorial intentionality to impose a deterministic reading upon every work in his canon" (4). It is never made clear why authorial intention produces "deterministic" readings, or why Gillespie's version of reader-response analysis should be considered less deterministic, or what is objected to in "determinism," a term remaining undefined.

This book is characterized by windy abstractions: "Wilde's artistic consciousness produces a creative multiplicity that fosters pluralistic associations with the conventional Victorian milieu" (3). If Gillespie means that Wilde's wit applied to a lot of different people for a lot of different reasons, it's not news. Gillespie claims to be building on the work of Jerome Buckley and David Daiches, Steven Marcus and Regenia Gagnier, highly disparate writers whom Gillespie characterizes as being aware of the immensely heterogeneous aspect of the Victorian age. But what Gillespie writes — that all these writers have shown "how often slippages and ambivalences disrupt the stability of assumptions governing conventional depictions of middle-class Victorian social mores" — fails to characterize any of them. "My book," Gillespie offers, "seeks to apply and extend those insights [that is, those of Buckley, Daiches, Marcus and Gagnier] to understand in particular the material impact of the later Victorian age — with all its complexities and contradictions — upon Wilde's artistic nature and upon the canon which that nature produced" (5).

Reading Gillespie's book, I could not get away from the impression that he dislikes Wilde. He often apologizes for Wilde or defends him. The very first line of the book offers a disparaging picture of Wilde: "Until his ill-considered libel suit against the Marquess of Queensberry brought him disgrace in 1895, Oscar Wilde excelled at playing upon the power of popular sentiment to enhance the public's favorable perceptions of his life and work" (1). This paints a picture of Wilde as a sly and deliberate trickster trying to pull one over on us, and inaccurately suggests that Wilde's chief activity consisted in "playing upon the power of popular sentiment" to make himself look good, when, in fact, he did something more interesting because it is more difficult to understand: he played upon the power of public sentiment to make himself look bad. He remarked that if you pretend to be good the world takes you very seriously, but if you pretend to be bad, it doesn't.

Gillespie's second sentence conveys the same disapproving tone, the need to excuse Wilde, to praise with faint damns: "Thus, regardless of the flip tone" of some of Wilde's epigrams, "they reflect the serious attention that Wilde gave to the evocation of conventional views and traditional cultural values" (1). Gillespie is on the wrong track. It is not despite, but because of, Wilde's "flip" tone — and it is not a flip, but a light, tone — that Wilde gets across a serious message. Wilde was the first to assume that what he joked about he took seriously, sometimes so seriously that he suffered more than he could bear, and so joked about painful things to relieve himself, or to help himself bear the seriousness of this thought. At numerous points in the book, Gillespie disapprovingly alludes to Wilde's "flip" tone. Nearly every formulation about Wilde begins with an apologetic "although" or "despite" for Wilde's "superficial glibness" or flippancy (41).

The introduction, "The Insistence of Pluralism: Wilde, the Reader, and the Elements of Composition," closes with a discussion of literary analysis that happens to contradict Wilde's main idea in his best-known work of criticism, "The Critic as Artist." Gillespie writes that "as one formulates a reading — of *The Picture of Dorian Gray*, for instance — given over to a particular ideology (Marxist, for example) factors suggesting alternative responses (new historical, feminist, homoerotic, and any and all combinations) will also inevitably register. The most sophisticated approach to this condition would recognize the reading to which we give preference while acknowledging the alternatives that also obtain" (15). By Gillespie's standards, Wilde was therefore unsophisticated when he wrote, "A critic cannot be fair in the ordinary sense of the word. It is only about things that do not interest one that one can give a really unbiassed opinion, which is . . . the reason why an unbiassed opinion is valueless" (*CW*, 1047). Of course, Gillespie need not adopt Wilde's belief, but a critic wed to pluralism, and one whose definition of sophistication diverges so widely from Wilde's, would be likely to find Wilde's way of thinking annoying.

Chapter one is entitled "Tame Essence of Wilde" — an insulting title, since "tame" was the reverse of Wilde's self-image and indeed of his public persona, not to mention his entire career. The chapter nominally concerns the evolution of Wilde's early writings, though Gillespie begins not with the poems, but with a product of Wilde's maturity, *The Picture of Dorian Gray*. The introduction, containing not a single concrete thought, is characterized by pronouncements like the following:

"The multiplicity inherent in Wilde's canon (alluded to at the close of the introduction) grows directly out of his process of composition, and the ethos of the late-nineteenth-century world that he inhabited largely shaped his approach to writing. Consequently, understanding the pluralistic nature of the cultural context from which Wilde's canon emerged becomes an essential step to full interpretation of his work." Gillespie then promises to examine "how Wilde's interaction with society shaped the imaginative structure of his works" (17).

In this chapter, Gillespie wishes to demonstrate that "the benefits that accrued from the initial success of Wilde's efforts to establish himself in an emblematic role similar to Dorian's threatened his creative endeavors over the long term: The way that Victorian society perceived Wilde set up collateral expectations for his art" (18). Gillespie's wording here — "benefits that accrued" — makes Wilde sound like a businessman or a banker, as does "collateral expectations." If what Gillespie wants to say is that Wilde's flamboyant personality provoked people to expect him to write about flamboyant characters, that is again not news, and what might prove interesting — the ways in which Wilde's public persona influenced ways in which audiences perceived his art — does not get clarified.

The chapter takes up the topic of "pluralism" in Wilde's fairy tales, but pluralism is never meaningfully defined. Discussing Wilde's tale, "The Devoted Friend," in which a selfless character dies while devoting himself to a selfish man, Gillespie focuses on the ending. Hans dies, and the tale's narrator — a Linnet — says "that's the end." He then reproaches the listener for not getting the moral of the story. The listener is enraged at the idea of there being a moral to the story at all, and leaves. Gillespie suggests that the "moral's content remains ambiguous: Should one live as Little Hans no matter what the reaction of others? Or should one not extend kindnesses to ungrateful friends?" (29) He claims that the ending "invites us to reconsider the implications of fairy tales by affirming the view of the inherent danger in producing any story with a moral" (29). Stories without morals were the kind that Wilde liked to tell; this is old stuff. The tale can be fruitfully read as a comment on his own life, on his own self-sacrificing ways, especially with young men whom he knew to be using him. But biographical reading is what Gillespie wishes to avoid.

In chapter two, "Cultural and Aesthetic Responses in Wilde's Essays," Gillespie suggests that in the essay-dialogues — "The Decay of Lying"; "Pen, Pencil, and Poison" (which he mistakenly refers to as "A Pen, Pencil, and Poison,"); "The Critic as Artist"; and "The Portrait of

Mr. W. H.," Wilde addresses "concerns that directly shaped the composition of *The Picture of Dorian Gray*." He adds that Wilde "assumed that readers of his novel would exercise an interpretive freedom ranging well beyond the prescriptive responses of critics who were seeking to impose a dogmatic consistency upon his compositions" (36). Alas, "a dogmatic consistency" dominates Gillespie's own formulations, for he goes on to subject a charming maxim of Wilde's — "Certainly we are a degraded race, and have sold our birthright for a mess of facts" — to an overused formulation: "Despite such apparent flippancy . . . the essay's broad comments on aesthetics articulate views far less whimsical then its best-known apparent non sequitur: nature imitates art" (38).

It is not nature but *life* that imitates *art* in Wilde's formulation in the context of his essay, "The Decay of Lying," and he is observing, among other things, the ways in which fashion follows trends in art, as, for instance, when women adopt pre-Raphaelite dress. Without a word about this, Gillespie produces a non sequitur all his own: "although observations in this essay have the aphoristic flavor common to much of Wilde's writing, they also highlight an ongoing theme in his work: The individual imagination holds supremacy over the habituation of convention, and one betrays one's intellect by surrendering that supremacy to follow without question expected patterns of thought" (38). It is a sad state when an educated man suggests that *although* a piece of writing is aphoristic, it illuminates a theme. Isn't aphorism defined by power of illumination?

The chief problem of this chapter is that of the entire book, the attempt to perceive Wilde as a thinker who ought to have been systematic, and to fault him for avoiding the limitations of system. Hence, Gillespie remarks of "The Critic as Artist," "Wilde the critic is demanding that Wilde the artist acknowledge the concept that the determination of meaning rests at least in part with each reader who encounters the work" (45). Wilde the artist and Wilde the critic remain inseparable. Wilde is direct on the point of meaning, arguing that the reader produces it. The "at least in part" formulation arises from Gillespie's discomfort with Wilde's idea.

Discussing "The Portrait of Mr. W. H.," Gillespie asserts that to respond to the essay by "questioning whether or not Wilde actually believes the theory of the sonnets" articulated therein "simply misses the point" (47). The reverse is true. The essay's point is that Wilde does and does not believe what he is saying, or that he wants to believe his own theory, tries and succeeds in doing so, and then loses faith again. But Gillespie prefers to believe that Wilde's intention is to provide a "strategy of reading." It's true that Wilde's historically minded piece provides an ideal strategy, that of the detective working with slim circumstantial evidence to construct a plausible theory, but the essay has many other intentions as well, including Wilde's intention to reveal himself and to be understood and accepted. In the essay, at least one man kills himself to validate his theory of the sonnets, and Wilde wanted the reader to sense, without knowing, his own urgency. Perhaps he did not himself understand why he felt so urgent, but his subsequent self-destructive behavior shows that something drove him to model himself on his ill-fated characters.

In this chapter, Gillespie covers Wilde's reactions to charges of immorality that various periodicals and newspapers brought against *The Picture of Dorian Gray*. Gillespie considers "Wilde's overall response" to these charges, which strike him as "particularly important in terms of our perception of the relation of intra- and extratextual forces shaping both the composition and the interpretation of his novel." This is followed by Gillespie's assertion that Wilde didn't want to let his writing be dictated by conventional taste, but even so he "attended to public feelings to prevent resentment from developing across a broad segment of society" (53). On the contrary, Wilde did his best to foster resentments, as his tragic end reveals.

Chapter Three, "Picturing Dorian Gray," and subtitled, "Resistant Readings in Wilde's Novel," begins with a cliché — "an aura of ambivalence and ambiguity . . . mediates relations among Wilde, his writing, and his readers" (57) — but includes one original remark: "As we read through *The Picture of Dorian Gray*, it becomes evident that an insistent nostalgia continually informs the images of Dorian created in the minds of both Basil and Henry. Each retains a retrospective view of Dorian's nature remarkably close to the judgments reached in Basil Hallward's studio . . ." (67), but the observation is never developed. Gillespie slips back into vagaries about Wilde's "pluralism," and lamely ends the chapter with this: "In *The Picture of Dorian Gray* the numerous alternatives for reading disrupt easy categorization" (74). This suggests that it is Gillespie who feels disrupted by not easily being able to pin down or categorize the work.

Chapter four, "The Force of Conformity," concerning Wilde's plays of the early nineties, opens with another variation on the vagaries closing the preceding chapter: "As the previous two chapters have shown, the exotic discourse of *The Picture of Dorian Gray* easily lends itself to the interpretive multiplicity and the deferral of closure that I have advocated as the best approach to a full appreciation of Wilde's canon"

(75). The term "deferral of closure" seems to mean never deciding on an interpretation, let alone articulating one. Gillespie's message of this chapter appears to be that Wilde's social comedies "have the capacity to sustain similarly diverse readings" (75).

This is not news, and at this point, halfway through the book, one would hope to find Gillespie attempting some readings, any readings at all, let alone diverse ones. Mentioning only that "some readers" see Wilde as bordering on plagiarism in his plays, Gillespie priggishly comments, "A more precise view of the situation sees in the plays a continuing effort to elaborate topics already familiar to Wilde's readers in a fashion that both reflects and caricatures the enthusiasms, needs, and fears of his age" (77). If only Gillespie would touch on some of these topics! He does offer a few plot summaries, mentioning, for instance, that *Lady Windermere's Fan* is on the surface "a rather unpretentious melodramatic tale, broadly analogous in plot and exposition to contemporary plays such as Sir Arthur Wing Pinero's *The Second Mrs. Tanqueray*." But he doesn't say anything more about this well-known fact than that Wilde's work, unlike the melodramas, "invites reconsideration along dialogic lines of the deeper, more ambivalent attitudes that define it" (86).

Chapter five, "The Victorian Impulse in Contemporary Audiences," concerning the "Regularization" of *The Importance of Being Earnest,* nominally concerns the efforts of literary critics to "enforce their interpretations by focusing on selected distinguishing features" of the comedy that "support a specific central concern without extending full consideration of the play's pluralistic potential" (100–101). But actually, it seems Gillespie would like to "regularize" productions of the play to suit his tastes. He asserts that the elements of the play allow "performance . . . from a number of equally valid points of view," but that "Unfortunately, despite the play's combination of familiarity and innovation . . . particular productions of *The Importance of Being Earnest* often fail to address the play's pluralistic scope" (100).

The phrase "equally valid" would make Wilde wince. "Pluralistic" is a word that never gets defined. But the chapter does include one interesting observation that hints at the meaning of pluralism. Advocating "a response" to Wilde's title that is "more suited to the mutability of his language," and "explores the ambivalence of the title by incorporating pluralism into one's initial linguistic response," Gillespie suggests that "Being" in *The Importance of Being Earnest* could "be synonymous with both 'Seeming' and 'Becoming'" (101). One hardly needs a term like "pluralism" to make this point, but at least now we know that pluralism means something like open-mindedness.

In this chapter, Gillespie displays some awareness of the degree of vagary to which he subjects the reader. Declaring that any interpretation "that circumscribes the play's imaginative breadth by excluding multiple alternatives from simultaneous consideration would find itself operating outside the work's own epistemological parameters," he admits, "This may seem as rather nebulous interpretive charge" (105).

Chapter six, "From Beau Brummell to Lady Bracknell," concerns the figure of the dandy in *The Importance of Being Earnest*. The chapter begins with the claim that "despite the sense of extravagant and exuberant ambiguity" in the play, "readings . . . have too often tended to blend restraint and detachment to distill a tame essence of Wilde." This dubious claim is followed by the idea that the "pluralism" — surely an overused term by now — "manifests itself through the personalities of its diverse characters rather than its plot" (115). Why exclude the plot? That point is never made clear.

What follows is this definition of dandy: "while acknowledging the coercive power and the definitive linearity of the dominant social institutions of the period, the dandy forgoes complete conformity and actively cultivates the digressive relativity of pluralism. Although he embraces the most radical forms of self-indulgence, the dandy in general (and Wilde's version in particular) assiduously offers nominal submission to principles of public respectability" (116).

I wonder what it means to "actively" cultivate the digressive relativity of pluralism? As opposed to passively cultivating it, that is.

Chapter seven, "The Salome of Wilde and Beardsley," begins by noting that the "compositional format" of the play differs from Wilde's other plays, and "from the standard fare (melodramas and Ibsen-influenced tragedies) that dominate the late-Victorian stage. The expressionistic discourses and the polyphonic interaction of the play, complemented by the stylized illustrations that Aubrey Beardsley did for the first English edition, offer readers imaginative experiences very different from those that other works by Wilde may have led them to anticipate" (134).

Gillespie goes on to complain that the "creative dissonances" of the play have "prompted many scholars to seek certitude through clearly articulated polemical aims," which Gillespie thinks is bad, since such approaches "enforce the primacy of a single perspective that dominates their interpretive response" (136). Gillespie's goal appears to be to have no point of view whatsoever, although there is the unstated one of showing a certain dismay over, if not disregard for, Wilde.

The title of the final chapter, "The Failure of Solipsism," (subtitled "Wilde's Late Work") again reveals this contempt. Closing the book on a note of failure can suggest only this. Accusing Wilde of solipsism is at best ignorant, even in reference to what many consider to be his least well written work, *De Profundis,* produced under the strain of his prison sentence. The first paragraph of the chapter even accuses Wilde of changing his "process of composition" in such a way that he created "an environment that frustrates efforts to apply the approaches that worked so well in reading earlier portions of his canon" (155). Poor Wilde, frustrating Gillespie-as-reader!

The book's final paragraph offers a warning to the reader that displays either an ignorance of Wilde's critical ideas or a desire to ignore them: "unless one approaches the bulk of [Wilde's] canon with the inherent acceptance of the simultaneous validity of even contradictory alternative readings — a hypostatic perceptiveness — interpretations cannot progress beyond the rudimentary level." Since Wilde devoted his considerable energies to embracing contradictory readings, Gillespie's message here can only be read as disapproval.

Works Cited

Gillespie, Michael Patrick. 1996. *Oscar Wilde and the Poetics of Ambiguity.* Gainesville, Florida: UP of Florida.

Wilde, Oscar. [1891] 1986. "The Critic as Artist." *Complete Works of Oscar Wilde.* Ed. Vyvyan Holland. New York: Harper & Row.

5: Irish Ethnic Studies and Cultural Criticism

THE 1990S MAY COME to be known as the decade of Wildean identity politics: a number of well-researched books and essays have appeared, tracing Wilde's Irish roots, describing their indelible influence
on his life and work, arguing for an Irish Wilde, and marshaling evidence to prove that Wilde has been mislabeled "English" or "British"
for a variety of reasons, including his desire to make a name for himself
among the British. Among the best are essays by Dierdre Toomey,
Davis Coakley, and Jerusha McCormack; an essay collection edited by
McCormack; and a new biography of Wilde by Davis Coakley. Since
some of Coakley's best ideas appear in an essay, I include a discussion
of that rather than his biography.

Also included in this section are essays showing Wilde's influence on
popular culture: Mary Blanchard's excellent study of Wilde's impact on
American society is included here, as well as Pia Brinzeu's brief article
concerning Wilde and cyberculture.

Davis Coakley

Davis Coakley, in "The Neglected Years: Wilde in Dublin," discusses
biographical aspects of Wilde's life, such as the influence of the diversified members of the Irish School of Medicine upon his early development. Oscar Wilde's father, Sir William Wilde, was "one of the most
brilliant and diversified members of the Irish school," and was married
to the poet Jane Francesca Elgee, whose involvement with the revolu-
tionaries of 1848 had made her famous.

While discussing what Sir William and Lady Wilde read to their
children at bedtime — often patriotic verses of the Young Ireland poets
— Coakley makes an interesting observation that I have never come
across before: Wilde "reverted to the ballad form of the Young Ireland
era in *The Ballad of Reading Gaol*. The meter that he adopted was used
by the poet Denis Florence MacCarthy, to express Ireland's distress
under English rule, in a short poem entitled 'New Years Song' . . ."
(53). Coakley quotes lines from the poem, comparing them to lines in
Wilde's ballad, convincingly demonstrating that "New Years Song" was
a likely influence. Much work has been done on English sources of the

poem by authors like Coleridge, A. E. Housman, and Tennyson; this new source is an interesting one.

Coakley moves to other cultural influences, mentioning that when Oscar was ten years old the National Gallery was opened, and that many of the themes of paintings held there were biblical: "I think it was worth noting, in view of Oscar's subsequent interest in Salome, that two of the paintings which the gallery bought depicted Saint John the Baptist in the wilderness and a third depicted the beheading of the saint" (54). The latter was acquired in 1864, that is, when Oscar was ten years old.

Coakley has done interesting nook-and-cranny work, digging up rather obscure early influences on the conversational prowess of Oscar Wilde. The physician Sir William Stokes was a frequent guest at Wilde dinners, and was known as a great talker. John Pentland Mahaffy, Wilde's mentor at Trinity, was influenced by Stokes and wrote a book on the art of conversation. In that book, and in his obituary of Stokes, he said that "a witty talker" had proclaimed that the "golden rule of conversation" is "to know nothing accurately" (55–56). This was elaborated by Mahaffy, and later by Wilde in "The Decay of Lying." Coakley's article closes with a remark in Vyvyan Holland's memoir, *Son of Oscar Wilde*: "It has frequently been said that Ruskin molded my father's character at Oxford, but it would be more accurate to say that Ruskin watered the seed that had been sowed by Mahaffy" (60).

Roy Rosenstein

Roy Rosenstein, in "Re(dis)covering Wilde for Latin America: Martí, Darío, Borges, Lispector," looks at "several critical high points in Wilde's reception in Latin America over more than a century" (349). José Martí, Cuba's national hero, a journalist and critic, was in 1882 the first to recognize Wilde's importance, while in the 1890s Nicaragua's Rubén Darío, "the most influential poet Spanish America has yet produced," and in the twentieth century Argentina's Jorge Luis Borges and Brazil's Clarice Lispector have all paid homage to Wilde for Latin America (349).

Rosenstein reports that José Martí, whose dates, 1853 to 1895, make him almost an exact contemporary of Wilde, was in New York to hear Wilde speak. Martí remarked, "Look at Oscar Wilde! Listen to Wilde! [He] has purchased with his economic independence the right to intellectual independence" (350). According to Rosenstein, Martí saw in Wilde "a brother who champions artistic independence, the key word for the Cuban who will devote his life to freeing his country from colonial domination." Martí was "fatally wounded leading his troops into battle in 1895 . . . in the same year Wilde also fell" (350).

Rosenstein goes on to mention that Martí and Darío were making their literary marks around the same time that Wilde hit his zenith. Wilde had first been recognized in 1888 with "The Happy Prince," while in the same year Darío published *Azul* in Chile. Characterizing Darío as comparable to Swinburne, Rosenstein remarks that Darío's praise of Wilde "must have seemed remarkably supportive in the 1890s amid the widespread condemnation that surrounded Wilde in life and after his death" (351).

Other Spanish-speaking writers were not so tolerant of Wilde: Unamuno attacked him as "the apostle of decadence," following Max Nordau, as did other Continental Spanish writers (351). In his 1912 *Autobiography*, Darío writes that "now, in England and everywhere, [Wilde's] glory is reestablished." Rosenstein points out, "Thus, substantially before Wilde's adoption by Spanish readers at the time of World War I or by Russian modernists as soon as 1904, Darío, who would give *modernismo* its name, had embraced Oscar Wilde" (351).

Rosenstein goes on to discuss Borges's many "salutes to Wilde" (352), among them Borges's translation of "The Happy Prince," which became Wilde's first appearance in Latin America. His lifelong interest in Wilde culminated in the judgment that Wilde is "almost always right" (353). Finally, Rosenstein discusses "the culmination of Wilde's penetration and assimilation in Latin American culture," when *The Picture of Dorian Gray* was introduced and championed by the poet Clarice Lispector.

Neil Sammells

Neil Sammells, in "Rediscovering the Irish Wilde," attempts to define the nature of Wilde's Irishness, which lies in various conflicting or, as he writes, "sliding" identifications: "His penchant for the green carnation buttonhole is symptomatic: it is the badge of a homosexual coterie, a demonstration of the self-consciously modern and refined taste which prefers the artificial to the natural, and a declaration of national allegiance which refracts and politicises both. It is in effect, a languidly insistent and coded declaration of difference. As Wilde said, on the banning of *Salome:* 'I am not English. I am Irish, which is quite another thing'" (363).

Sammells goes on to say that the nature of Wilde's Irishness sets the editors of *The Field Day Anthology of Irish Writing* (1991) "at odds with themselves and with each other." He cites Christopher Murray and others "finding Wilde's work compromised by his English context" (364). Seamus Deane also wrote that in all of Wilde's work "the subversive, even radical, critique of society that is implicit in what he has to say, finds no release within the linguistic conventions which he mocked but by which he remained imprisoned" (364). Wilde stands accused of conceding to English, rather than Irish, arbiters of taste.

Sammells sides with those writers who, like Declan Kiberd, see Wilde's Irishness as a "function of *difference*" that is "defined — not demeaned — by his English context. The Irish Wilde . . . expresses himself in a series of subversive literary strategies . . . which are the response of a colonial subject to discourses which, as Terry Eagleton puts it, are 'on the side of Ceasar'" (365). Shaw, Sammells writes, "recognises both the nature and the importance of Wilde's Irishness most clearly" (365).

Discussing ways in which Irish writers deal with the English language, Sammells states that Wilde "outenglishes" English. His characters speak with an "elegance and an almost extraterritorial precision that exploits English to its own destruction. Wilde's consciousness of his foreignness informs his parodic engagement with language; as an Anglo-Irishman he contrives to 'distance himself within' English, thus registering his paradoxical position in the colonial power-structure between England and Ireland" (367).

Sammells sums up this way: "Wilde's textual strategies display difference in order to deny it. The same is true of his adroit manipulation of his Irishness. Wilde is, to quote Owen Dudley Edwards, 'at once the metropolitan sophisticate and the loyal son of the Celtic periphery'" (369). His Irishness is for Sammells "not defeated by his Englishness." Instead, the Irish Wilde is "defined both by and against the English Wilde" (369).

Jerusha McCormack

Jerusha McCormack, in "Oscar Wilde: The Once and Future Dandy," explores the meanings of the term "dandy," in the context of Wilde's remark: "The future belongs to the dandy. It is the exquisites who are going to rule" (269). As McCormack points out, he was wrong, "in the sense that few today would even know what a dandy was, much less recognize in him a figure of power." She traces the origins of the term dandy — wrongly perceived by most people as "merely a man of fashion, albeit one who made an almost heroic commitment to style" (269). In Charles Baudelaire she finds a definition of dandyism as "an institution outside the law" (269). Dandyism is closely linked, Baudelaire remarks, to periods "of transition when democracy has not yet become all powerful, and when aristocracy is only partially weakened and discredited" (270).

McCormack shows the connection between Wilde and the tradition of the dandy clearly, stating that the dandy performs "a kind of psychic jujitsu — he 'throws people' by using the force of their attitude to defeat them. In effect, by means of his performance the dandy gets his audience to share his contempt for itself" (270). Wilde and his dandies in this context "anticipate the Dada principle of provocation or the procedures of the Theatre of Cruelty." McCormack draws a connection to Mohandas Gandhi, observing that he came to London from India in October 1888 to study law at the Inner Temple, and that like Wilde, he "had taken note of the work of the Fabian Society and was to be crucially influenced by the work of John Ruskin" (270). He, like Wilde, "refashioned himself as a dandy" (270).

Both Wilde and Gandhi, McCormack says, were "from the margins of the British Empire" — that is, as outsiders, they had reason to wish to become more British than the British, and with the zeal of converts to transform themselves into British gentlemen, or at least British dandies. Hence, "Wilde used the figure of the dandy to register protest in much the same way as Gandhi registered his" (271). Both engaged in a kind of "ritual provocation that effectively hands control over to the audience. Apparently innocuous ('nonviolent' in Gandhi's terms), their strategy of protest is designed to elicit powerful response" (271).

McCormack brilliantly sums up what looked at first to be an unlikely comparison: "Wilde's target [like Gandhi's] was equally the doublethink of the Empire at home: 'It is the spectator, and not life,' he asserted, 'that art really mirrors.' By turning the audience's language upon itself, Wilde's dandy engages in a mime of its ritual cant which exposes it as cant. By its laughter, Wilde's audience betrays recognition while denying implication" Thus, in laughing at Wilde's dramas and making them a success, the audience felt itself to be a success, as Wilde pointed out. "When it turned on Wilde, his audience did so with the ferocity of those betrayed by a figure of their own making: to use Wilde's own phrase in another context, their reaction was the 'rage of Caliban seeing his own face in a glass'" (272). Her final sentence is particularly shrewd, and an inspired conclusion to an original and very convincing argument: "Until [Wilde's] dandyism is interpreted in terms of protest and provocation and even in terms of larger political dissent, it may not be possible to understand the full implications of Wilde's claim that he stood in symbolic relations to the art and culture of his age" (272).

Jerusha McCormack, ed.

Wilde the Irishman, a collection of seventeen essays and an introduction by the editor, aims to repossess and redefine Wilde as an Irishman. "For nearly a century," the dust jacket announces, "Oscar Wilde has been seen primarily as a 'British' writer — an experience that ignores his Irish parentage and the experience of the first twenty years of his life." The essays are divided into two sections, "Appropriations" and "Continuities," which are designed to explore the difference between understanding him as primarily an Irishman and understanding him as primarily a British writer. The editor, Jerusha McCormack, sums up the situation with a Wildean formulation: "Given a choice between being English or Irish . . . Wilde chose both . . . [he was] born into a class known as the Anglo-Irish, at once the pillar of a rotting imperial regime in Dublin and more Irish than the Irish themselves." He was therefore born "into an oxymoron, and doomed to live out his life as paradox," becoming "adept at living on both sides of the hyphen" (1).

Jerusha McCormack's short, lively introduction articulates the complexities of defining Wilde, investigating those aspects of Wilde that he himself continually investigated: "To say that Wilde is Irish . . . is to define him in terms of a question: what does it mean to be Irish? How many things does it include? And what must it . . . exclude? . . . Wilde was inventing Ireland as he proceeded to invent himself, and, in inventing himself, helped to invent what is now modern Ireland" (2). Her approach to the problem of Wilde's Irishness is informed by definitions of Irishness expressed in Wilde's time: "Wilde's identification with Ireland had perhaps less to do ultimately with historical fact or party-political affiliation than a consistent cultural identification with what he called 'Celtic.' The Celt, as defined by Ernest Renan and Matthew Arnold, was not merely Irish, but also Breton, Scottish and Welsh; he was of the oppressed peoples which embodied all that was alien and rejected by the English; in turn the Celt rejected what Wilde called the 'inherited stupidity' of the master-race: its common sense, its philistinism, its puritanism" (2).

McCormack is sensitive to the inherent conflicts underlying competing definitions of Irish identity with which Wilde struggled: "What Wilde's life demonstrates is that to be Irish is to have multiple, and divided, loyalties: to be both colonizer and colonized, native and official, within the Pale and beyond it: to inhabit a space where contraries meet and are transvalued into something else, a something which by definition escapes definition: to be in a provisional and mutating state, not a recognized state but a state of mind . . . Precisely because Ireland is still a question, it is appropriate that Wilde should now be made part of it, and its destabilizing energies in turn destabilize and transmute our interpretation of him" (3).

The book is, she sums up, "an exercise . . . in crossing borders [and] in blurring and even eliminating them," bringing up an area that is more and more examined in cultural and post-colonial literary criticism today. Finally, she points out that for "the first time since his death, Wilde is being recognized as Irish" (5). The book's intention is to "reinstate his spirit back in its own hunting grounds: to relocate its origins and its effect in its native Ireland and in that spiritual territory that Wilde himself understood as home to the collective unconscious of his race" (5).

This sets the tone for a collection of intellectually sound, clearly written essays, and for the most part the collection lives up to it. The essays are always readable, even when they are wrong-headed, and that readability, in the current critical climate, is a virtue to be prized. I've summarized many, though not all, of McCormack's selections.

The first essay, Declan Kiberd's "Oscar Wilde: The Artist as Irishman," offers original insights into Wilde's perception of himself as an Irishman as well as of British reactions to the Irish. At the same time, the essay covers familiar biographic material with charm and Irish wit. Discussing Wilde's eccentric, ambitious mother, for instance, Kiberd writes, "She had longed for a girl and so, when the boy-child arrived like an uninvited guest, she was somewhat miffed" (9).

When not relating Wilde to the Irish, Kiberd's interpretations are sometimes weak. In quoting one of Wilde's epigrams from *The Importance of Being Earnest* — "All women become like their mothers. That is their tragedy. No man does. That's his." — Kiberd degradingly refers to it as a "wisecrack." Adding insult to injury, he writes, "The loutish sexism of the first half of the proposition is fully retrieved by the sharp intelligence of the conclusion" (10). At least Kiberd thinks the conclusion shows intelligence, but the fact is, the intelligence of the conclusion only exists combined with the first half of the epigram. Where is the loutishness? Where is the sexism? Is it not simply a truth, sometimes painful and sometimes pleasant, that women tend to hear their mother's voices in their own when speaking to their children, see their mother's faces when they look in the mirror, and find themselves approving or disapproving of the very things that their mothers approved or disapproved of?

Kiberd ignores the confession in the second half of the epigram — that it is a man's tragedy not to become like his mother. Certainly this was one of Wilde's personal tragedies. He had a warlike mother, who called herself "Speranza," and envisioned herself as the hope of Ireland in troubled times. An "ardent feminist," full of "strident patriotism," as Kiberd notes, she penned inflammatory articles and poems for "nationalist journals" (9). A mother envisioning a "hundred thousand muskets" glittering in the sun, all pointed at Great Britain, demanded the same macho stance from her favorite son, and her favorite son's ambitions differed. He proved to be a subtle nationalist, not a strident one, and he struggled to meet her standard. She held him to that standard even, or especially, when she knew it would ruin him, as when she announced that if he stayed in London during his trials he would always be her son, but if he left, she would never speak to him again. Her martial attitudes hit home, especially since Wilde's father — anything but a fighter — was in many ways overshadowed by her.

Although much of the biographic information Kiberd offers is not new, some of his interpretations of Wilde's development as a young man hit the mark. As a college student and after graduation he began to shape himself: "he busied himself with the task of arranging a pose based on the art of elegant inversion. All the norms of his childhood were to be reversed. His father had been laughed at by society, so he would mock society first. His mother had been unkempt, so he would be fastidious" (10).

Returning to the essay's main theme, Wilde's Irishness, Kiberd has a knack for revealing British envy and unease around the Irish, remarking that "Wilde's entire literary career constituted an ironic comment on the tendency of Victorian Englishmen to attribute to the Irish those emotions which they had repressed within themselves . . . Wilde saw that the image of the stage Irishman tells far more about English fears than Irish realities, just as the 'Irish joke' revealed less about Irishmen's innate foolishness than about Englishmen's persistent and poignant desire to say something funny" (11).

On the subject of Wilde trying to be more English than the English, Kiberd observes "a comprehensive suppression of personality" on

Wilde's part," a "step toward selfhood" taken at too great cost, for "the more he suppressed his inherited personality, the more it seemed to assert itself" (11–12). Kiberd understands the complex contradictions involved in Wilde's development toward selfhood: Wilde wanted to "become a very Irish kind of Englishman, just as in Ireland his had been a rather English kind of Irish family. The truth, in life as well as in art, was that whose opposite could also be true" (13).

Throughout the essay, Kiberd maintains a Wildean acceptance of contradiction and paradox, which enhances his understanding: "The Wildean moment is that at which all polar oppositions are transcended" (16). Perhaps it is his sympathetic understanding of Wilde that leads him to invoke the theories of the psychoanalyst Otto Rank to explore the double self in Wilde. Rank has often been used to explore Wilde's *Picture of Dorian Gray,* less often Wilde's conflicting inner selves or his conflicting national selves. Kiberd writes, "There could hardly be a more convincing psychological explanation of the strange oscillation between conciliation and coercion in imperial policy towards Ireland than Rank's report on the tactics employed in the making of the double. The notion of the 'innocent' and 'spontaneous' Irish may have been an emotional convenience to those Victorians who were increasingly unable to find satisfaction for feelings of guilt in universally accepted religious forms. The myth of an unspoilt peasantry, in Cumberland or Connemara, was, after all, a convenient means of emotional absolution from guilt in a society for which natural instinct was often tantamount to a vice" (17).

Wilde's *Importance of Being Earnest* is therefore, Kiberd suggests, "a parable of Anglo-Irish relations and a pointer to their resolution." Kiberd expands on these politics, exploring ways in which Wilde behaved like the colonizers, "becoming a sort of urbane, epigrammatic Englishman," and at the same time subversively "pointed to a subterranean radical tradition of English culture which might form a useful alliance with Irish nationalism and thus remain true to its own deepest imperatives" (18). *The Importance of Being Earnest* fits into this scheme by subtly opposing imperial aims: "The hierarchical view of humankind, on which imperialism justified itself, led to a purely instrumental view of the English working class, but that class would never rise in revolt, since the empire also reduced class tensions by opening up careers overseas to talented members of the lower orders" (19). *The Importance of Being Earnest,* however, is made up of characters who are "nothing less than the revolutionary ideal of the self-created man or woman." Kiberd discusses the republican politics of the play, and why "in order to deal with Ireland, a play such as *The Importance of Being Earnest* had to be set in England. Wilde had discovered that an Irishman came to consciousness of himself as such only when he left his country. Wearing the mask of the English Oxonian, Wilde was paradoxically freed to become more 'Irish' than he could ever have been back in Ireland" (21).

The next essay, Dierdre Toomey's "The Story-Teller at Fault: Oscar Wilde and Irish Orality," concerns Wilde as "an excellent talker," in Yeats's phrase, and explores the importance of the Irish oral tradition in Wilde's oeuvre. Beginning with Yeats's memories, in which Wilde's stories were ruined as soon as Wilde wrote them down and "spoiled" them with "the verbal decoration of his epoch," Toomey moves to a crucial comparison: "Yeats himself manifested a productive tension between extreme endorsement of oral culture . . . and extreme concern with the text elaborately realized in an object, the book. In contrast, the tension between writing and talking for Wilde was a hostile symbiosis. He told a journalist that there should be a more satisfactory way of 'conveying' 'poetry to the mind' than by printing it, and he frankly told Gide that writing bored him" (25).

To my knowledge, no one has made this point before, nor examined its implications so well. Toomey points out that even though many members of Wilde's audience had no "Irish context in which to place his orality" they still "valued his oral tales over their written versions" (25). Wilde always preferred talking to writing, and his attitudes toward his talk, Toomey demonstrates, typify those of oral cultures: "Wilde lacked any strong sense of ownership in his oral tales — an identifying characteristic of oral cultures, in which the text belongs to the whole community" (26). Toomey characterizes oral texts as "by their very nature, contextualized and responsive to a particular audience" (26).

Toomey then turns to the work of Walter Ong, who suggests that in oral cultures, words are "events," or as Toomey puts it, "not *things*, dead, 'out there' on a flat surface, as they are to literates living in a chirographic-typographic culture," but "magical, penetrative, and internalized" experiences. She adds that Ong's ideas are "perfectly realized" in chapter two of *The Picture of Dorian Gray*, when Dorian thinks to himself, "Words! Mere words! How terrible they were! How clear, and vivid, and cruel! One could not escape from them. And yet, what a subtle magic was in them! They seemed to be able to give a plastic form to formless things . . . Mere words! Was there anything so real as words?" (27).

Toomey's analysis continues with more characteristics of oral cultures: "Gesture and the somatic element are vital in oral cultures and related to the physicality of the story-telling mode" (27). Other traits she lists include "the agonistic structure found in 'The Decay of Lying' and 'The Critic as Artist,' the lack of a hierarchy between text and interpretation (a profound element in Wilde's aesthetic)" and "Wilde's love of the aphorism." She then makes a very good point, casting new light on approaches to Wilde's borrowings from other writers, which are sometimes referred to disparagingly as plagiarism, but which I had always seen as intentional re-writing, parodic or serious. Toomey writes: "Another sphere in which oral culture differs absolutely from literate culture is in its attitude to cliché, stereotype and plagiarism. These cardinal sins of literacy are cardinal virtues of orality. Originality in an oral culture consists not in inventing an absolutely new story but in stitching together the familiar in a manner suitable to a particular audience, or by introducing new elements into an old story" (28). Charges of plagiarism against Wilde fail to take into consideration his intentions, which were often not those of literate culture.

Toomey goes on to cite instances of oral literature in Wilde's works, specifying his "major cycle of biblical tales" (29). She then turns to Yeats as "alone of Wilde's friends" the only one who "had the Irish nationalist context in which to place a valuing of the oral over the written, and to understand the larger cultural and political implications of such a stance" (32). She summarizes Yeats's recollections in his *Autobiographies* of controversy over the Irish language, remarking that even as late as 1899, a Professor Robert Atkinson, the Todd Professor of Celtic Languages in the Royal Irish Academy and Professor of Sanskrit and of Romance languages at Trinity College, Dublin, was arguing "that modern Irish was not an authentic language and that Irish folk tales were disgusting and worthless." Yeats and others saw Atkinson's pronouncements as "essentially political," Toomey writes, Atkinson's hostility deriving from the role of modern Irish in the nineteenth century as "primarily an oral language" (33). She suggests also that "Atkinson's neurotic fear of the 'low,' the 'primitive,' and pre-literate seems to indicate a construction of oral and folk texts as dangerous and expressive of uncontrollable unconscious forces" (33).

Toomey finishes this highly readable and informative article with details about ways in which Wilde's oral tales drew on tales collected in the West of Ireland by his parents.

In the next article, "Hunting Out the Fairies: E. F. Benson, Oscar Wilde and the Burning of Bridget Cleary," Angela Bourke explores a little-known but important piece of the Wilde story: E. F. Benson's "coded commentary" — as Bourke aptly puts it — on the Wilde trials. Naturally, "Fairies" is meant in a double sense. The situation she describes, gay men fleeing Britain in the wake of Wilde's conviction, is well known, but the piece of writing by Benson that she interprets is not, and offers a window into the world of a sensitive, intellectual, closeted gay contemporary and friend of Wilde.

E. F. Benson, a son of the Archbishop of Canterbury, made a sensation with his first novel, *Dodo*, published in 1893, which made him rich and famous and gave him access to the Wilde circle. Knocking around Cairo with Lord Alfred Douglas in 1894, Benson was in a circle of young men who quoted bits from *The Picture of Dorian Gray* while floating up the Nile to Luxor, as Richard Ellmann relates. Bosie was a good friend, but one Benson never dared to bring home to his family.

Angela Bourke has discovered that "for all his caution," Benson "did publish one article which reads like a masked or coded commentary on Wilde's fate," which she deduces partly from its date of publication — June 1895, "just as Wilde was beginning a two-year-sentence of imprisonment with hard labour in Pentonville for acts of gross indecency." The subject of Benson's article, a sensational tragedy of rural Ireland widely reported in newspapers, was "not the sort of subject in which Benson usually expressed interest," Bourke notes (36).

The story Benson reports is that of Bridget Cleary, burned to death by her husband and other relatives in her kitchen in Ballyvadlea, near Clonmel, County Tipperary, on the night of 15 March 1895. Reports of the event appeared during the week that the "Marquess of Queensberry stood trial for libeling Oscar Wilde, and Wilde himself was arrested and charged," that is, in April 1895 (36–37). Bourke writes, "Several articles offered analyses of the Cleary case, but Benson's was unusual. It appeared while the prisoners were still on remand and the case was *sub judice,* and argued that the defendants merited clemency. This intervention in the court's business did not go unnoticed; in December of the same year, an article in the journal *Folk-Lore* rapped Benson firmly over the knuckles. Even without mentioning Oscar Wilde, therefore, he was taking a risk. He added to it by invoking a story which obliquely paralleled the Wilde case, with its public humiliation of an Irish male defendant and its theme of folklore and magic."

The Bridget Cleary case had many political implications. Like the Parnell case (in which Charles Stewart Parnell, named as co-respondent in the divorce of Captain O'Shea, lost all hope of instituting Irish Home Rule), the Cleary case could be exploited by opponents of

Home Rule to portray the Irish as primitive bumpkins incapable of governing themselves. Bridget Cleary had been burned as "an apparent attempt to banish a fairy changeling, believed to have been left by the fairies." Those present at the burning believed themselves to be "hunting out the fairies" (37). Benson and others deplored the "primitive and savage superstition" of those involved.

Oscar Wilde's downfall was as Bourke rightly points out "another sort of witch-hunt . . . It can also be fairly described as a case of 'hunting out the fairies.' 'Fairy' may have been in use to denote a male homosexual as early as the sixteenth century." Moreover, although "the stories of Oscar Wilde and Bridget Cleary rest on different senses of the word 'fairy,' they share a body of imagery that reveals much about how societies deal with their marginal members: rendering them invisible; driving them underground; consigning them to wild or barren areas of the shared landscape; punishing them viciously when they refuse to disappear" (38).

Therefore, Bourke suggests, "it is as though the space consciously left blank for Oscar Wilde has been occupied by Bridget Cleary" in Benson's essay, "so that the account of her death masks an unspoken preoccupation with Wilde. Wittingly or unwittingly, in drawing attention away from Wilde and towards the Cleary case, Benson has given us a refracted picture of Oscar as Irishman, as story-teller and misunderstood victim" (38).

Bourke goes on to explore ways in which the Bridget Cleary story and Benson's attitude toward it reveals his ambivalence toward Wilde. "A changeling, or person 'in the fairies' is someone who has changed, or a person who fails or is unwilling to fulfill society's expectations." Bridget Cleary had been married six years but had no children, was better off than her neighbors, and was a strong-willed woman whose husband had seen her talking with the "egg-man" near a "fairy-castle." Wilde's rupturing of society expectations as an openly gay man needs no discussion here (45). Bourke concludes, "Something of the same ambivalence Benson displayed about Wilde in his later book, *As We Were*, is already evident in his article on the Cleary case" (45). In the latter work, Benson referred to Wilde as a man who had given into perversions, but he wrote, "no decent man can feel anything but sheer pity and sympathy for one so gifted and so brittle and withal so lovable" (39).

The next article, "Impressions of an Irish Sphinx," by Owen Dudley Edwards, includes some canny, wise observations and speculations about Wilde. It begins, however, by meandering through a series of wrongheaded statements.

Quoting Wilde's long poem, "The Sphinx," Edwards suggests that Wilde "gave himself no aura of mystery such as that with which his political leader, Charles Parnell, surrounded *him*self" (48). Wilde's actions are well known as mysterious, in the sense that different interpretations of his decision to take legal action against the Marquess of Queensberry exist and are being invented every day. But "Wilde did not contrive his life, and indeed built it far less designedly than most of us," Edwards insists, despite an abundance of evidence to the contrary (48).

In fact, Wilde's plays read like blueprints for his trials and conviction, *The Importance of Being Earnest* and *An Ideal Husband* being among the more obvious examples of this phenomenon. In *The Importance of Being Earnest*, for example, solicitors arrive in one scene to arrest Algernon for debt and take him to Holloway prison (*CW*, 350–51). In *An Ideal Husband*, the scheming Mrs. Cheveley tries to blackmail Sir Robert Chiltern into handing over state secrets, warning him that "Scandals used to lend charm, or at least interest, to a man. Now they crush him. And yours is a very nasty scandal" (495). She goes on to paint a vivid portrait of the delight a journalist would take in raking Sir Robert over the coals. These are just a few examples of Wilde contriving his life.

Edwards faults Declan Kiberd for tying in Wilde "with a theory that the great men of the Irish Renaissance had fathers who were failures." The argument is impossible, Edwards insists, offering a foolish reason: "(a) because the Oedipus complex is far rarer than Freud imagined it (Oedipus himself being one of its numerous exceptions); (b) because Irish Protestants by definition could not be failures; (c) because Sir William Wilde combined the zenith of achievement in his time in demography, aural surgery, optical surgery, topography, ethnology, ethnography, medico-biography, public health and Irish character" (51). But all Sir William's immense intellectual and cultural achievements could not wipe out personal failures and private anguish that made him as well as others perceive him as a failure. His private life was a shambles of affairs and illegitimate children, and one lover stalked him and provoked a trial that ruined his reputation and impoverished him. All this is well known.

I did find in Edwards's article the interesting point that the Great Famine "and its revelation of human responsibility for human suffering were probably the greatest individual legacies in creative response which Wilde inherited from his parents" (55). Edwards makes another keen observation about the naming of Wilde and his elder brother Willie: "The eldest son was given firm forebear names: William Charles Kingsbury Wilde. The second — Oscar Fingal O'Flahertie Wilde — was a hostage to Irish cultural identity" (58).

One section of the essay deals with a rarely touched upon subject, the influence of Wilde's young sister Isola upon his writings. Isola died when she was nine and Oscar was eleven, and he mourned her loss all his life, carrying a lock of her hair with him wherever he went. Edwards writes, "Of the family in Wilde's Irish life, the one who seems to have made the greatest impact on his fictional creativity is the one whom we know least: his sister Isola" (60). He offers Isola's short, sad history — born in 1857, died in 1867 — and discusses in detail the designs Wilde drew on the envelope of her hair, and the poem devoted to her, "Requiescat," written during Wilde's first year at Oxford.

Edwards suggests, as I have done elsewhere, that Wilde was "haunted by the idea of Isola's survival" in various of his works (61). Wilde's tale "The Canterville Ghost," Edwards observes, includes the idea of a young girl's "redemptive power" and "her love transcending the death she risks." Edwards speculates brilliantly that Dorian Gray, "the boy who never grows old as Isola never grew old," could be a male version of her" (63).

The final section of the essay usefully discusses the kind of education that the young Oscar Wilde received at Portora Royal School in Enniskillen. Providing humorous examples of old exam questions that ranged from the ambitious to the arcane to the trivial, Edwards points out that they concerned English history exclusively. Irish history was not taught, and this, Edwards maintains, "explains why the Union was doomed: any society which educates its future ruling class in ignorance of the country it rules has abdicated" (64). He adds that Robert Harborough Sherard, Wilde's friend and first biographer, recognized that "Wilde's very Irish-conscious family background made for his hopeless alienation" (66). The ways in which the school forced Wilde to deny his identity are vivid in much of Wilde's work, Edwards believes, pointing particularly to Wilde's story "The Star Child," which "seems the most profoundly influenced by this enforced denial of identity" (67). The Star Child's "real parents, beggar and leper, who turn out to be king and queen, would typify Wilde's Irish heritage, including that of the Famine. The wicked magician who enslaves the child and beats him for giving alms to the starving leper could be England, or the headmaster of Portora, or the spirit of cosmopolitan sophistication"

(68). This is speculation at its best, revealing Wilde's Irishness and its meaning.

The next article, Fintan O'Toole's "Venus in Blue Jeans: Oscar Wilde, Jesse James, Crime and Fame," proves to be an eye-opening tour through little-known Irish-American history.

During Wilde's American tour of 1882–83, he wrote to Helena Sickert about the execution of Jesse James, noting of inhabitants of the Missouri town of St. Joseph, where James had lived, "the whole town was mourning over him and buying relics of his house." O'Toole compares James to Wilde, observing that "the themes" of a popular cartoon of James, "the glamour of wickedness and the corruption of the young — would become, in due course, central to the fate of Oscar Wilde." And like Wilde, "Jesse James ascended into Heaven with all the trappings of the saint. He was betrayed by a friend before being martyred" (71).

Returning to Wilde, O'Toole remarks that he "may have considered his own performance in America to be original, but in fact it was a re-play of a familiar role. To take just one example of an educated Irish-man arriving on the western frontier to civilize the native, there is another Oscar and Trinity College Dublin graduate, Oscar J. Goldrick, who electrified the town of Auroria (now Denver) with his arrival in 1858." Goldrick dressed as a dandy in "a shiny plug hat, polished boots, an immaculate linen shirt, lemon-colored kid gloves, a Prince Albert coat, and a waistcoat embroidered with lilies of the valley, rose-buds, and violets" (72). O'Toole adds, "Though he may not have known it, Wilde did not invent the role of Irish dandy as American re-former."

This would not be so convincing were it not for other examples of-fered, notably that of Billy the Kid. Remarking on Wilde's visit to a prison in Lincoln, Nebraska, after which he wrote the haunting words, quoted often after his imprisonment and death, "I should hate to see a criminal with a noble face," O'Toole adds, "Wilde's visit to Lincoln prison took place just nine months after another strange parable of Ire-land and America, of fame and infamy, had played itself out there. A young Irishman, born twenty-one years earlier in a tenement in New York to a woman, Catherine McCarty, who had fled the Famine in Ireland, was gunned down by a sheriff named Pat Garrett. By the time Wilde arrived in London, no fewer than five biographies of the young man, Henry McCarty, better known as Billy the Kid, had appeared" (75).

O'Toole adds, "The blurring of the distinction between fame and notoriety, which is so much a part of the afterlife of Jesse James and Billy the Kid, and which would become so much a part of the life of Oscar Wilde, also explodes the distinction between civilization and barbarism, and indeed between art and life, which was meant to be central to Wilde's American tour" (76). Wilde identified himself with the wild west — O'Toole doesn't mention how Wilde enjoyed his name as an adjective — but does quote him praising the "Far West with its grizzly bears and its untamed cowboys" over the "inexpressibly tedious" cities of America.

Turning to the "great American myth" of "the taming of the wilderness, the conquering of the uncivilized Indian by the civilized white man," O'Toole notes that at "the same time as the West of America is being opened up, British colonial language is using the savagery of the Indian tribes as a convenient analogue for the native Irish" (77). The Native Americans were frequently compared to the Irish peasants, the genocide of the American Indian compared favorably in an 1865 editorial of the *Irish Times* to the emigration of the Irish: "A Catholic Celt will soon be as rare on the banks of the Shannon as a Red Indian on the shores of the Manhattan." Once the Irishman had arrived in America, of course, the picture looked different: "the Irish cease to be the Indians and become the cowboys. They are the Indian killers and the clearers of the wilderness. They are the mythic outlaws. Jesse James's grandfather comes from Kerry; Billy the Kid is a child of the Irish Famine." And, O'Toole adds, "of course Billy himself was killed by another Irish-American, Pat Garrett" (78). Billy is both "the wild Irish savage" and the "rugged white American."

Comparing the careers of James and Billy the Kid to Wilde, O'Toole suggests that the "self-conscious theatricality" of all three is "close to the centre of Wilde's career, because it is the meaning of exile itself. Exile is a form of self-dramatization, the assumption of a role, the tailoring of one's personality to an alien audience. Exile makes things that are unconscious — language, gesture, dress, the accouterments of nationality — conscious. It forces the exile to become a performer" (79). Wilde's ambiguity and ambivalence grow, then, out of his exile.

The next article, Jerusha McCormack's "The Wilde Irishman: Oscar as Aesthete and Anarchist," tackles in a clear, lively style some of the elusive connections between Wilde's politics and his art. The paper builds on her earlier work, especially "The Once and Future Dandy," published in *Rediscovering Oscar Wilde*.

In "The Wilde Irishman," McCormack stresses the ways in which anarchism is an essential part of Wilde's art and of his being. His divided identity spawns this controlled chaos in his life and work: he was "a figure with a public who came to recognize in him a parody both of the Irishman and the proper English gentleman. The Irishman was straight out of the Celtic stereotype — wild, anarchical, imaginative, witty, passionate and self-destructive. The Englishman, a straight aristocratic prototype — cool, elegant, contemptuous, manipulative, obsessed with position and its signs in dress and manner. At some point, both colluded: the Irishman was lazy, the aristocrat leisured; the Irishman paradoxical; the aristocrat systematically rude — contradicting others as the Irishman contradicted himself — the Irish bull rendered as an English snob." Wilde managed — and in this lay his genius, McCormack argues — to create himself as "a figure who was a terrorist by another name, a dandy who chooses not to nail himself to a cross but to nail others with his cross-talk . . . an *agent provocateur*" (85).

McCormack then turns to Wilde's first play, *Vera*, concerning Russian nihilism, and remarks, "Being a literary invention, the Nihilist could not exist outside art, or rather he imported the values of art into political action. In the history of anarchism, the Nihilist's appearance coincided with an aestheticizing of terrorism" (85). She recounts several examples of aesthetes who became anarchists, mentioning anarchists as literary characters in Stevenson, Henry James, and Joseph Conrad, as well as "the comic saboteur in Wilde's own 'Lord Arthur Saville's Crime'" (85). Turning then to Wilde's essay, "The Soul of Man Under Socialism," McCormack offers an intriguing new reading, suggesting that it is not about socialism at all, but about anarchy. Pointing out that Matthew Arnold defined anarchy as "doing as one likes" — and Wilde's affinity for Arnold is well known — she remarks that Wilde "argues for nothing less than the abolition of all authority since 'all authority is quite degrading. It degrades those who exercise it, and degrades those over whom it is exercised.'" He goes on to write, "Disobedience . . . is man's original virtue," and to praise disobedience and rebellion as the source of progress (86).

McCormack moves then to a subject treated in her earlier essays, the dandy as "a leisured outsider who conceives of himself (in the words of Baudelaire) as 'establishing a new kind of aristocracy'" (89). She moves to examples of the dandy in Wilde's plays, suggesting that the disruptiveness or "psychic jujitsu" — a term employed in her earlier essay on the dandy — are exploited by them to force his audience to share his contempt for it. Thus, in *An Ideal Husband,* Lord Goring recognizes the double standard in the supposedly moral Lady Chiltern, who demands that her husband tell her the terrible truth of his past but also begs him to lie to her about it. Lord Goring, McCormack observes, "is able to save [Lady Chiltern's husband] precisely because he understands that the single, integrated 'moral' self is a fiction . . . Lady Chiltern does not really care about the truth of the matter (she does, after all, beg her husband to lie to her)" (91). Wilde, as McCormack has elegantly argued elsewhere as well, "perfects the dandy as one with the power of exposing empire-speak so as to reveal its forked tongue and the actual spiritual anarchy on which it rests" (91).

The next piece, "Wilde and Parnell," by W. J. McCormack, ranges ramblingly over details of Wilde's life and approaches to Wilde before arriving at the surprising thesis that "in noticing with Sherlock-Holmes-like keenness that the name of Parnell is never to be heard in Wilde's journalism or in his available correspondence, we must surmise that what has occurred here is nothing less than a forceful repression" (100). Charles Stewart Parnell dominated Irish politics in the 1880s, as the leader of the Irish Party supporting Home Rule. He was charged in 1880 with conspiracy growing out of Land League activities. Over the next years he was in and out of political hot water, and personal hot water poured in by 1886, when, McCormack notes, the *Pall Mall Gazette* alluded to his affair with Kitty O'Shea, wife of Captain William Henry O'Shea. O'Shea filed for divorce — years after the beginning of his wife's affair — in 1889, naming Parnell as co-respondent. As Davis Coakley remarks in his excellent biography, *Oscar Wilde: The Importance of Being Irish*, "Where lies and forgeries did not succeed, Victorian Prudery proved triumphant. Parnell fell from his political pinnacle and he was hounded to his death shortly afterwards at the age of forty-five" (Coakley 195).

McCormack's article looks for connections between Wilde and Parnell, noting, for instance, that the first time the papers mentioned Parnell's affair with Kitty O'Shea, Wilde was at the same time signing George Bernard Shaw's petition supporting the American anarchists at the center of Chicago's Haymarket Riots, and "at some not exactly identified date, was initiated into homosexual practice by Robbie Ross" that same year. Parnell was, no doubt, an inspiration to Wilde, who admired him, and McCormack is wise to draw attention to "Wilde's unquestionable awareness of Parnell's fate," but as he points out, "No neat correlation of Parnellite and Wildean chronologies can be tabulated" (99). Still, the point he makes at the end of his article — that it is possible to see in Charles Stewart Parnell "an objective correlative whose career Wilde observed and suppressed" (102) adds a new dimension to Wilde's careful crafting of his own life as a hero and a martyr to Ireland.

Alan Stanford's "Acting Wilde" is a wise and highly original exposition of the difficulties involved in acting Wilde for Irish audiences, as well as a shrewd analysis of Wilde's position as a member of the envied and rejected Anglo-Irish class.

Stanford begins by saying that although he uses the same style for English and Irish audiences, "Irish audiences have never really understood Wilde." He justifies this startling remark with a convincing analysis of differences in Irish and English class structures. The Irish don't understand Wilde, he adds, "because they are so damned middle class." While it has been said that England boasts of its class system, America denies having one, and Ireland doesn't know what its class system is, Stanford has observed a class system based on "merit," that is, on money and power. Ireland has, in reality, "two classes only: those in the middle and the underdogs . . . no aristocracy, and the aristocracy we did have, the Anglo-Irish, we have always refused to accept, considering them to be foreign and imposed rather than an integral part of the Irish identity." Because the Irish have "spent hundreds of years suppressing the notion that the Anglo-Irish were part of the Irish tradition," they now have "no national relationship with the idea of an upper, or self-regarding superior, class. Hence," he adds provocatively, "the Irish audience has no real notion of where Wilde is coming from" (152).

Mentioning that Wilde grew up around the Irish middle class, who were the guests at his mother's well-known salons, Stanford remarks that Lady Bracknell of *The Importance of Being Earnest* is not the British aristocrat she is often taken for but a middle-class social climber. The point has been made before, but not so well: "She is a classic Wilde character, not because she is funny, but because she is dangerous. She understands power and the way it is deployed. She is possibly Wilde's greatest creation in his war on the authority of a pompous upper class. She is almost anarchic in her exposure of pomposity in rank" (153). Anarchy is actually her métier; she is the one who worries about the "worst excesses of the French Revolution" (*CW*, 334) just because she is ready to be anarchic in her own socially manipulative shenanigans.

Stanford goes on to argue that Wilde's artistry lies in his understanding of power, specifically power "that has to do with manipulating systems and people rather than overthrowing them." Ireland is, he asserts, a shame, not a guilt, culture, so that wrongdoers worry only about being found out, not about their inner moral wrongness: "Oscar the Irishman understood the importance of the dirty secret as the wellspring of power" (153).

Stanford turns to an explication of Patrick Mason's production of *The Importance of Being Earnest,* which modernized Wilde, with Lady Bracknell as Margaret Thatcher and Gwendolen and Cecily as Sloane Rangers, that is, British preppies. Mason's production was a "brilliant" satire on a dying empire, Stanford writes, but went "too far" by imposing Oscar Wilde's personal tragedy on the final lines of the play, so that Ernest's last line is interrupted by a "taped voice that says loudly, 'Oscar Wilde, you have been found guilty of . . .' and so forth" (154). This destroyed the essential aim of the play, Stanford believes: "If we start being sincere about Wilde, we are all in trouble." But the Irish have a tendency to do that, he adds, pointing out that "Only an Irishman, a Dubliner from the days when Dublin still felt that it was the second city of the empire, could view England with such a cynical eye; and an Irishman, of the Anglo-Irish class, Wilde could recall seven hundred years of being an outsider who was also the insider; he was, if you wish, the enemy within" (155).

Stanford closes by commenting on the force of Wilde's personality, such that "The sense of his presence" for actors of his plays "is overwhelming." Actors are anxious about how Wilde would react to their version of his lines, and "You can hear his voice in every line" (156).

In the next article, "Women of No Importance: Misogyny in the Work of Oscar Wilde," Victoria White offers the thesis that "while Wilde's conscious self may have been in favour of women's advancement, it is clear that he also feared it; his women are either lily-like virgins, whores or honorary men, who invert all the convention of their roles, as when Gwendolen drawls that home is 'the best place for a husband'" (160). This seems on target, as does her next observation, that there is "just one kind of woman who has no place in Wilde's cosmology, and that is a mature, sexually active, reproductive woman" (160). As she notes, Wilde felt disgusted by his own wife's pregnancies. Her explanation is psychoanalytic and plausible: Wilde saw himself as a child, especially in relation to his mother, and he feared being "engulfed" by her body.

This seems reasonable, but it is also possible that as a gay man he felt repulsed by his wife's pregnant body because once Constance was pregnant, he could no longer fantasize about her as being "really" a man. Long passages in *Dorian Gray* about the actress, Sibyl, and in *Lord Arthur Savile's Crime,* reveal fantasies about women who are, under their costumes, really boys. A pregnant woman could only be a woman, that is, she is missing a penis, and can be of no sexual interest to a gay man. While Wilde sympathized greatly with women about political, social, and cultural problems concerning them, he could not help but find them inferior sexually by virtue of his not being attracted to them. He should not be blamed for what was, after all, only a matter of taste. White mentions my book, including my theory that Isola Wilde, Wilde's young sister who died, may have inspired his "great search for the innocent and the beautiful," inspiring his love of boys. To explain Wilde by calling him 'homosexual,' and to explain his fear of women by referring to his homosexuality, is "a ridiculous simplification," she argues rightly. Still, these facts are small pieces of a huge and complicated puzzle; they should not be discarded, but put in their proper place.

Mary Blanchard

Oscar Wilde's America: Counterculture in the Gilded Age, is a beautifully written book, filled with rare and revealing illustrations of Wilde and other figures in the aesthetic movement. It brilliantly demonstrates how Wilde shaped gender roles in nineteenth-century America during the Gilded Age, the post-civil war period of hectic acquisitiveness that takes its name from the novel "The Gilded Age" by Mark Twain and Charles Dudley Warner. Blanchard's study provides more about Wilde's influence than about his life and work but weaves in a number of astute observations about him. In the process of delineating a cultural history of the aesthetic movement in the United States, she shows that Oscar Wilde proved to be a prophet of regeneration. She advances an original and interesting thesis: Wilde rescued America from the post-civil war doldrums, offering especially women new ways of thinking about their lives and social roles: "Indeed, as Wilde had immediately perceived . . . the time had come for Americans to take a cultural position that differed from the position of the heroes of war and battle. 'I think you have taken quite enough motives from war,' he told Americans as he toured the nation's capital. 'You don't want any more bronze generals on horseback. . . . Suppose you try the motives that peace will give you now'" (xii).

In five chapters, a prologue and an epilogue, Blanchard explores Wilde's impact on a nation still recovering from the terrible shock of the Civil War and Reconstruction, and the ways in which women who took up his message challenged prevailing views of female roles, eventually becoming so much of a threat to these views that Aestheticism as a movement foundered.

The prologue gives the book's most complete picture of Wilde's performances and their impact on Gilded-Age Americans. Conjuring up Wilde's visit to San Francisco, where many members of the audience came to gawk at his velvet jacket and knee-breeches as much as to hear his message, Blanchard writes: "For months, newspapers throughout America [had] been filled with descriptions of these improbable items of aesthetic dress, and now the very incarnation of aestheticism" stood preaching "a living art, a new truth, that could transform their lives." And "the transformative power of beautiful surroundings on the thousands upon thousands of Americans ultimately would be enormous" (xii).

Blanchard then makes a key point: "the visionaries of American aestheticism were women" (xiii). Aestheticism offered them a way out of domesticity: "Overshadowed by such celebrated male artists as Louis Comfort Tiffany and John Lafarge, the little-known or neglected female artists of American aestheticism realized the deeper cultural promise of the aesthetic movement. For what these women saw in aestheticism was its power of liberation." These women visionaries, Blanchard continues, "recognized in aestheticism an escape from Calvinist orthodoxy, an evasion of tyrannical fathers and ineffective husbands, and an opportunity to advance in the social and business worlds of the Gilded Age." Female artists in particular felt inspired by "the occult, the fantastic, and the symbolic," as they appeared through aesthetic forms and ideas. But "in the end . . . it was precisely this liberating power of aestheticism that would bring down upon the American women a repressive reaction. As female artists championed professional careers for women beyond conventional domesticity, less visible middle-class housewives explored alternative identities opened to them by the aesthetic quest," and dressed in uncorseted aesthetic dresses, shocking their Victorian contemporaries (xiii).

It was this subversive transforming of restrictive female dress, along with other trappings of aestheticism — its promotion of individualism and of opium smoking, its exotic backgrounds — that awakened "deep anxieties." Oscar Wilde's appearance increased these anxieties, since some saw him as a man with "strong, square shoulders and manly waist and hips," Blanchard writes, quoting contemporary observers, and others wrote that he was "womanish," that there was something "unmanly" about him, that he was a "Mama's boy" (xiv). It "was unsettling enough that Wilde's aesthetic costume seemingly bordered on female attire, but it was even more disturbing when American men began to take up oriental robes for themselves or artistic furnishings for their rooms . . . No longer the virile citizen/soldier of the Civil War years, was the male now an artist/decorator of feminine space? Were the American heroes of the battlefield to be replaced by dandies and interior designers?" (xiv).

As much as people worried about a "gender reversal" among men, they worried that aesthetic women might be dangerously "bohemian," or engage in "forbidden sexualities." Blanchard points to William Dean Howells's novel, *The Coast of Bohemia* (1893), as an example of these concerns. She concludes that as soon as people realized that "the feminization of American men was the price of the cultural success of aestheticism, a powerful reaction set in. The stage was set for the reemergence of conventional identities in the 1890s: the maternal domestic female and the strong masculine man. Once Oscar Wilde had been convicted of 'gross indecency' in 1895, the claims that aestheticism would lead to a higher, finer spiritual life came to seem grotesque and were suddenly discredited" (xiv). It was not long before the return of the soldier-hero icon that Wilde and aestheticism had begun to discredit, for the Spanish-American war began in 1898, and then the "female visionaries of American aestheticism faded into historical oblivion" (xiv–xv). Blanchard finishes the chapter by observing that in America, "aestheticism was the story of the feminine and domestic world . . . The sudden celebrity and abrupt eclipse both of the decorative arts and of the female visionaries who popularized them were crucial to the ultimate meaning of the American gilded age" (xv).

Chapter one, "Oscar Wilde, Aesthetic Style, and the Masculine Self," explores reasons for Wilde's great appeal to Americans on the tour he undertook to promote the American production of Gilbert and Sullivan's *Patience,* the operetta that spoofs aestheticism. He was, Blanchard notes, "a surprising success" by any standard. She suggests one reason for his success was that "Wilde's flamboyant dress, his breaking of gender codes, spoke to a nation that was beginning to explore style, not to expose social nonconformity but to create alternate identities." She speculates that Americans liked to "flirt with difference," to borrow selectively from aesthetic style, and that the popular press indicated "an emergent anxiety not only about the new aesthetic ideology but, more dangerously, about the celebrated and stylized masculine self" (3).

Blanchard remarks that the new male popularized by Wilde was "in dialectical relation to a more persistent and visible ideal — the man as soldier." The military metaphor was everywhere in the national history, from freedom fighter to the soldier/citizen of the Civil War and even in social reform — the Salvation Army also typified the "prevailing template of the manly soldier" (4). Blanchard then points out that "a variety of historical developments" — industrialization, the rise of a professional class, the recurrent cycle of depressions, and the growth of urban centers — and the aftermath of the Civil War led to transformations of gender roles. Ulysses Grant, for instance, emphasized the "womanly sentiment of compassion" in his civil war memoirs of 1885 (5).

In a section entitled "Style and the Homosexual Subject," Blanchard connects Wilde's effeminacy with homosexuality, taking a different — and more plausible — stand from that of Alan Sinfield in his book, *The Wilde Century*, reviewed in these pages. She writes, "to wary Victorians, the charge of effeminacy connoted the usual nineteenth-century caricature of male homosexuality. Warnings were everywhere: 'His face is so very womanish,' ran one typical comment" (10). She notes that the concept of the invert or male homosexual "was an emerging concept during the 1880s" (11), alluding to Karl Ulrich's work on the subject, but makes it clear that effeminacy was typically considered an earmark of homosexuality: "In America at the time of Wilde's visit, homosexuals were 'bound together by a sort of magnetism [to] recognize one another,' noted one 'unfortunate' informant to the medical press. Perhaps Wilde was publicly perceived by some journalists as one of these unfortunates, just as he was blatantly named a homosexual in private memoirs. One member of the Century Club in New York asked, when Wilde was expected, 'Where is *she*? Well, why not say 'she'? I understand she's a 'Charlotte Ann.'" Blanchard adds that in California, members of a Bohemian club referred to Wilde as a "Miss Nancy" (12).

Wilde's effeminacy and homosexuality were treated with levity by the popular press. "A sympathetic cohesion seemed to exist between the aesthetic model and the middle class," Blanchard explains, since "Wilde's lectures on the decorative arts were popular and prestigious events throughout the country," and he was therefore "a symbolic icon of both Victorian domesticity and aesthetic and homosexual proclivities" (17).

The rest of the chapter details Wildean connections to prominent American men, in particular, Mark Twain — that "Twain equated creativity with violation of sexual taboos, an ideology similar to Wilde's" (19) — and that Twain also broke gender boundaries, by wanting to dress in "a loose and flowing costume made all of silks and velvets resplendent with stunning dyes" (20). Sanford White, the architect, liked aesthetic interiors and was "known for his homoerotic proclivity" (24). Aesthetic style was "compatible with ideas of masculinity in the 1870s and 1880s," but the "intrusion of feminine detail into the smoking room and library was also common" (24). But with this feminizing of the culture, Wilde was also "to a surprising degree . . . applauded as 'manly'" (27).

This alliance between aesthetic style and the masculine self "provoked attacks from some Victorian men unsure of their own gender orientation," Blanchard observes (27). She adds that the "intrusion of Wilde's teachings into the ideological foundations of the new American market place only signaled new alarms to a hesitant nation. For Wilde, shrouded in the mystique of the feminine aesthetic, extolled manly labor at the same time as he subverted its iconography" (32). What he did, Blanchard suggests, was to transform "America's yeoman artisan hero into a homoerotic object d'art" (33).

At the same time, women were becoming a significant part of the movement. "The sense of women competing in the same artistic professions as men was a subcurrent of the whole aesthetic ideology . . . If Wilde could be castigated as homosexual, yet endorsed as manly, and if a workman could become a beautiful object d'art while women received acclaim as woodcarvers, painters, and scroll carvers, then Victorian society was fundamentally adrift" (35). Wilde, she concludes, had raised the status of aesthetic style, "but this was corollary to a more important controversy in Gilded Age America — the definition of the manly citizen and his relationship to these new forms of art" (35).

The tide turned, however, in the 1890s, with the "recovery of the soldier/hero," for which Theodore Roosevelt was in part responsible: "Roosevelt's continual flirtation with death, his exposure on the western prairies and his bravado on the battlefield, reminded Americans that the heterosexual fighter, both the giver and taker of life, was the requisite corrective to the androgynous aesthete" (39).

The next few chapters deal more with Wilde's influence on particular women than with Wilde himself, so will not be summarized here in detail. Chapter two, "Candace Wheeler's Search for the Aesthetic Life," explores the career of a textile artist and painter who was greatly influenced by Wilde, and who once met him when he visited her studio on his American tour (46). Chapter three, "The Aesthetic Parlor, The Object D'art, and the Sedated Self," begins with Wilde's seeking a means in the decorative arts to "alleviate cultural disarray" (85), and then turns to women aesthetes, especially Mary Louis McLaughlin, an artist. Chapter four, "Bohemian Boundaries, The Female Body, and Aesthetic Dress," begins with Wilde's remark about the "ignoble quality" of modern dress: "I do not know a greater heroism than that which opposes the conventionalities of dress" (137). And dress affected the moralities of the day: "Victorian women who chose to wear artistic dress (and research indicates that many middle-class and lower middle-class women participated in this vogue) used Wilde's option to surrender to one's impressions, to challenge the moralists, to use their bodies to flirt with forbidden bohemian boundaries" (138). A few women were even arrested when in 1884, "Louisville police were ordered to 'suppress' aesthetic costumes in public" (153). One of the photos in this chapter, incidentally, presents one Hattie Fels Owen as the New Woman in 1908. In a white suit and straw boater, she looks like a young Oscar Wilde. The final chapter, "The Catholic Icon, the Popular Press, and the Aesthetic Virgin," deals with ways in which aesthetic style replaces Christian moralism.

In her epilogue, Blanchard traces transformations in aestheticism, which was "buried in America by 1918," although aesthetic experiments "survived in mutated formats in the twentieth century" (235). She adds that "By 1900, Wilde's tour, and the movement that he represented, can be seen as part of a new dialectic — not as a culmination or crystallization of a process marked as female, but as part of a modern backlash against the uses or claims that women had increasingly made upon male professionalism in the arts" (241).

Pia Brinzeu

Pia Brinzeu's article, "Dorian Gray's Rooms and Cyberspace," is devoted to the intriguing thesis that "cyberspace offers a hitherto unimagined chance for the study of space representations in literature," and "space relations are perhaps one of the most clearly structured dimensions of meaning in a text, especially in novels in which the writers insistently describe the story-space, turning the main focus of their narrative to the cities, villages or houses that shelter the characters and novels" (21–22). Seeing the rooms of the novel in cyberspace has allowed Brinzeu to conclude that "every chapter is situated within a different closed space, arranged in concentric circles around the very portrait of Dorian Gray" (22), and that "all the chapters begin and finish with the characters' entering or leaving a room," with the sole exceptions of the beginnings of chapters eleven and nineteen. This device, she suggests, "gives rhythm and movement to an otherwise completely static novel, links rather disparate places, and refreshes the stifling atmosphere of the interiors with glimpses of street landscape" (25).

Brinzeu brings up a number of technical possibilities for cybernetic readers, such as the transformation of linguistic structures into mental images and the reduction of "all the settings of the book to one single room" (27). Virtual reality, she remarks, "also offers the possibility of a change in the point of view," that is, from the third person narration of the novel to the "feelings and impressions of Dorian" (28).

Works Cited

Blanchard, Mary Warner. 1998. *Oscar Wilde's America: Counterculture in the Gilded Age*. New Haven: Yale UP.

Brinzeu, Pia. 1994. "Dorian Gray's Rooms and Cyberspace." *Rediscovering Oscar Wilde*. Ed. C. George Sandulescu. Princess Grace Irish Library: 8. Gerrards Cross: Colin Smythe.

Coakley, Davis. 1994. "The Neglected Years: Wilde in Dublin." *Rediscovering Oscar Wilde*. Ed. C. George Sandulescu. Princess Grace Irish Library: 8. Gerrards Cross: Colin Smythe.

———. 1995. *Oscar Wilde: The Importance of Being Irish*. Dublin: Town House.

Ellmann, Richard. 1988. *Oscar Wilde*. New York: Vintage.

McCormack, Jerusha. 1994. "Oscar Wilde: The Once and Future Dandy." *Rediscovering Oscar Wilde*. Ed. C. George Sandulescu. Princess Grace Irish Library: 8. Gerrards Cross: Colin Smythe.

———, ed. 1998. *Wilde the Irishman*. New Haven: Yale UP.

Rosenstein, Roy. 1994. "Re(dis)covering Wilde for Latin America: Marti, Dario, Borges, Lispector." *Rediscovering Oscar Wilde*. Ed. C. George Sandulescu. Princess Grace Irish Library: 8. Gerrards Cross: Colin Smythe.

Sammells, Neil. 1994. "Rediscovering the Irish Wilde." *Rediscovering Oscar Wilde*. Ed. C. George Sandulescu. Princess Grace Irish Library: 8. Gerrards Cross: Colin Smythe.

Sandulescu, C. George, ed. 1994. *Rediscovering Oscar Wilde*. Princess Grace Irish Library: 8. Gerrards Cross: Colin Smythe.

6: Biographic Studies

BIOGRAPHY IS OF SPECIAL importance to Oscar Wilde, because he remains a writer whose work can neither be fully understood nor completely appreciated without knowledge of the degree to which he attempted to craft his life as a work of art, perceived his life as a part of his art, and in a sense exploited his art to craft blueprints for his life. In my book, *Oscar Wilde: A Long and Lovely Suicide,* I argue that biographers worship or condemn their subjects just as children worship or condemn their parents. Oscar Wilde, in *A Woman of No Importance* (*CW,* 457), said, "Children begin by loving their parents. After a time they judge them. Rarely, if ever, do they forgive them." Such insights resulted from his inclination toward self-analysis and psychologically based interpretation of biographical information, which I followed in my book by examining the ways in which conscious and unconscious wishes fit together in the mosaic of Wilde's life. Psychoanalytic and psychologically based criticism offer methods of piecing together interests and motivations of a subject that seem unrelated, often bizarrely unrelated or contradictory, especially with a subject like Wilde. Such methods do not necessarily avoid hagiography or demonizing of a subject. They may, however, provide reasons for a biographer to reflect on extreme love for or loathing of the subject, and to increase awareness of personal responses as well as those of his or her surrounding culture. Again, following Wilde in his rejection of "objectivity," the personal becomes the biographical, in the sense that the critic deals intellectually as well as emotionally with private, political, or cultural reasons that he or she feels drawn to the subject.

Whatever method a biographer uses, what remains essential is an interest and a belief in personality in the traditional sense as the unique fingerprints of the soul. All of the selections below show this interest.

The second part of this chapter, Biography and Censorship, concerns the difficulties biographers and critics, including myself, have had in gaining free access to Wilde's unpublished writings and quoting them. Merlin Holland, whose work is excerpted in this section, is Oscar Wilde's grandson and literary executor. His control over the Wilde estate, until unpublished letters and papers enter the public domain, is therefore of great concern to any Wilde biographer or critic.

Part One: Biographic Essays and Criticism

John Stokes

John Stokes, in "Wilde the Journalist," covers the least known area of Wilde's career, namely his more than seventy unsigned book reviews for the *Pall Mall Gazette*, written between March 1885 and May 1990, and Wilde's editorship of *The Woman's World* between November 1887 and June 1889. In this witty, well-written essay, the only thing missing from Stokes's account is Wilde's opinion of journalism. Wilde made a number of remarks that reveal his basic attitude toward it: "Modern journalism, by giving us the opinions of the uneducated, keeps us in touch with the ignorance of the community" ("The Critic as Artist," *CW*, 1048). Also: "In the old days men had the rack. Now they have the press" ("The Soul of Man Under Socialism," *CW*, 1094).

Stokes observes that Wilde "saw anonymous journalism as a way of mapping out his personal literary territory, even if the hidden pattern can sometimes look like a maze." He set out to be the kind of writer who could cover many different subjects: "From romantic novels to cookbooks, from every kind of translation to musicology, Wilde took pride in attempting the unlikely" (69). A number of his interests can be deduced from his journalism, for instance, "that he had a considerable enthusiasm for Russian literature" (69). He reviewed Dostoevsky's novel *Insult and Injury*, and in that review spoke very highly of *Crime and Punishment*, which he had also reviewed for the *Pall Mall Gazette*. Stokes points to moments in the reviews when Wilde took advantage of his anonymity to joke about his friend Robert Sherard's book of poems, *Whispers*, in the midst of favorable remarks about Sherard's novel, and to praise his mother's work in a "shameless puff" (70).

Stokes notes that "Habits of self-reference and self-plagiarism reappear when Wilde is writing about women in general" (71). Suggesting that because the "woman writer" was increasingly a figure of interest in the late nineteenth century, Stokes writes that Wilde was "anxious to capitalize on the phenomenon, and, prompted perhaps by the example of his mother, to demonstrate a personal interest. Admiration for women writers could be combined with his own aesthetic and political preferences" (71). Stokes notes that literature in the mid-nineteenth century was something that supposedly led women astray and threatened men's masculinity, and that Wilde worked toward the "erosion of this doctrine" by "voicing his own enthusiasm for women writers and

by helping in the supply of intelligent publications for the female con-
sumer" (71). He covers Wilde's editorship of the *Woman's World,* remarking that his approach to his editorship "shares some of the
widespread contradictions of the period" (72). He quotes Laurel
Brake's study of Wilde's editorship, in which she states that women are
constructed as serious readers who want education, and that qualities
seen as unsuitable for them, like tastes, triviality, dress, and gossip, are
instead indulged in by Wilde.

An interesting point is that Wilde began writing for the *Pall Mall
Gazette* just at the time when its editor, W. T. Stead, began the
"Maiden Tribute" campaign designed to protect young girls from
prostitution and abduction, a campaign resulting in scandal and "in the
new indecency laws under which Wilde himself was eventually to be
prosecuted" (73). As Stokes rightly says, "We might look for a connection between these events, and expect Wilde's journalism in some way
to reflect the circumstances of its production, the public and private
spheres that were now for a homosexual man inextricably involved one
with the other" (73). He gives some instances of what he terms
"games-playing . . . with erotic overtones," for instance the ways in
which Wilde discusses Chatterton and Keats, and Keats and Saint
Sebastian, calling Saint Sebastian "a lovely brown boy, with crisp, clus-
tering hair and red lips" (76).

But Stokes hesitates to call such language "gay discourse," as do
some scholars, because it was common enough to have been used by
many non-gay writers: "To make the point rather differently: to know
that the anonymous reviews were by Wilde would not necessarily dis-
close the truth about him, assuming that the truth was simply sexual"
(77).

Stokes closes a very informative article by mentioning that when
Wilde was "finally in a position to give up journalism he did so quite
easily, turning to genres where he could be more forthcoming about
deception" (78).

Masolino D'Amico

Masolino D'Amico's article, "Oscar Wilde in Naples," concerns the final years of Wilde's life, when he left Berneval-sur-Mer, a small French
village, to live in Naples with Lord Alfred Douglas. The article contains
new and interesting information about Wilde's various residences in It-
aly and what the Italians thought of him. D'Amico reports that Wilde
and Alfred Douglas first checked into a posh hotel, the *Hôtel Royal des*

Etrangers, where they ran up a bill for sixty-eight pounds in a fortnight. They later lived in Posillipo, where their villa "is still visible at what is now 37, via Posillipo" (76).

D'Amico remarks that Wilde cut "a rather conspicuous figure," because of the scandal associated with him, and that his literary excellence "was a matter of hearsay, as none of his works was available to an Italian audience" in translation (77). The author dug up comments in the local Italian gossip columns about Wilde's presence in Naples, some of them malicious and misinformed, while others, as he modestly puts it, "add a few brushstrokes to the portraits we have of Wilde in his Italian exile" (78). One paper discovered that Alfred Douglas was living with Wilde and commented, "[he] adds so little honour to the name of one of the greatest historical families of Great Britain" (78). Another paper managed to barge in on Wilde and get a confused interview. The interviewer said, "And you have left England for a long time," a question that stopped Wilde dead in his tracks. The interviewer goes on: "I repeated my question but to no avail. England must have had a strange effect on the superman's nervous system: he widened his eyes as if I had asked him to square the circle, and stood there dumbly, motionless, as if he were pursuing faraway memories long since dormant" (79).

These snapshots and snippets provide new and valuable biographical information, as well as a road map to Wilde's former residence in Naples.

Norman Page

Norman Page, in "Decoding *The Ballad of Reading Gaol*," explores autobiographical elements of the long poem Wilde wrote after getting out of prison in 1900. His last major work, it is, as Page remarks, "a surprise ending to his literary career" (305). The style — the ballad form, in which he remarked he was "out-Henleying Kipling," alluding to writers for whom he had not expressed anything like wholehearted praise, certainly was not what anyone might have expected, and Page investigates why.

His arresting answers are convincing. He suggests that the poem has a "precise biographical context" that Wilde tries to hide with the "impersonality" of the ballad form. Wilde was, Page adds, writing the ballad as a product of a specific moment: "the first days of his freedom, embittered by the realization that his family life, and especially his relationship with his sons, had been destroyed forever" (306). But as Page shrewdly points out, "What we find on turning to the poem . . . is not a direct confrontation of this personal tragedy but an objectifying and displacing of his experience" (306). Influences mentioned include Kipling's ballad *Danny Deever*, also about a soldier sentenced to be hanged for murder. The man hanged in Wilde's poem was a wife murderer, with whom, Page says, Wilde identified: "to identify himself with a wife-murderer would have called for no great imaginative leap on Wilde's part, since he had before him Constance's letter reminding him that he had destroyed his domestic and family life." With the refrain of the poem, "each man kills the thing he loves," Wilde is, Page believes, "writing his personal history in a simple code" (309). He had killed his relationship with Constance and his family life.

Page also mentions the "separateness" of the condemned man in Wilde's poem from the other prisoners as "all important." This "necessarily reduces the narrator, which most readers will be ready to identify with Wilde himself, to the status of an observer" (310), which is a good way of distancing himself from painful personal experience. As a closing note, Page remarks that "a last unexpected touch" is that of all Wilde's works, it is the ballad that furnished the inscription for his tomb in Père Lachaise.

Kerry Powell

Kerry Powell, in "Wilde & Two Women: Unpublished Accounts by Elizabeth Robins & Blanche Crackanthorpe," has succeeded in the extraordinary — finding new, unpublished manuscript material about Wilde. "Bound together in Fales Library of New York University" (312) are a typescript copy of an 1895 letter from Blanche Crackanthorpe to Elizabeth Robins, and a memoir about Wilde by Robins. Both women were well-educated and supported feminist causes; Crackanthorpe advocated birth control and reproductive rights, and had authored a play. Robins, who, like Crackanthorpe, dared to support Ibsen, introduced *Hedda Gabler* to England (312–13).

The two women had been friendly with Wilde until the time of his trials, when they became ambivalent towards him. Powell finds in the documents left by these women a "mixture of sympathy and tension between Wilde and what might be called late-Victorian feminism" (313). Crackanthorpe wrote to Robins sympathetically about Wilde's plight during his trials, calling him a "tortured, hunted animal," but also expressed considerable concern for Constance Wilde, "and in general for standards of morality which must be upheld at any cost" (313). Her letter makes it clear that she is in favor of the police rounding up homosexuals: "nothing would do so much to purge schools and universities — and sorely they need it — as sentences which should strike terror and dismay into the hearts of the offenders" (314). For years after Wilde's trials, she "still found it unsettling to look back on the catastrophe that engulfed Wilde in 1895" (314).

Elizabeth Robins' memoir relates how Wilde visited her late in 1894 or 1895. She felt estranged from him, and was at first glad when he got up to leave. It was pouring rain, however, and she urged him to stay, whereupon he began to tell stories: "On and on, the pure diction, the delicate imagery" (317). They were better than anything he had ever written, and by comparison she found his written fables to be "mannered exercises . . . Cold? They were dead" (317).

These fascinating memoirs are indeed a worthy find, offering glimpses of Wilde and his wife that are new, and that reveal the sorrows of each.

Denis Donoghue

Denis Donoghue, in "The Oxford of Pater, Hopkins, and Wilde," begins with a concise, informative description of Pater's undergraduate career at Queens College, which he spent "discarding his Anglican faith, showing off his newly acquired agnosticism, and learning enough German to read Hegel." He took a poor Second, "not even a gentleman's Third," and so proved a much less distinguished student than either Hopkins or Wilde (94). Describing Pater's interests, Donoghue remarks on his membership in Old Mortality, a discussion group for undergraduate fellows who were mostly agnostics; his probationary fellowship in Classics at Brasenose, whose students were "distinguished only on the playing fields" (95); and his eagerness "to show off his irreligious character as a token of his modernity . . . He enjoyed breathing the thin air of speculation" (95).

Moving to Pater's career as a tutor, Donoghue discusses Hopkins, sent to Pater by Benjamin Jowett in 1866. The young Hopkins, well respected as a student, endured a personal life that was "in other respects . . . often a torment. Mainly but not exclusively attracted to young men, he worried over his susceptibility to beauty in any form," Donoghue notes, adding that in one of his diaries, "he found himself," in ten months, "guilty of 1,564 sins, an average of five a day: 238 of these were sexual" (96). Nocturnal emissions and masturbation preoccupied him, so he fasted and performed other penances. Pater, "talking two hours against Xianity," Hopkins notes in his journal, must not have allayed his anxieties, although Donoghue writes that Hopkins "was immune to Pater's two hours of agnosticism. No church was high enough for him" (96–97). He converted to Catholicism.

Meanwhile, Hopkins wrote essays for Pater, including "The Origin of Our Moral Ideas," in which he attacked utilitarianism. When he converted, the relationship between him and Pater was suspended for a few months, but mended eventually. Hopkins entered the Jesuit novitiate, but even after that saw Swinburne and met the artist Simeon Solomon, known to the cognoscenti as a homosexual.

Donoghue notes Hopkins's kinship to Ruskin as a writer and his continued "mild friendship," grounded in "art, aesthetics, and homoerotic sentiment," with Pater, before moving on to transformations in Pater's career, in particular the ways in which he got himself into "endless trouble," though his "own life was virtually colorless" (101). Publishing an account of Winckellmann's life in January, 1867, in which he discussed Winckellmann's "fervid friendships with young men," fanned the flames of scandal.

Moving to Wilde's relationship with Pater, Donoghue writes that in "his first term at Magdalen College, Oxford, Wilde read *Studies in the Histories of the Renaissance*," the book that he claimed "had such a strange influence over my life" (103). Either it or Huysmans's notorious *A Rebours* seduced Dorian Gray "on his progress to immorality" (103).

Under the influence of Ruskin for at least his first two years, Wilde met Pater in his third, after sending him an article on the Grosvenor Gallery that he had written, which included a "few references to Greek islands, handsome boys, and Correggio's paintings of adolescent beauty" (103).

Donoghue notes that the friendship between Wilde and Pater flourished, but that "Pater never really liked Wilde, he thought his charm somewhat vulgar." Wilde also thought Pater "too timid for not living up to the daring of his prose." Starting in June, 1887, they began to write about each other's work (104). By 1889, Wilde was working on "The Critic as Artist," which he would publish in September 1890 and in *Intentions* a year after, and in which "Pater's practice as a critic is the main justification for Wilde's theory of criticism as creation" (105). Pater inspired the basic theory of Wilde's great essay.

Yet "the friendship between Pater and Wilde virtually came to an end in the winter of 1891. While *The Picture of Dorian Gray* was still in manuscript and before he started serial publication of it in July 1890 in *Lippincotts Monthly Magazine,* Wilde showed it to Pater" (106).

Donoghue sees the book as "pure Pater, a celebration of music and the uselessness of art. It is not clear what part of the book Pater took exception to" (106). But wasn't that just it? A certain envy, both of Wilde's mind, of his ability to be more like Pater than Pater, and of his daring? The review Pater wrote, from which Donoghue quotes, suggests this. Pater remarks that the "wholesome dislike of the commonplace" leads Wilde "to protest emphatically against so called 'realism' in art," and Donoghue observes that it is strange "to find Pater holding out the possibility that 'the commonplace' might not be justly identified with the habits and tastes of the bourgeoisie" (107). Pater said this himself, but since Wilde borrowed the idea, he wanted to dissociate himself, Donoghue observes.

Although the friendship between Wilde and Pater lapsed, Wilde remained interested in him all his life, reading his books in prison. The Oxford "of Pater, Hopkins and Wilde was," after all, "a homosexual sanctuary." Donoghue covers these writers "in relation to the rhetoric of modern literature and criticism" (114), including Q. D. Leavis's views of Pater, her association of him with "the genteel tradition," and her view of him as unserious, a view clearly not accepted by Donoghue.

Melissa Knox

In my article, "Losing One's Head: Wilde's Confession in *Salome*," I argue that the surface action in *Salome* conceals hidden meanings. Why did the Irish poet write it in French? Why did he transform the politically motivated execution of John the Baptist into a sexually perverse lust murder by a young girl who has tried to seduce the prophet? The story of Salome's wish to seduce the religious prophet, a man denouncing women and their sexuality, a man obviously not inclined toward heterosexual adventures, seems improbable, and so leads to the feeling that it needs to be understood as a symbolic expression of thoughts that Wilde wanted to remain hidden, even as he appeared to be expressing them with shocking vividness and candor. Salome herself cannot be easily understood: sometimes she seems the naïve child wondering why anyone wouldn't want to kiss her, then she tastes the bloody lips of the severed head with every sign of vengeance and sexual relish.

Wilde remarked that he lived "in terror of not being misunderstood" (*CW*, 1016), a quip that can be taken as an epigraph for *Salome*, his drama of operatic fame. His strong desire to conceal and yet to reveal everything expressed itself in witty ambiguities, verbal conundrums that amused, yet confused his audiences, and made him a master of the quotable but impenetrable epigram. He lived in fear of being understood. He knew that in every line he wrote he revealed the secrets of his soul, "for out of ourselves," he observed, "we can never pass, nor can there be in creation what in the creator was not" (*CW*, 1045). Indeed, it fits his *Salome* when he remarked, "Man is least himself when he talks in his own person. Give him a mask and he will tell you the truth" (*CW*, 1045). The Byzantine setting of the play, the strange, biblical language borrowed from the *Song of Songs*, the utterings of Delphic obscurity lifted from various Old Testament prophets, mask a confession that he feared would be all too easily understood. The more the characters in the play question the meaning of Jokanaan's strange prophecies, the more Wilde hints at his fear: the public will recognize his own confession behind his mask of wit or obscurity. The play reveals, in one bloody statement, a confession that he wanted to make, even though he knew that to confess it would destroy him.

My main point is that the play's many interpreters have not considered the sexually voracious Herodias and Herod as disguised portraits of figures in Wilde's early life, but the many publicized sexual escapades of Wilde's father, the well-known eye surgeon, and the salacious remarks of his mother at her weekly salons, seem to have inspired in a distorted form the creation of the Herod family. In this constellation, Wilde's loss of his young sister Isola when she was nine and he was eleven, a sister dearly loved by him, cannot be ignored.

The family resonances, not easily discerned, can be discovered in aspects of the story that are not easy to understand. When Salome, who is introduced as a young and beautiful girl, tells Jokanaan that she would like to kiss him, he rebuffs her with great disgust. Why is she interested in this strange man covered with filth and rags? Curiously, although he denounces women and their sexuality, she appears not to hear or to understand him, guilelessly announcing herself: "I am Salome, Daughter of Herodias!" (*CW*, 558). Why does she want this man so isolated from the outside world, and who appears to be feared by her parents? With a child's impetuosity, she just wants him. Unconcerned with his responses — indeed, she hardly hears them — she is concerned with her desires. Do you ask a doll whether it wants to be kissed? He is a doll for her, an important one because her parents fear him, and because he rejects her, and so he seems more desirable.

Jokanaan, the prophet imprisoned in the dark, dirty cistern, resembles Wilde because he feels no sexual attraction to women. Unlike Wilde, he is easily able to resist sexual temptation. Wilde, who boasted,

"I can resist anything except temptation!" (*CW,* 388) admired the ability of Jokanaan to say "no" to Salome. In *De Profundis,* his long prison letter to his lover, Lord Alfred Douglas, he summed up his own weakness in yielding to the influence of Lord Alfred with this significant statement: "I lost my head." Like Jokanaan, Wilde considers himself a prophet, announcing a new way of life for believers. Certainly he is a kind of John the Baptist, in the sense of being both a martyr and a mascot for gay rights.

Once we have recognized Wilde in Jokanaan and his parents in the salacious behavior of Herod and Herodias, it is possible to see other connections. The Wildes had a daughter, a younger sister of Oscar, whom he adored. When she died at the age of nine, he kept a lock of her hair in an envelope that he had lovingly dedicated. Years later, reciting to a friend a memorial poem composed to Isola when he was twenty, he remembered her "dancing like a golden sunbeam about the house" (Sherard 250).

Isola played a crucial role in his life. In many poems, he associates young girls and their deaths with erotic longing or seduction. That childish seductive behavior probably took place between the very young Oscar and his sister would be quite normal. The chaotic family background of the Wilde home suggests that the parents were too preoccupied to give their children enough care and affection. Oscar and Isola, I assume, turned increasingly to each other for love and emotional support, which would have quickly ripened into a childish sexual intimacy. This kind of erotic activity, when practiced by adults, has the flavor of perversion and in the case of Wilde can be found glorified in his drama *Salome.* Salome, with her "little feet" and hands and her childish wish for the eyes in Jokanaan's severed head to open and look at her, behaves like a child of four or five, much younger than her approximate age of fourteen. Childhood relationships, distorted or disguised, reappear in the later relationships of the adolescent and the adult. Wilde appears to have had a dim sense that such early experiences indelibly stamped him. In a letter of early 1886 he wrote: "Our most fiery moments of ecstasy are merely shadows of what somewhere else we have felt, or of what we long some day to feel" (*Letters,* 185) — a remark that invites us to look for a model of Salome in his early life. Oscar's intensity of grief for Isola, that lasted all his life, derived from the guilt he felt as a young boy. He had allowed himself to be seduced by his little sister — had probably agreed to infantile sexual play — and then she was the one who — as Wilde must have felt — was punished by death.

Salome ultimately demands and gets Jokanaan's severed head, and Wilde certainly lost his head more than once in his life. His quip, "I often betray myself with a kiss" (*Letters*, 373), is a hint that helps to unravel the secret of the play. If Freud is right in suggesting that relationships often begin and end with identifications, we might surmise that Wilde's early attachments to his overwhelming mother and seductive younger sister got stuck in the phase of identifying with them because they could not be developed in reality, or, if they were partially developed, the resultant guilt would have become unbearable. The relationships therefore had to end. He retreated into an unconscious feminine identification: like his mother and sister, he too would be sexually approachable by a male.

Just before writing *Salome,* he had met Lord Alfred Douglas, the fatally attractive young man for whom Wilde martyred himself, who prepared the way for Wilde to crucify himself. This blonde, beautiful boy, twenty years younger than Wilde, revived, by his childlike appearance and impulsive behavior, Wilde's earlier love for the little sister who died, and in letters Wilde frequently addressed him as "Child," "my delicate flower, my lily of lilies," language very reminiscent of *Salome* and the *Song of Songs,* whose language Wilde appropriates in *Salome.* From prison, Wilde promised in a letter to Lord Alfred that "even covered with mud" — we can understand that to mean in the grave, or from the cistern — "I shall cry to you" (*Letters*, 397–98). Such words, such intense worshipful love as this, are reminiscent of the feelings he expressed for his sister. "Romance lives by repetition," Wilde wrote, "we can have in life but one great experience at best, and the secret of life is to reproduce that experience as often as possible" (*CW,* 149).

Part Two: Biography and Censorship

The following selections are from *The Cambridge Companion to Oscar Wilde,* ed. Peter Raby, and from C. George Sandulescu, *Rediscovering Oscar Wilde,* respectively.

Merlin Holland

Merlin Holland's "Biography and the art of lying" opens with an anecdote about Wilde's last days in the Hotel D'Alsace, during which the proprietor asked about his life in London, and according to Holland, Wilde answered, "Some said my life was a lie but I always knew it to be the truth; for like the truth it was rarely pure and never simple." At the very end of Holland's essay, in his penultimate footnote, he writes, "See also opening anecdote to this chapter which I confess to fabricating to illustrate the point" (17).

Holland uses this fabricated remark as a springboard for a discussion about the difficulties of writing the biography of such a rich, contradictory figure: "Some who have tried to pin him down have found that he turns to quicksilver in their fingers" (3), especially since Wilde himself said that he lived in terror of not being misunderstood. "Too many" of Wilde's biographers have, according to Holland, "come to him with an agenda of their own or a depth of personal feeling which limits their view and somehow dilutes the richness of his character" (5). It would be understandable for Wilde's grandson to have an agenda of his own and a depth of personal feeling which limits his view, but not necessarily one that dilutes the richness of Wilde's character. As mentioned, it was Wilde who elaborated on the idea that such personal investments must exist in order to make criticism — and that includes biography — possible.

Holland's attitude towards Wilde's major biographers is indeed negative: "Richard Ellmann's blade was certainly sharp enough but his untimely death prevented the follow-through of a clean cut. His predecessors, with the notable exception of Hesketh Pearson, for the most part took rough aim with a meat cleaver" (5). As a biographer of Wilde myself, I can't agree. Contemporary accounts of Wilde remain valuable, even, or especially, when they may seem inaccurate. Holland himself concedes that for all their faults — Robert Sherard's factual errors, for instance, that Wilde was imprisoned in Wandsworth — "these early biographers of Wilde knew the man in person" (8).

Nonetheless, he feels that the early biographers as a group, mainly Wilde's friends, provided "essentially impressionistic personal views . . . technicolour elements in a grey world of facts" (9–10). Now that another sixty years have gone by since the publication of the first biographies, all those who knew Wilde personally are dead. The likelihood of "sensational new source material passing through the sale-rooms is slight" (10), Holland asserts, and accuses biographers today of inventing them. First he takes to task Richard Ellmann, who in his masterly *Oscar Wilde* (1987), acclaimed as the best, most complete biography to date, mistakenly published a photograph of what he believed to be Wilde in costume as Salome, when it has turned out to be an Hungarian opera singer, Alice Guszalewicz.

Holland devotes nearly a page to this mistake and the manner in which it occurred, the photo being separated from its caption in an archive, and so on. But as Holland himself points out, Wilde had been caricatured dressed as a woman in a contemporary drawing by Alfred Bryan, which appears in Ellmann's biography on the page preceding the Alice Guszalewicz photograph. That he was perceived by even one contemporary as wanting to be seen as a woman should not go uncommented upon. Wilde himself remarked, as I have elsewhere mentioned, that "all women become like their mothers. That is their tragedy. No man does. That's his" (*CW*, 335). Few have studied this remark for implications of Wilde's vision of himself as a woman, and his ability to empathize with women, which was grounded in his strong identification with his mother. Holland does not touch this subject, instead interpreting the caricature as pertaining only to Wilde's speech on the opening night of *Lady Windermere's Fan,* which he feels has nothing to do with Wilde being seen as — or wanting to be seen as — a woman.

Holland's wrath builds: "Less excusable, because certain facts were manipulated to fit the theory and others blatantly ignored, was Ellmann's insistence on Wilde's death from syphilis" (12). As a matter of fact, Ellmann did not insist that Wilde died of syphilis. Although he writes that Wilde "contracted syphilis, reportedly from a woman prostitute" (Ellmann 88, note), he makes it clear that there exists no medical evidence for his claim, but only strong anecdotal evidence, and that opinions differ strongly on the cause of Wilde's death. He adds: "My belief that Wilde had syphilis stems from statements made by Reginald Turner and Robert Ross, Wilde's close friends present at his death, from the certificate of the doctor in charge at that time, and from the fact that the 1912 edition of Ransome's book on Wilde and Harris's 1916 life (both of which Ross oversaw) gives syphilis as the cause of death" (88). Turner, Ross, and Harris were all devoted to Wilde, in the best position to know what his ailments were, and with sympathies entirely on Wilde's side. None of them would ever wish to state that Wilde suffered from a disease which had — and still has — a terrible stigma. And although no medical history of Wilde's illnesses remains extant, except for the record of a urinalysis performed in Paris in his last year (in the William Andrews Clark Memorial Library, Los Angeles), which proves only that Wilde suffered from dehydration, the doctor who attended him during his last days said that Wilde's ear infection, a suppurative otitis media, resulted from "a tertiary symptom of an infection he had contracted when he was twenty" (546), which was, Robert Ross said, the legacy of syphilis. In sum, Ellmann makes it clear that although the final illness was an ear infection, it was "almost certainly syphilitic in origin." Syphilis, if Wilde had it, neither improved Wilde's health nor helped him recover from the ear infection.

Next, Holland criticizes my biography, *Oscar Wilde: A Long and Lovely Suicide*. Believing that he has scotched Ellmann's interpretation, Holland writes: "Informed discussion post-Ellmann does not seem to have deterred more persistent sensationalists intent on discovering new skeletons in the Wilde cupboard. A recent 'psychoanalytic' biography of Wilde by Melissa Knox bows before the weight of medical opinion and accepts that he did not die from the disease but attempts to make a case for syphilitically determined life largely from Sherard conjectures, which themselves relied on the false premise of his death from syphilis as a starting point. Even allowing for this hiccup in logic, she overlooks the fact that Sherard's information was all second-hand; that he espoused the syphilis cause principally to attack Harris, Gide, and Renier; and that as a convert he is a fanatic and a totally unreliable source . . . The Knox strain is nothing if not contagious; by the end of the book 'possibly, even probably, Wilde's two sons have it, his wife has died of it, and the Canterville ghost has it by implication. The only one to escape, curiously, is Bosie Douglas'" (14).

It is sad to see a man so desperate to avoid the taint of a disease that he cannot bear to acknowledge its crucial role in Wilde's history. Fear of syphilis can cause considerable harm, and Wilde certainly lived in terror of the disease and fell prey to his fears that he had contracted it. For the record, I did not state that Wilde had syphilis or died of it, nor did I rely exclusively on Robert Sherard. I discussed differing statements made by Arthur Ransome, who initially stated that Wilde died of syphilis and then retracted his earlier statement. I remarked on Wilde's treatment with mercury. I then wrote: "For my purpose it is not so important that Wilde had contracted this dread disease as that he appears to have believed he had . . . Evidence of his fear of the disease exists in a number of his writings" (*Oscar Wilde: A Long and Lovely Suicide*, intro., xx). I discuss the well-known influence of Joris Karl Huysmans's novel on Wilde's *The Picture of Dorian Gray*, particularly remarks made by the main character, Des Esseintes, regarding his fear of contracting syphilis and his projection of his fears onto the world surrounding him. Staring at his hothouse flowers, Des Esseintes remarks, "Most of them, as if ravaged by syphilis or leprosy, displayed vivid patches of flesh mottled with roseola . . . It all comes down to syphilis in the end" (intro., xx).

Merlin Holland appears to be nearly as offended by the attempts of biographers to document Wilde's first homosexual encounter as he is by the research on Wilde and syphilis: "Trying to establish when Oscar Wilde's first homosexual encounter took place, preferably before his marriage, has become another of the new sensationalist pursuits" (14). Another page follows about "shoddy research" in this area. But the issue seems a red herring. Wilde's emotional life, his inner wishes, which he may or may not have acted on, are documented in his letters, which Holland himself praises as giving "an entirely new impetus to Wilde studies and a much greater understanding of the complexities of his character. They also, most importantly, help to corroborate or disprove certain facts or statements about him made posthumously by his friends and contemporaries" (5). And in those letters Wilde reveals himself to be well aware of homosexual urges, which he accepts as a matter of course, in July 1876, that is, some eight years before his marriage, which took place in 1884. In the July 1876 letter, which he wrote as a twenty-year old Oxford student, he tells his close friend William Ward how he almost missed an exam: "While lying in bed on Tuesday morning with Swinburne (a copy of) I was woke up by the Clerk of the Schools . . ." (*Letters*, 15). Imagining himself lounging in bed with Swinburne, "the first English poet to sing divinely the song of the flesh" (Chesson 204), a man who specialized in painting lurid portraits — for instance, of Sappho's sadomasochistic lesbian lust for Anactoria — Wilde coyly invites Ward to approve, or perhaps share, some kind of erotic life. A reader need only dip into *The Letters of Oscar Wilde* (1962) and its companion volume, *More Letters of Oscar Wilde* (1985) for more examples.

At the very end of Merlin Holland's essay he asserts that the "wealth of material" now available, "makes Wilde's life more contradictory and complicated than ever. The inherent duality lives on, now more of a plurality . . . It will remain so until we accept that our view of Wilde must always be a multicoloured kaleidoscope of apparent contradictions in need not of resolution but of appreciation" (16). Surely resolving certain issues in Wilde's life need not oppose, but rather increase, appreciation of his life and art.

The following paper, "Plagiarist or Pioneer?" by Merlin Holland, is included for the light it throws on Holland's attitudes toward his grandfather as well as for his feelings about biographers. Holland begins this way: "If [Wilde's] relentless self-promotion during his life as a dandy, wit, conversationalist and writer of comedies has outlived any reputation he may have had as a scholar and a thinker, it is just as he would have wished it to be, the life taking precedence over the works, the genius as he saw it, over the talent" (193). This seems unfair to

Wilde, whose letters and epigrams make it clear that he wanted to be remembered as a scholar and thinker, even if much of the time he needed to obscure his brilliant thought. Holland comments that the general public knows Wilde for his novel, fairy tales, and comedies, not for his scholarship.

He then moves to Wilde's early ambitiousness, revealed in friends' contemporary accounts, Wilde's letters, and poems that he wrote and sent to eminent persons, Lord Houghton and William Gladstone, in obvious hope of being noticed and making a name for himself. In London two years later, in 1879, he courted leading actresses of the day and made his way into society, with great skill.

Much of the first part of this article is familiar, although well and accurately told. The meat of the article, the best, although the saddest part, is Merlin Holland's justification for the acts of censorship he is empowered to make as the executor of the Oscar Wilde estate, which allows him to control both access to manuscripts and use of them by scholars. He never uses the term censorship; I write as one whom he tried to censor. He remarks only, "I did not know my grandfather, and cold logic tells me that I have no more reason to defend or criticise him than my neighbour; and yet there is an intangible link perhaps vicariously through my father' suffering as a child which is difficult to ignore" (197). Holland then quotes from his father's moving 1954 autobiography, *Son of Oscar Wilde,* in which Wilde's younger son, Vyvyan, complains that the longer people have been dead, the more people "hack them about" when they write about them, "to make them fit a pattern of their own making until no flesh or blood remains. This is especially true of Oscar Wilde" (197).

One sympathizes with the son's desire not to have his father's image "hacked about," but Wilde would more likely have laughed and said, "Of course!" I think he would have been delighted to see his own theories of criticism as creation so clearly demonstrated. He would have laughed, even he who once said biographers were merely the body-snatchers of literature. But neither his son nor his grandson can laugh about what was, after all, their family tragedy.

Instead, Holland tells a tale of being approached by "two American scholars," wanting photocopies from the William Andrews Clark Memorial Library in Los Angeles, the largest repository of Wilde manuscripts in the world. The scholars wanted the notebooks Wilde kept at Oxford, Holland reports, clearly referring to the book that became *Oscar Wilde's Oxford Notebooks,* edited by Smith and Helfand. Holland is suspicious, although there seemed "no good reason to refuse *for there was little in them which could be sensationalized in the manner which was characteristic of all too many books about my grandfather around that time"* (198) [my italics]. This shows his interest in suppressing material that he deems sensational. He confesses to a "nagging fear" that the book might "show Wilde up in an unfavourable light" (198). In practice this has meant, from my own experience and that of scholars I know, attempts to suppress anything about Wilde's possible infection with syphilis or his homosexuality. A good treatment of this problem is Susan Balée's "Reply to Merlin Holland" in *Victorian Studies* (see introduction).

Holland confesses that he is ashamed to have harbored the thought that to put "such a ragbag of diffuse scribblings" as *Oscar Wilde's Oxford Notebooks* "was to serve up barrel scrapings as haute cuisine instead of leaving them to be tipped, as I believed properly, into the stock pot" (198). But Wilde's Oxford notes *are* haute cuisine, not scraps. Holland's remarks, curiously, show a tendency to denigrate his grandfather, as well as a fear that others will denigrate Wilde. Otherwise, it would not occur to him to think of Wilde's undergraduate notebooks as pieces in a "ragbag," or as "barrel scrapings." In reality, rare indeed is the scholar who denigrates Wilde, although material about Wilde's life that Holland dislikes is often perceived by him as denigration of his grandfather. Certainly the days of seeing Oscar Wilde as an intellectual lightweight are long gone, and it is strange that Holland still feels that Wilde is underrated as a thinker and philosopher.

In the end, Holland came to value the *Oxford Notebooks*, and allowed the book to be written, but his initial suspiciousness is sad to discover.

Holland turns to the topic of Wilde and plagiarism, opposing again the terms plagiarist *or* pioneer. Wilde, of an Hegelian turn of mind, would have said *and,* not *or.* To see Wilde's obvious, artful plagiarisms as unoriginal is to fail to recognize an important component of his creativity. Holland moves through well-worn details about the comments made when Wilde's poems were published, the obvious echoes of Keats, Wordsworth, "Swinburne and water," as one reviewer caustically wrote. Holland declines to see the intentional parody and delight Wilde took in his ostentatious borrowings, castigating him for "signs of a tendency to lift whole phrases if not paragraphs from writers more established than he" (200). But Wilde himself said, that he never read "Flaubert's *Tentacion de Saint Antoine* without signing my name at the end" (Beerbohm 36). It is Wilde's deliberate plagiarism, his art of appropriation, that is worth exploring — not a lazy sneaking around, which is what one usually associates with the term "plagiarism."

Holland offers many a tale of "plagiarism," but little interpretation beyond saying that "Wilde was a literary magpie with a love of glittering language. Mundane considerations of 'respect' for the origins of a phrase or a plot yielded before the potential which they offered" (208). Calling Wilde a mere "magpie" insults him and ignores his creative and original use of the texts he appropriated. Holland then inadvertently reveals his mistrust of Wilde: "I am not implying that he was intellectually amoral, but more that he seemed to believe in a sort of communism of language and ideas . . ." (208). If Holland is "not" saying it, why does he say it? What comes across is bewildered disapproval, not an attempt to see the brilliant borrowing that fueled some of Wilde's best work. Wilde lived the idea that "great writers steal," and lived it most successfully, rendering new each "stolen" item until it belonged more to him than to its originator.

Holland's conclusion does not depart from the faintly suspicious contempt in which he appears to hold his grandfather. Telling us that Wilde the thinker and scholar must eventually take his place beside that of Wilde the entertainer and jester — a commonplace idea — he expresses a fear that no one could possibly believe him: "The literary establishment will scoff and the public will object . . ." (211). But this is the furthest thing from what is happening now. The current explosion of scholarship and popular interest suggests that Oscar Wilde can only increase in stature as we enter the new millennium.

Works Cited

Beerbohm, Max. 1964. *Letters to Reggie Turner*. Ed. Rupert Hart-Davis. London: Soho Square/Richard Clay.

Chesson, Wilfred Hugh. 1985. "A Reminiscence of 1898." *More Letters of Oscar Wilde*. Ed. Rupert Hart-Davis. New York: Vanguard Press.

D'Amico, Masolino. 1994. "Oscar Wilde in Naples." *Rediscovering Oscar Wilde*. Ed. C. George Sandulescu. Princess Grace Irish Library: 8. Gerrards Cross: Colin Smythe.

Donoghue, Denis. 1994. "The Oxford of Pater, Hopkins, and Wilde." *Rediscovering Oscar Wilde*. Ed. C. George Sandulescu. Princess Grace Irish Library: 8. Gerrards Cross: Colin Smythe.

Ellmann, Richard. 1998. *Oscar Wilde*. New York: Vintage.

Holland, Merlin. 1994. "Plagiarist or Pioneer?" *Rediscovering Oscar Wilde.* Ed. C. George Sandulescu. Princess Grace Irish Library: 8. Gerrards Cross: Colin Smythe.

———. 1997. "Biography and the art of lying." *The Cambridge Companion to Oscar Wilde.* Ed. Peter Raby. New York: Cambridge UP.

Holland, Vyvyan. 1954; rpt 1988. *Son of Oscar Wilde.* New York: Oxford UP.

Knox, Melissa. 1994. "Losing One's Head: Wilde's Confession in *Salome.*" *Rediscovering Oscar Wilde.* Ed. C. George Sandulescu. Princess Grace Irish Library: 8. Gerrards Cross: Colin Smythe.

Page, Norman. 1994. "Decoding *The Ballad of Reading Gaol.*" *Rediscovering Oscar Wilde.* Ed. C. George Sandulescu. Princess Grace Irish Library: 8. Gerrards Cross: Colin Smythe.

Powell, Kerry. 1994. "Wilde & Two Women: Unpublished Accounts by Elizabeth Robins & Blanche Crackanthorpe." *Rediscovering Oscar Wilde.* Ed. C. George Sandulescu.

Raby, Peter, ed. 1997. *The Cambridge Companion to Oscar Wilde.* New York: Cambridge UP.

Sandulescu, C. George, ed. 1994. *Rediscovering Oscar Wilde.* Princess Grace Irish Library: 8. Gerrards Cross: Colin Smythe.

Sherard, Robert. (n.d., ca. 1915). *The Real Oscar Wilde.* Philadelphia: David McKay.

Stokes, John. 1997. "Wilde the Journalist." *The Cambridge Companion to Oscar Wilde.* Ed. Peter Raby. New York: Cambridge UP.

7: Summary and Future Trends

FOR CRITICS COMMITTED to intensive biographic scrutiny as a first step in literary analysis of Oscar Wilde, the criticism of the 1990s examined in this book offers hopeful trends. Ethnic Studies — an offshoot of Cultural Studies — shows a renewal of interest in social and familial influences in the development of a writer's personality, and in the complex interactions between culture and the individual. If the last decade provides any indication, the field of Irish Ethnic Studies and Cultural Criticism seems likely to grow, and with it, the interest in Oscar Wilde as a personality with a unique impact on his surrounding culture, as opposed to a writer who primarily expressed that culture's economy, social stratification, prejudices, and beliefs.

Exploring the meaning of British and Irish identity, Irish Ethnic Studies has done much to expose stereotypes, to explore the psychology and politics of colonial and post-colonial Ireland, to define ways in which cultures, like individuals, have personalities, to delineate ways in which cultures influence the expression of personalities, and to reveal ways in which behaviors that look to an outsider like quirks of a particular personality may be the expression of an ethnically specific style. For instance, Deirdre Toomey's essay, "The Story-Teller at Fault," explores inner tensions in Yeats and Wilde as Anglo-Irishmen caught between competing cultures, between the oral story-telling traditions of Irish culture and the written tradition of Great Britain. Likewise, Jerusha McCormack brilliantly retells the old story of Wilde as a dandy, placing it in the context of Wilde's political and personal investments in England and Ireland. Rejecting the old idea of the dandy as "merely a man of fashion," she develops Baudelaire's idea that dandyism is linked to shifting political sands, to times when democracy is growing but the old aristocracy retains some power. Pioneering writers in this field include Davis Coakley, Jerusha McCormack, and Declan Kiberd.

Another area likely to continue influencing Wilde criticism is Gay, Queer and Gender studies. The last ten years have seen an explosion of interest in gender as a field of research, in the political uses and abuses of the terms "gay" and "queer," and in sociobiological research on the history of the science behind the long-accepted divisions of heterosexual and homosexual. Representative of this research and likely to shape future Wilde scholarship as well as Gay, Queer, and Gender Studies is *Sexing the Body: Gender Politics and the Construction of Sexuality*, by Anne Fausto-Sterling (New York: Basic Books, 2000). An interesting debate may continue to evolve between "Constructionists" — those who perceive cultures and societies as the authors of forms of sexuality as well as of the labels given to it, and "Essentialists," those who find it more plausible that certain forms of sexuality, among them homosexuality, have existed in comparable if not identical forms in virtually all societies, and may be deemed innate features of human nature or the various human natures, "nature" being the expression of internal, that is emotional, physiological, and biological states.

Although the task of investigating Wilde's sexuality and the relationship between sexuality and culture is an exciting and continually growing field, much of currently available Gay, Queer, and Gender criticism of his life and work, especially those works from the 1990s dealt with above, remains under the sway of moral idealism, namely vigorous resistance to homophobia, advocacy of acceptance of many sexualities that a number of cultures have traditionally rejected or harshly penalized, and the indictment of the ways in which cultures have marginalized sexualities deemed "transgressive." Even though these are laudable goals for a socially just universe, they remain moral ideals rather than investigative efforts. Wilde's observation that morality is "the attitude we adopt towards people whom we personally dislike" can be taken as a useful critique of such criticism, because he understands morality as a defensive attitude, one that can get in the way of literary analysis no matter how useful it may prove in other areas. Today's morality goes by other names, but what it lacks, and what Wilde had and advocated in his criticism, is open-mindedness, a willingness to entertain new ideas. This is not the same as "objectivity," which Wilde disliked as much as he considered it to be impossible to achieve; one can remain relatively open to ideas and still have strong opinions. To be "objective" in Wilde's terms would involve not having opinions to begin with, not caring enough about the subject to want to take a position. But to begin a literary investigation with hardened notions of good and evil usually results in a polemic, not a discovery. For Wilde, the critic and the artist involved themselves in a perpetual search for that will o' the wisp, truth, and the search had to remain uncontaminated by good intentions or moral precepts.

A form of criticism that seems unlikely to shape future Wilde scholarship in the same way as Ethnic and Gender studies is Reader Response criticism. Only one full-length volume identifying itself as

Reader Response criticism has appeared on Wilde in the 1990s. The field has neither the political nor the psychological power of Ethnic or Gay, Gender and Queer Studies, and it has been practiced in highly disparate ways by different critics. Stanley Fish and Michael Gillespie both self-identify as Reader Response critics, but others might label them differently. Rejecting New Criticism, Reader Response criticism offers none of the possibilities provided by other forms of criticism utilized by Wilde scholars of the 1990s, for instance, the value of studying Wilde's ethnic identity and conflicts about it, the value of studying his sense of himself as a man primarily attracted to other men, but whose letters and remarks suggest also one who questioned his sexuality as he questioned everything else, and who either felt a sexual attraction to his wife or believed that he did, or should. Theories of ethnicity and gender seem to offer more ways of studying how Wilde did or did not fit into his culture to the Wilde scholar than does Reader Response criticism.

Because the desire to define identities in cultural, ethnic, and political ways continues to shape current criticism, ideas about personality and biography that have sometimes been rejected in a critical climate influenced by the idea of the death of the author seem destined to play an important role in future Wilde studies. Close readings owing allegiance to no one school of theory, Theater criticism, forms of New Historicism and biographic studies are in no danger of dying out. Wilde's personality demands them, and his way of remaining endlessly interpretable almost guarantees continued biographic interest in his life and work.

Works Cited

Fausto-Sterling, Anne. 2000. *Sexing the Body: Gender Politics and the Construction of Sexuality.* New York: Basic Books.

Hart-Davis, Rupert, ed. 1962. *The Letters of Oscar Wilde.* New York: Harcourt, Brace and World.

———, ed. 1985. *More Letters of Oscar Wilde.* New York: Vanguard Press.

Haynes, Todd. 1998. *Velvet Goldmine.* New York: Miramax.

Holland, Merlin. 1996. Comments on Susan Balée's Review of *Oscar Wilde: A Long and Lovely Suicide,* by Melissa Knox. *Victorian Studies* 39.4: 539–41.

Ingleby, Leonard Cresswell [Cyril Arthur Gull]. 1907. *Oscar Wilde*. London: T. Werner Laurie.

Jackson, Holbrook. [1913] 1966. *The Eighteen-Nineties: A Review of Art and Ideas at the Close of the Nineteenth Century*. New York: Capricorn.

Knox, Melissa. 1994. *Oscar Wilde: A Long and Lovely Suicide*. New Haven: Yale UP.

Nassaar, Christopher. 1974. *Into the Demon Universe: A Literary Exploration of Oscar Wilde*. New Haven: Yale UP.

Pearson, Hesketh. 1946. *Oscar Wilde: His Life and Wit*. New York: Harper and Bros.

Ransome, Arthur. 1912. *Oscar Wilde: A Critical Study*. London: Martin Secker.

Richards, I. A. [1929] 1956. *Practical Criticism: A Study of Literature*. New York: Harcourt, Brace.

Sandulescu, C. George, ed. 1994. *Rediscovering Oscar Wilde*. Princess Grace Irish Library: 8. Gerrards Cross: Colin Smythe.

Small, Ian. 1993. *Oscar Wilde Revalued: An Essay on New Materials & Methods of Research*. North Carolina: ELT Press.

Smith, Philip E., and Michael S. Helfand. 1989. *Oscar Wilde's Oxford Notebooks*. New York: Oxford UP.

Wilde, Oscar. [1891] 1986. "The Critic as Artist." *Complete Works of Oscar Wilde*. Ed. Vyvyan Holland. New York: Harper & Row. (References to this work will be cited in the text as CW.)

Woodcock, George. 1949. *The Paradox of Oscar Wilde*. London: T. V. Boardman.

Works Cited

Balée, Susan. 1995. Review of *Oscar Wilde: A Long and Lovely Suicide*, by Melissa Knox. *Victorian Studies* 38.2: 319–21.

———. 1996. "Reply to Merlin Holland." *Victorian Studies* 39.4: 542–43.

Barthes, Roland. 1977. "The Death of the Author." *Image — Music — Text.* Trans. S. Heath. New York: Hill & Wang.

Beerbohm, Max. 1964. *Letters to Reggie Turner.* Ed. Rupert Hart-Davis. London: Soho Square/Richard Clay.

Behrendt, Patricia Flanagan. 1991. *Oscar Wilde: Eros and Aesthetics.* London: Macmillan.

Blanchard, Mary Warner. 1998. *Oscar Wilde's America: Counterculture in the Gilded Age.* New Haven: Yale UP.

Brinzeu, Pia. 1994. "Dorian Gray's Rooms and Cyberspace." *Rediscovering Oscar Wilde.* Ed. C. George Sandulescu. Princess Grace Irish Library: 8. Gerrards Cross: Colin Smythe.

Bristow, Joseph. 1997. "'A Complex Multiform Creature': Wilde's Sexual Identities." *The Cambridge Companion to Oscar Wilde.* Ed. Peter Raby. New York: Cambridge UP.

Brooks, Cleanth, John Thibaut Purser, and Robert Penn Warren, eds. 1975. *An Approach to Literature.* Englewood Cliffs, NJ: Prentice-Hall.

Brown, Julia Prewitt. 1997. *Cosmopolitan Criticism: Oscar Wilde's Philosophy of Art.* Charlottesville and London: The UP of Virginia.

Chesson, Wilfred Hugh. 1985. "A Reminiscence of 1898." *More Letters of Oscar Wilde.* Ed. Rupert Hart-Davis. New York: Vanguard Press.

Coakley, Davis. 1994. "The Neglected Years: Wilde in Dublin." *Rediscovering Oscar Wilde.* Ed. C. George Sandulescu. Princess Grace Irish Library: 8. Gerrards Cross: Colin Smythe.

———. 1995. *Oscar Wilde: The Importance of Being Irish.* Dublin: Town House.

Cohen, Ed. [1987] 1991. "Writing Gone Wilde: Homoerotic Desire in the Closet of Representation." *Critical Essays on Oscar Wilde.* Ed. Regenia Gagnier. New York: G. K. Hall.

———. 1993. *Talk on the Wilde Side: Toward a Genealogy of a Discourse on Male Sexualities.* New York: Routledge.

Coleridge, Samuel Taylor. [1817] 1983. *Biographia Literaria*. Ed. J. Engell and W. J. Bate. Vol. 7, *The Collected Works of Samuel Taylor Coleridge*. Ed. Kathleen Coburn. Bollingen Series 75. Princeton, NJ: Princeton UP.

Craft, Christopher. 1991. "Alias Bunbury: Desire and Termination in *The Importance of Being Earnest.*" *Critical Essays on Oscar Wilde*. Ed. Regenia Gagnier. New York: G. K. Hall.

D'Amico, Masolino. 1994. "Oscar Wilde in Naples." *Rediscovering Oscar Wilde*. Ed. C. George Sandulescu. Princess Grace Irish Library: 8. Gerrards Cross: Colin Smythe.

Danson, Lawrence. 1994. "Each Man Kills the Thing He Loves: The Impermanence of Personality in Oscar Wilde." *Rediscovering Oscar Wilde*. Ed. C. George Sandulescu. Princess Grace Irish Library: 8. Gerrards Cross: Colin Smythe.

———. 1997. *Wilde's Intentions: The Artist in his Criticism*. Oxford: Clarendon Press.

Dever, Carolyn and Marvin J. Taylor, eds. 1995. *Reading Wilde, Querying Spaces: An Exhibition Commemorating the 100th Anniversary of the Trials of Oscar Wilde*. New York: Fales Library, New York U.

Dollimore, Jonathan. [1988] 1991. "Different Desires: Subjectivity and Transgression in Wilde and Gide." *Critical Essays on Oscar Wilde*. Ed Regenia Gagnier. New York: G. K. Hall.

Donoghue, Denis. 1994. "The Oxford of Pater, Hopkins, and Wilde." *Rediscovering Oscar Wilde*. Ed. C. George Sandulescu. Princess Grace Irish Library: 8. Gerrards Cross: Colin Smythe.

Ellmann, Richard. 1988. *Oscar Wilde*. New York: Vintage.

Eltis, Sos. 1996. *Revising Wilde: Society and Subversion in the Plays of Oscar Wilde*. Oxford: Clarendon Press.

Fausto-Sterling, Anne. 2000. *Sexing the Body: Gender Politics and the Construction of Sexuality*. New York: Basic Books.

Foldy, Michael. 1997. *The Trials of Oscar Wilde: Deviance, Morality, and Late-Victorian Society*. New Haven: Yale UP.

Foucault, Michel. [1969] 1977. "What is an Author?" *Language, Counter-Memory, Practice*. Trans. D. F. Bouchard and Sherry Simon. Ithaca, NY: Cornell UP.

Gagnier, Regenia, ed. 1991. *Critical Essays on Oscar Wilde*. New York: G. K. Hall.

Gillespie, Michael Patrick. 1996. *Oscar Wilde and the Poetics of Ambiguity*. Gainesville, Florida: UP of Florida.

Gopnik, Adam. 1998. "The Invention of Oscar Wilde," *The New Yorker*, May 18. 78.

Greenblatt, Stephen Jay. 1982. Introduction to "The Forms of Power and the Power of Forms in the Renaissance." *Genre* 15: 1–2.

———. 1990. *Learning to Curse: Essays in Early Modern Culture*. New York: Routledge.

Harris, Frank, ed. Gallagher John F. 1963. *My Life and Loves*. New York: Grove Press.

Hart-Davis, Rupert, ed. 1962. *The Letters of Oscar Wilde*. New York: Harcourt, Brace and World.

———, ed. 1985. *More Letters of Oscar Wilde*. New York: Vanguard Press.

Haynes, Todd. 1998. *Velvet Goldmine.* New York: Miramax.

Hoare, Philip. 1997. *Oscar Wilde's Last Stand*. New York: Arcade.

Holland, Merlin. 1994. "Plagiarist or Pioneer?" *Rediscovering Oscar Wilde*. Ed. C. George Sandulescu. Princess Grace Irish Library: 8. Gerrards Cross: Colin Smythe.

———. 1996. "Comments on Susan Balée's Review of *Oscar Wilde: A Long and Lovely Suicide,* by Melissa Knox." *Victorian Studies* 39.4: 539–41.

———. 1997. "Biography and the art of lying." *The Cambridge Companion to Oscar Wilde*. Ed. Peter Raby. New York: Cambridge UP.

Holland, Vyvyan. [1954] 1988. *Son of Oscar Wilde*. New York: Oxford UP.

———. 1986. Introduction to *The Complete Works of Oscar Wilde*. London: Collins.

Hyde, H. Montgomery, ed. 1962. *The Trials of Oscar Wilde*. New York: Dover.

Ingleby, Leonard Cresswell [Cyril Arthur Gull]. 1907. *Oscar Wilde*. London: T. Werner Laurie.

Jackson, Holbrook. [1913] 1966. *The Eighteen-Nineties: A Review of Art and Ideas at the Close of the Nineteenth Century*. New York: Capricorn.

Kaufman, Moises. 1999. *Gross Indecency: The Three Trials of Oscar Wilde*. New York: Dramatists Play Service.

Knox, Melissa. 1994. "Losing One's Head: Wilde's Confession in *Salome*." *Rediscovering Oscar Wilde*. Ed. C. George Sandulescu. Princess Grace Irish Library: 8. Gerrards Cross: Colin Smythe.

———. 1994. *Oscar Wilde: A Long and Lovely Suicide*. New Haven: Yale UP.

Mason, Stuart [Christopher Millard]. 1920. *Oscar Wilde and the Aesthetic Movement*. Dublin: Townley Searle.

McCormack, Jerusha. 1994. "Oscar Wilde: The Once and Future Dandy." *Rediscovering Oscar Wilde*. Ed. C. George Sandulescu. Princess Grace Irish Library: 8. Gerrards Cross: Colin Smythe.

———. 1998. *Wilde the Irishman*. New Haven: Yale UP.

Murray, Isobel. 1994. "Oscar Wilde in His Literary Element: Yet Another Source for Dorian Gray?" *Rediscovering Oscar Wilde*. Ed. C. George Sandulescu. Princess Grace Irish Library: 8. Gerrards Cross: Colin Smythe.

Nassaar, Christopher. 1974. *Into the Demon Universe: A Literary Exploration of Oscar Wilde*. New Haven: Yale UP.

Page, Norman. 1994. "Decoding *The Ballad of Reading Gaol*." *Rediscovering Oscar Wilde*. Ed. C. George Sandulescu. Princess Grace Irish Library: 8. Gerrards Cross: Colin Smythe.

Paglia, Camille A. 1991. "Oscar Wilde and the English Epicene." *Critical Essays on Oscar Wilde*. Ed. Regenia Gagnier. New York: G. K. Hall.

Pearson, Hesketh. 1946. *Oscar Wilde: His Life and Wit*. New York: Harper and Bros.

Powell, Kerry. 1990. *Oscar Wilde and the Theatre of the 1890s*. Cambridge: Cambridge UP.

———. 1994. "Wilde & Two Women: Unpublished Accounts by Elizabeth Robins & Blanche Crackanthorpe." *Rediscovering Oscar Wilde*. Ed. C. George Sandulescu.

Raby, Peter. 1994. "Wilde and European Theatre." *Rediscovering Oscar Wilde*. Ed. C. George Sandulescu. Princess Grace Irish Library: 8. Gerrards Cross: Colin Smythe.

———. 1997. *The Cambridge Companion to Oscar Wilde*. New York: Cambridge UP.

Ransome, Arthur. 1912. *Oscar Wilde: A Critical Study*. London: Martin Secker.

Richards, I. A. [1929] 1956. *Practical Criticism: A Study of Literature*. New York: Harcourt, Brace.

Rohmann, Gerd. 1994. "Re-Discovering Oscar Wilde in Travesties by Joyce and Stoppard." *Rediscovering Oscar Wilde*. Ed. C. George Sandulescu. Princess Grace Irish Library: 8. Gerrards Cross: Colin Smythe.

Rosenstein, Roy. 1994. "Re(dis)covering Wilde for Latin America: Marti, Dario, Borges, Lispector." *Rediscovering Oscar Wilde*. Ed. C. George Sandulescu. Princess Grace Irish Library: 8. Gerrards Cross: Colin Smythe.

Sammells, Neil. 1994. "Rediscovering the Irish Wilde." *Rediscovering Oscar Wilde*. Ed. C. George Sandulescu. Princess Grace Irish Library: 8. Gerrards Cross: Colin Smythe.

Sandulescu, C. George, ed. 1994. *Rediscovering Oscar Wilde*. Princess Grace Irish Library: 8. Gerrards Cross: Colin Smythe.

Sherard, Robert. (n.d., ca. 1915). *The Real Oscar Wilde*. Philadelphia: David McKay.

Sinfield, Alan. 1994. *The Wilde Century: Effeminacy, Oscar Wilde and the Queer Moment*. New York: Columbia UP.

Small, Ian. 1993. *Oscar Wilde Revalued: An Essay on New Materials & Methods of Research*. North Carolina: ELT Press.

Smith, Philip E., and Michael S. Helfand. 1989. *Oscar Wilde's Oxford Notebooks*. New York: Oxford UP.

Stokes, John. 1996. *Oscar Wilde: Myths, Miracles, and Imitations*. Cambridge: Cambridge UP.

———. 1997. "Wilde the Journalist." *The Cambridge Companion to Oscar Wilde*. Ed. Peter Raby. New York: Cambridge UP.

Tydeman, William and Steven Price. 1996. *Wilde: Salome*. Cambridge: Cambridge UP.

Varty, Anne. 1998. *A Preface to Oscar Wilde*. London and New York: Longman.

Wellek, René. 1965. *A History of Modern Criticism*. Vol. 4: 1750–1950. Cambridge: Cambridge UP.

White, Hayden. 1989. "New Historicism: A Comment." *The New Historicism*. Ed. Harold Veeser. London: Routledge.

Wilde, Oscar. [1891] 1986. "The Critic as Artist." *Complete Works of Oscar Wilde*. Ed. Vyvyan Holland. New York: Harper & Row. (References to this work will be cited in the text as CW.)

Woodcock, George. 1949. *The Paradox of Oscar Wilde*. London: T. V. Boardman.

Zhang, Longxi. [1988] 1991. "Oscar Wilde's Critical Legacy." *Critical Essays on Oscar Wilde*. Ed. Regenia Gagnier. New York: G. K. Hall.

Index